MEDITATIONES DE PRIMA PHILOSOPHIA
MEDITATIONS ON FIRST PHILOSOPHY

René Descartes

Meditationes de prima Philosophia

Meditations on First Philosophy

A BILINGUAL EDITION

Introduced, edited, translated
and indexed by
George Heffernan

UNIVERSITY OF NOTRE DAME PRESS
NOTRE DAME   LONDON

©1990
University of Notre Dame Press
Notre Dame, Indiana 46556
All Rights Reserved
Manufactured in the United States of America

Library of Congress Cataloging-in-Publication Data
Descartes, René, 1596–1650.
    [Meditationes de prima philosophia. English & Latin]
    Meditations on First Philosophy = Meditationes de
prima philosophia / René Descartes ; edited, translated
and indexed by George Heffernan. — Bilingual ed.
    p. cm.
    Includes bibliographical references.
    ISBN 0-268-01380-2   —ISBN 0-268-01381-0 (pbk.)
    1. First philosophy—Early works to 1800. 2. God—
Proof, Ontological—Early works to 1800. 3.
Methodology—Early works to 1800. 4. Knowledge,
Theory of—Early works to 1800. I. Heffernan, George.
II. Title. III. Title: Meditationes de prima philosophia.
B1853.E5H44 1990
194—dc20   89-40751

Meinen Kollegen,
den Mitgliedern des Philosophischen Seminars
der Université de Notre Dame du Lac,
gewidmet:
Denn was könnte unwissender sein als zu glauben,
man wisse das, was man nicht weiß?
Und was könnte unphilosophischer sein als zu meinen,
man sei philosophisch, wenn man es nicht ist?

CONTENTS

Introduction to René Descartes'
Meditationes de prima philosophia

Descartes' Youth, Education and Early Years

René Descartes, the celebrated "Continental rationalist" and arguably the very first philosopher to try to realize the ideal of epistemic foundationalism by grounding the theory of "rationality" rigorously and systematically in the notion of "evidence", was born on March 31, and baptized on April 3, 1596, at La Haye (now "Descartes"), near Tours, France. Although he had the advantage of being born into an old and well-established family — his father Joachim, for example, was a parliamentary counsellor at Rennes —, so that he would never have to earn a living, he also had the disadvantage of having shaky health as a child — as a student at La Flèche, for example, he was to receive special permission to "lie in" until quite late in the day —, so that he would later report that doctors did not even expect him to live long enough to reach adulthood.

While the exact dates are not known with any real reliability, Descartes attended the Jesuit "Collège Royal" at La Flèche in Anjou from 1606 to, probably, 1614, motivated by, as he would put it in the *Discours de la méthode*, the desire to acquire "a clear and assured knowledge of all that which is useful for life" ("une connaissance claire et assurée de tout ce qui est utile à la vie" [I, § 6]). In the "First Part" of the *Discours*,

1

which also contains a highly interesting 'portrait of the philosopher as a young man', Descartes praised the school itself as "l'une des plus célèbres écoles de l'Europe" (§ 6), yet blamed some of the things that he claimed to have learned there, including "that philosophy provides the means to speak seemingly truly about all things and to let oneself be admired by the less wise" ("que la philosophie donne moyen de parler vraisemblablement de toutes choses, et se faire admirer des moins savants" [§ 7]). It was at La Flèche, by the way, that Descartes also acquired that proficiency in the Latin language which was later to make it possible for him to write his major philosophical works in that medium, that is, the *Regulae ad directionem ingenii,* the *Meditationes de prima philosophia* and the *Principia philosophiae.*

One event in particular cannot but have made a deep impression on the young Descartes during his schooldays at La Flèche. For the "Collège" had been founded in 1603/04 by King Henry IV of France (1589–1610 [a convert to Catholicism {1593}]), who on April 13, 1598, had issued the Edict of Nantes, thereby giving the Huguenots (French Protestants) equal political rights with the Catholics, but by no means guaranteeing them unqualified freedom of religious worship. On May 14, 1610, Henry was assassinated by a fanatical Catholic. On June 4 of that year the dead King's heart was ritually transferred to the college at La Flèche. On June 6, 1611, there were ceremonies at the school commemorating the anniversary of that occasion. In that connection there took place the recitation of a memorable poem — "On the Death of King Henry and on the Discovery of some New Planets or Stars Revolving around Jupiter, made the previous Year by Galileo . . ." — marking both the death of the Founding King and some of the astronomical advances of Galileo Galilei (1564–1642), who in 1610 had published *Sidereus nuncius* ("*The Starry Messenger*"), recording his discovery of four satellites revolving around the planet Jupiter. Already the signs seemed to indicate that Descartes would live during a time of substantial religious as well

as scientific — and that meant philosophical — change and, *maybe*, even of progress. But at the time one just could not yet know whether, as there had been a Renaissance and a Reformation, there would also be an Enlightenment, that is, an Age of Reason.

To conclude his formal education Descartes took a *baccalauréat* as well as a *licence* in law at the University of Poitiers (November 9–10, 1616). One of the most important things that Descartes appears to have learned during his academic education, however, was precisely the lesson expressed by Seneca's ironic remark that "non vitae, sed scholae discimus" (*Epistulae ad Lucilium*, CVI, 12). Disillusioned by theoretical studies to the point of despairing of the originally sought "clear and assured knowledge" — ". . . de penser qu'il n'y avait aucune doctrine dans le monde qui fût telle qu'on m'avait auparavant fait espérer . . ." (*Discours*, I, § 6) —, and resolving henceforth to turn his attention to himself and to the world in order to find such knowledge — ". . . de ne chercher plus d'autre science que celle qui se pourrait trouver en moi-même, ou bien dans le grand livre du monde . . ." (*ibid.*, § 14) —, he left France and embarked on his travels in 1618. The first place he went was Holland, where he became acquainted with the respected mathematician Isaac Beeckman, who got him interested in mathematical as well as in scientific and philosophical matters.

There Descartes also composed his first work, a short treatise on music, namely, the *Compendium musicae* (December, 1618), which remained unpublished during his lifetime.

Descartes' Dreams and Philosophical Mission

Now this was the time of The Thirty Years' War (1618–1648 [cf. *Discours*, II, § 1: ". . . l'occasion des guerres qui n'y sont pas encore finies . . ."]), and the Catholic Descartes, still in Holland, first joined the forces of Prince Maurice of Nassau (he did so under an assumed name, "M. du Perron", "Perron"

being the name of a small fief that he owned in Poitou). But then, having traveled to Germany, Descartes was associated with the army of Duke Maximilian I of Bavaria. In 1619 he went to Frankfurt to attend the coronation of King Ferdinand of Bohemia as *Kaiser* Ferdinand II of the *Heiliges Römisches Reich Deutscher Nation* (August 28). The official festivities of this occasion lasted from July 20 to September 9. Upon trying to return to Bavaria, he found himself held up by the bad weather of the approaching winter, and on November 10 he was staying in the now famous *poêle* or "stove-heated room" somewhere, probably, in the vicinity of Ulm on the Danube River (cf. *Discours*, II, § 1: "J'étais alors en Allemagne . . ."; cf. *ibid.*, III, § 6) — with no one and nothing between himself and his *pensées* (*ibid.*).

It was then and there that Descartes had a vision of a new mathematical, scientific and philosophical system. According to his biographer, Adrien Baillet (*La vie de Monsieur Des-Cartes* [Paris: Horthemels, 1691; Hildesheim: Olms, 1972 {Photographic Reprint}], Book I, Chapter 1 [supposedly based on material from Descartes' early notebooks]), Descartes had — following a day of very intense philosophical meditation which left him in a state of great mental agitation (". . . j'étais rempli d'enthousiasme . . .") — three consecutive dreams in one night (November 10–11), dreams that he regarded as having been sent by God and that he would understand as having bestowed a sense of philosophical mission on his life. While the details of the dreams are not unimportant, let it suffice here and now to note that the question that was put to Descartes in the dreams — more precisely, in the last one — was: "Quod vitae sectabor iter?" ("What way of life shall I follow?") The same dream provided its own answer, to wit: "Est et non." ("It is and it is not.") Descartes interpreted the question as being one concerning what ought to be the "occupation" of his own future life, and the answer as being that he ought to pursue truth and to avoid falsity in the sciences: ". . . je pensai que je ne pouvais mieux que de continuer en celle-là même où je me trou-

vais, c'est-à-dire, que d'employer toute ma vie à cultiver ma raison, et m'avancer, autant que je pourrais, en la connaissance de la vérité . . ." (*Discours*, III, § 5; cf. *ibid.*, I, § 3 ["la recherche de la vérité"]). Having made a vow in connection with his three dreams, Descartes probably fulfilled it by going to Italy and making a pilgrimage to the shrine of the Virgin at Loretto sometime during the next few years.

Return to France and Years in Paris: Descartes and Mersenne

Having left the military, Descartes returned to France in 1622, spending some time during the years immediately following in Paris, but also traveling extensively in Germany, Holland and Italy (remaining in the latter country from September, 1623, to May, 1625). From 1625 to 1627 Descartes lived in Paris and was involved in various circles literary and learned. It was then and there that Friar Marin Mersenne, a Franciscan (1588–1648), was one of his intimates. When Descartes moved from France to Holland at the end of the decade 1620–1630, Mersenne was to function as a kind of 'philosophical agent' for him, corresponding with him on philosophical topics, acting as an intermediary between him and other philosophers and helping him to get his works published and recognized — for example, the *Meditations on First Philosophy*.

The *Regulae ad directionem ingenii*

Toward the end of that decade, in the years 1627–1628, Descartes was writing his first important work, the *Regulae ad directionem ingenii* or *Rules for the Direction of the Mind* (*Oeuvres de Descartes*, Vol. X, pp. 359–469), a text whose basic program consists of extending geometrical algebra into a *sapientia universalis* ("universal wisdom") capable of encompassing all of the sciences. Anticipating the foundationalist preoccu-

pation with the connection between evidence, on the one hand, and truth, on the other hand, which would come to be so characteristic of his later writings, the author of the *Regulae* defines "scientia" ("knowledge in the strict sense of 'science' ") as "cognitio certa et *evidens*" ("certain and *evident* cognition" [emphasis added]) and proposes that one believe only those things which are "perfectly known and cannot be doubted" (*Regulae*, II, § 1). While it was, among other things, Descartes' interest in exploring new ways of knowing such as "intuitus" ("intuition" [cf. *Regulae*, III, §§ 4–5 ff., etc.]) and "inductio" ("induction" [cf. *ibid.*, VII, §§ 4–5, 7, XI, § 2, etc.]) — which had been relatively neglected due to the traditional Scholastic preference for the "deductio" ("deduction") more fitting both to the "disputatio" ("disputation") of the *quaestiones disputatae* or *quaestiones quodlibetales* and to the "interpretatio" ("interpretation") of the textual commentaries (Francis Bacon [1561–1626] had just published the *Instauratio magna* [1605], Vol. II of which was the *Novum organum* [1620], Bk. II of which *organon*, in turn, introduced the new method of induction into the explanation of nature) — that motivated his concern with the problem of evidence, this topic did remain, nonetheless, rather underdeveloped in this work; for example, the turn of phrase "clare et distincte intellegere" ("to intellect clearly and distinctly") — which explicitly and thematically lets "clarity" and "distinctness" as dyadic modes of evidence occur together as members of a pair and which was later to become the standard Cartesian terminology — is to be found at only a single *locus* therein (*Regulae*, XI, § 2). Indeed, the *Regulae* were kept remarkably free of those very features which would come to be regarded as peculiarly characteristic of the fully developed Cartesian position on the relationship between evidence and truth. First and foremost lacking in this early work is in particular perhaps the view that it would turn out to be God who would have to fulfill the epistemic function of guaranteeing the universality and necessity of the connection between the clarity and distinctness of perceptions, on the one hand, and the certainty of them, on

the other hand (on *Deus* in the *Regulae*, see III, § 9, XII, §§ 17 and 20 [?], and XIV, § 1).

In the fall of 1628 Descartes visited Holland — seeing, for example, Beeckman at Dordrecht —, and in the spring of 1629 he took up permanent residence in Franeker (later Amsterdam and then Leiden) in the same country, where no later than the winter of 1628–1629 he formulated the "last" version of the *Rules for the Direction of the Mind*. The *Rules* were neither completed (only 21 of the projected 36 *regulae* are given [cf. *Regulae*, VIII, § 7, and XII, § 27]) nor ever published during his lifetime.

"The Hidden Life" in Holland: Scholarly Interests in Physiology and Anatomy

During the early years of the decade 1630–1640 Descartes visited various universities in Holland and thus made the acquaintance of many distinguished mathematicians, doctors of medicine and philosophers. One of his most highly cultivated interests became the study of physiology and anatomy. Indeed, for a while he resided in the Kalverstraat — that is, the "street of calves" — (Amsterdam), where he could both regularly witness the activity of the butchers and purchase as many animal carcasses as he needed for the dissections that he deemed indispensable to his scientific investigations. The result was a firsthand knowledge of the phenomena which could never have been gained by reading books on the subjects — although he did not at all neglect to study what Vesalius (e.g., *De humani corporis fabrica libri septem* [1543]) and other leading researchers in the field had written on these topics — as well as a firm conviction that any and every theory about such matters ultimately had to be confirmed by experience and experiment before it could ever have any chance at all of being regarded as true. Of course, some people were so resentful of his 'hands on' approach to the things themselves that they found fault with his activi-

ties by accusing him of "going through the villages to see pigs killed" (cf. Baillet, *La vie de Descartes*, I, pp. 196–197).

Descartes would live in Holland until 1649 and change his address frequently. The relatively tolerant intellectual atmosphere of the Protestant country may have motivated the former, and the desire for the tranquility and solitude of the withdrawn life, the latter. Indeed, all indications are that Descartes desired very much to live, as a matter of habit, according to the motto "Bene vixit, qui bene latuit.", in other words, "(S)he has lived well, who has been hidden well." (See "Letter to Mersenne" [April {?}, 1634]. The *locus classicus* for the saying appears to be Ovid's *Tristitiae*, 3, 4, 25; the reference to Epicurus' maxim "Lathe biosas." or "Live hiddenly." is obvious [see H. Usener, *Epicurea*, Fragment 551].) For Descartes, in any case, philosophy always seemed to remain something that he himself preferred to do essentially alone (cf., e.g., *Discours*, II, § 1 [". . . seul . . ."] ff., *Meditationes*, I, § 1 [". . . solus secedo . . ."], III, § 1 [". . . meque solum alloquendo . . ."] ff., etc.).

"*Le Traité du monde*"

Already by 1629 Descartes' interests in mathematics, science and philosophy had led him to form the idea for a comprehensive treatise which "instead of explaining only one phenomenon" would "explain all of the phenomena of nature — that is, all of physics" ("Letter to Mersenne" [November 13, 1629]). In other words, his intention was to develop a cosmology founded on a physics of such universal validity that it could explain things as apparently diverse as inanimate objects and human beings. By 1633 Descartes was ready to publish the whole work, only parts of which, namely, the beginning — *Le monde ou le Traité de la lumière*, that is, *The World or The Treatise on Light* (*Oeuvres de Descartes*, Vol. XI, pp. 3 ff.) — and the end — *Le Traité de l'homme*, that is, *The Treatise on the Human Being* (*ibid.*, pp. 119 ff.) —, have survived, under the title "*Le*

Traité du monde", that is, *The Treatise on the World*. (The last section, by the way, incomplete physiological essay that it would remain, represented the very first scholarly attempt to explain the functions of the human body in a thoroughly and explicitly materialistic and mechanistic manner.) However, the formal condemnation of Galileo by the Inquisition in Rome (June 22, 1633) for that scientist's having adduced evidence in the *Dialogo sopra i due massimi sistemi del mondo, ptolemaico e copernicano* (1632) for the superiority of the Copernican over the Aristotelian-Ptolemaic *Weltbild* — more precisely, for having argued that the earth moves both by rotating on its axis and by revolving around the sun — caused Descartes, consistent with the extremely prudential *maximes* of his "provisional morality" based on obedience to the authority of the Church and of the State (cf. the "morale par provision" of *Discours*, III, § 1 ff. [especially § 2: "La première était d'obéir aux lois et aux coutumes de mon pays, retenant constamment la religion en laquelle Dieu m'a fait la grâce d'être instruit dès mon enfance, et me gouvernant, en toute autre chose, suivant les opinions les plus modérées, et les plus éloignées de l'excès, qui fussent communément reçues en pratique par les mieux sensés de ceux avec lesquels j'aurais à vivre."]), to defer to "personnes, . . . dont l'autorité ne peut guère moins sur mes actions que ma propre raison sur mes pensées" (*Discours*, VI, § 1), that is, to the 'powers that were', by deciding to abandon plans to publish *The World*. After all, one of the very things that Descartes himself had explained in the *traité* was nothing other than the doctrine of the movement of the earth. Although *Le monde* was then never published in his lifetime, something of a summary of certain parts of it can be found in the "Fifth Part" of the *Discours* (to which compare especially William Harvey's [1578–1657] *Exercitatio anatomica de motu cordis et sanguinis in animalibus* . . . [1628] and *Exercitationes duae anatomicae de circulatione sanguinis* . . . [1649]).

The *Discours de la méthode*

Yet in his commitment to the theoretical life as being the happy life Descartes was nothing if not "resolute" (cf. *Discours*, III, § 3: "Ma seconde maxime était d'être le plus ferme et le plus résolu en mes actions que je pourrais, et de ne suivre pas moins constamment les opinions les plus douteuses, lorsque je m'y serais une fois déterminé, que si elles eussent été très assurées."), and on June 8, 1637, he published — for reasons that are best set forth in the "Sixth Part" of the same (i.e., he could not have kept his thoughts on 'la recherche et la connaissance de la nature' or on "la physique" ['research in physics'] secret without violating the law concerning the common good of humanity ["sans pécher grandement contre la loi qui nous oblige à procurer, autant qu'il est en nous, le bien général de tous les hommes" {§ 2; cf. §§ 3–4}]) — his first work, the *Discours de la méthode pour bien conduire sa raison, et chercher la vérité dans les sciences* or *Discourse on the Method of rightly Conducting one's Reason and of Seeking the Truth in the Sciences* (the correctly abbreviated English title of which can *only* be "*Discourse on THE Method*" [*Oeuvres de Descartes*, Vol. VI, pp. 1–78]), that modern masterpiece of self-effacement and dissemblance, together with *La dioptrique* or *The Optics* (investigating the principles of refraction [*ibid.*, pp. 81–228]), *Les météores* or *The Meteorology* (including less controversial material from *Le monde* on such topics as rainbows [*ibid.*, pp. 231–366 ff.]) and *La géométrie* or *The Geometry* (laying the foundations for analytic geometry [*ibid.*, pp. 369–485 ff.]). One might describe the "dessein" (*Discours*, I, § 5) of the methodological introduction as being, in general, a protreptic — in other words, an exhortation to the reader to do philosophy — and as expressing, in particular, the demand that 'les hommes de bon sens ou de la raison' or 'the human beings of good sense or of reason' (cf. *ibid.*, I, § 1 ff., II, § 1, etc.), to whom it is addressed, do natural philosophy by applying "la lumière naturelle" (I, § 15) or "la raison naturelle" (VI, § 11) to the study

of "the book of nature" (cf. Galileo, *Il saggiatore* [1623]: nature or the universe apprehended as a text "written in the language of mathematics") and, especially, by engaging in observations and performing experiments ("expériences": cf. *Discours*, VI, almost *passim*, especially § 8 [". . . à cause d'une infinité d'expériences dont j'ai besoin . . ."]) in order to explicate "the grand book of the universe" — instead of merely trying to interpret it as it was "understood" (*lucus a non lucendo*) in, and filtered through, the great books of the ancients. This periagogical intention of the *Discours* also helps to explain, incidentally, why the author chose to write it not in Latin, but rather in French (it was, after all, at that time highly unusual to do philosophy "en langue vulgaire"): "Et si j'écris en français, qui est la langue de mon pays, plutôt qu'en latin, qui est celle de mes précepteurs, c'est à cause que j'espère que ceux qui ne se servent que de leur raison naturelle toute pure, jugeront mieux de mes opinions, que ceux qui ne croient qu'aux livres anciens." (VI, § 11)

The Rules Regulating the Relationship between Evidence and Truth

As far as philosophy has been concerned, of course, the methodological considerations contained in the *Discours de la méthode* — presented not as a *traité* ("Letter to Mersenne" [March {?}, 1637]), but rather only "comme une histoire . . . ou . . . comme une fable" (*Discours*, I, § 5) — turned out to be much more important than the "specimen essays" ("Qui sont des essais de cette méthode"). The author of the *Discours*, seeing the lack of progress in past philosophy, that is, "qu'elle [philosophy] a été cultivée par les plus excellents esprits qui aient vécu depuis plusieurs siècles, et que néanmoins il ne s'y trouve encore aucune chose dont on ne dispute, et par conséquent qui ne soit douteuse" (I, § 12), rendered a devastating judgment on "la philosophie" of his time (*ibid.*): ". . . je réputais presque pour faux tout ce qui n'était que

vraisemblable." In other words, "philosophy" had become anything and everything other than "science" as defined as "certain and evident knowledge" by the author of the *Regulae*. In
addition, due to the foundational function of philosophy in relation to the other sciences, the condition of the latter could
not possibly be any better than that of the former: "Puis, pour
les autres sciences, d'autant qu'elles empruntent leurs principes
de la philosophie, je jugeais qu'on ne pouvait avoir rien bâti,
qui fût solide, sur des fondements si peu fermes." (*Discours*,
I, § 13) Taking as his model those things which he regarded
as representing the best aspects of three arts or sciences, namely, logic, geometrical analysis and algebra (*Discours*, II, § 6),
Descartes proposed to reform philosophy (cf. *ibid.*, II, §§ 1–3)
by refashioning it into a rigorously *regulated* (i.e., rule-governed)
activity which would be capable of resulting in correspondingly rigorously *regulated* and, therefore, true propositions —
given, of course, sound foundations of the deepest sort (on "les
fondements" see *ibid.*, II, § 2, IV, § 1, etc.).

As a matter of fact, the task of finding a foundation for
knowledge which could be so epistemically basic that it would
not make any sense to demand something even more fundamental than it is almost as old as Western philosophy itself. Already
in the *Politeia*, for example, Plato lets the interlocuters engage
in a dialogue about, *inter alia*, the supposedly presupposition-
less beginning of all knowledge, which is ultimately not evidence (since there was no Greek word for it, one resorted to
light as a metaphor for evidence [cf. 506 e–509 c {"The Image
of the Sun"}]), but rather "the Good" or "the idea of the Good"
(cf. 509 d–511 e ["The Image of the Line"]). Accompanied by
certain tropes of his own — for example, "the Good" or "the
form of the Good" gets replaced by God —, Descartes stands
firmly in this tradition.

Accordingly, in the "Second Part" of the *Discours* are presented certain rules, more exactly, "les principales règles de la
méthode" which the author claims to (have) follow(ed) in "correctly conducting the reason and investigating the truth in the

sciences" (cf. *Discours*, 'Introductory Remarks', and *Meditationes*, "Praefatio ad lectorem", § 1), these rules being four in number (cf. §§ 7–10): "Le premier [i.e., la première règle] était de ne recevoir jamais aucune chose pour vraie, que je ne la connusse évidemment être telle: c'est-à-dire d'éviter soigneusement la précipitation et la prévention; et de ne comprendre rien de plus en mes jugements, que ce qui se présenterait si clairement et si distinctement à mon esprit, que je n'eusse aucune occasion de le mettre en doute." (See *ibid.*, § 7; the second rule has to do with division, the third with order and the fourth with enumeration.) In other words, this first rule — never to accept anything as true that one does not evidently know to be such, that is, never to include anything in one's judgments that would not present itself so clearly and so distinctly that it could not be doubted — intimately links evidence, knowledge and truth. Thus it has also usually been taken without very much doubt to be the most important rule that Descartes ever formulated. After all, what is, for example, "le premier principe de la philosophie" being sought by Descartes, to wit, ". . . *je pense, donc je suis* . . ." (*ibid.*, IV, § 1 [cf. § 3]; cf. *Meditationes de prima philosophia*, II, § 3 [". . . *ego sum, ego existo* . . ."], § 6 [". . . ego sum, ego existo . . ."], III, § 9, etc., and *Principia philosophiae*, I, § 7 [". . . *ego cogito, ergo sum* . . ."], § 10 [". . . *ego cogito, ergo sum* . . ."], etc.), other than a judgment expressing a fact which is so clearly and distinctly perceived, or so evidently intuited, that it is absolutely impossible to doubt the truth of it?

Ay, there's the rub, for this supposedly self-sufficient first principle of Descartes' new system of philosophy really does nothing more than to represent a particular instance of a universal phenomenon, and it is actually the latter — thematized in the midst of the "premières méditations . . . métaphysiques" (IV, § 1) of the "Fourth Part" on the existence of God and of the human soul as "les fondements de sa métaphysique" ('Introductory Remarks') — much more than the former which ought to command the epistemic interest of the reader as well as, for that

matter, of the author of the *Discours*: "Après cela, je considér-
ai en général ce qui est requis à une proposition pour être vraie
et certaine; car, puisque je venais d'en trouver une que je savais
être telle, je pensai que je devais aussi savoir en quoi consiste
cette certitude. Et ayant remarqué qu'il n'y a rien du tout en
ceci: *je pense, donc je suis*, qui m'assure que je dis la vérité,
sinon que je vois très clairement que, pour penser, il faut être:
je jugeai que je pouvais prendre pour *règle générale* [this emphasis added], que les choses que nous concevons fort clairement et fort distinctement, sont toutes vraies; mais qu'il y a seule-
ment quelque difficulté à bien remarquer quelles sont celles que
nous concevons distinctement." (IV, § 3) In other words, "a
general rule" is set up expressing the possibility of making an
inference from a past or present experience of a relationship
between *clarity and distinctness* and *certainty* in one given case
to future experiences of the connection between *evidence* and
truth in many — indeed, in all — other cases. (One notes, in
passing, that Descartes himself does not really seem to appreciate
fully the subtlety of the problem of induction with which he
is here being confronted. For the question is whether, respectively, how one can justifiably infer from the accepted fact that
clarity and distinctness here and now assure certainty in *this*
case in particular to the supposed fact that evidence would always and everywhere insure truth in *all* cases in general.) Now
part of what the passage just quoted means is that the most important rule to be formulated in the *Discours* is not at all *la
première règle de la méthode* of the "Second Part" of that writing. As a matter of fact, the truly crucial epistemic rule is not
even mentioned, let alone laid down in any canonical way, in
that part of the book. On the contrary, while the normative
rule of the method of the "Second Part" says that one should
resolve never to accept anything as true that one would not evidently know to be so or that one should resolve never to judge
about anything that would not present itself so clearly and so
distinctly that there could be no doubt about it, the descriptive
rule governing the relationship between evidence, on the one

hand, and truth, on the other hand, of the "Fourth Part" says something significantly different, to wit, that the things which one perceives very clearly and very distinctly are all true in the sense — to anticipate what will follow — that they *must necessarily* be true and *cannot possibly* be false. (It would seem to go hand in hand with this distinction that neither the fact that *Je pense, donc je suis.* nor the proposition that "*Je pense, donc je suis.*" is meant to provide *the primary and ultimate foundation* for Descartes' philosophy, for the evidence itself by means of which one intuits that from the fact that "I [am] think[ing]" it follows and, therefore, can be inferred that "I am" has to be epistemically more basic than the mere obtaining of the state of affairs or the truth of the judgment. That is, for the consistent and consequent foundationalist — i.e., for someone like Descartes — , if the inference is supposed to be validated by evidence, then the question quickly becomes: But what validates the evidence itself, e.g., what guarantees that it is genuine and not deceptive? [On this remark cf., e.g., *Meditationes*, III, § 9, where the "lumen naturale" {"natural light"} is explicitly described as being more epistemically basic than the *cogito* itself.]) As far as the relationship between the two rules is concerned, moreover, it is surely the case that neither "the general rule of truth" — as it will be called in the *Meditationes* — would follow from the methodological rule or procedural recommendation, nor *vice versa*.

Furthermore, the distinction between the first rule of the method and the general rule of evidence and truth was so obvious to Descartes himself that he was even convinced that he had to go so far as to offer the reader some kind of justification for the posited universal and necessary connection between clarity and distinctness, on the one hand, and truth, on the other hand — which he did then try to do in the following way (emphasis added): "*Car, premièrement, cela même que j'ai tantôt pris pour une règle, à savoir que les choses que nous concevons très clairement et très distinctement, sont toutes vraies, n'est assuré qu'à cause que Dieu est ou existe, et qu'il est un être*

parfait, et que tout ce qui est en nous vient de lui. D'où il suit que nos idées ou notions, étant des choses réelles, et qui viennent de Dieu, en tout ce en quoi elles sont claires et distinctes, ne peuvent en cela être que vraies. En sorte que, si nous en avons assez souvent qui contiennent de la fausseté, ce ne peut être que de celles qui ont quelque chose de confus et obscur, à cause qu'en cela elles participent du néant, c'est-à-dire, qu'elles ne sont en nous ainsi confuses, qu'à cause que nous ne sommes pas tout parfaits. *Et il est évident qu'il n'y a pas moins de répugnance que la fausseté ou l'imperfection procède de Dieu, en tant que telle, qu'il y en a que la vérité ou la perfection procède du néant. Mais si nous ne savions point que tout ce qui est en nous de réel et de vrai, vient d'un être parfait et infini, pour claires et distinctes que fussent nos idées, nous n'aurions aucune raison qui nous assurât qu'elles eussent la perfection d'être vraies.*" (*Discours*, IV, § 7) In other words, what is supposed to assure human and, therefore, imperfect beings that their clear and distinct perceptions are veridical, in the sense that the truth of ideas is understood to be one of these ideas' perfections, is the alleged fact that they have these, as they have everything else that they have, from God, who is supposed to be a perfect being. On the other hand, it would be contradictory to think of falsity or imperfection, as such, as coming from God. For Descartes, then, God, who is epistemically more basic than, because the source of, light or evidence (cf. *Meditationes*, IV, § 13, VI, § 15, etc. [he too employs light as a metaphor for evidence, the word "evidentia" occurring, as it does, *only a single time* in this work {*Oeuvres de Descartes*, Vol. VII, p. 4}]), is, in a certain sense, supposed to play pretty much the same epistemic role that "the Good", which was epistemically more basic than, because the source of, light ("evidence"), was meant to do for Plato in his account of the reliability of the claim of what purports to be knowledge really to be such.

The Problem of "The Cartesian Circle"

Naturally it would only be a matter of time before the more systematic version of this position would cause readers of the *Meditationes* to object that Descartes is here arguing in a circle, viz., by first making use of certain clear and distinct ideas or perceptions in particular to attempt to establish the truth of the claim that God exists, and by then turning around and appealing to God to try to substantiate the claim that all clear and distinct ideas or perceptions in general are true (where "first" and "then" are to be understood first and foremost not temporally, but rather logically) — after all, who would there be to guarantee the truth of those clear and distinct ideas or perceptions which one needs in order 'to reach God' epistemically in the first place? At least this seems to be one of the more commonly accepted ways of stating the supposed problem of "the Cartesian circle". It should be obvious to everyone, by the way, that there is indeed a circle here. Actually, the only serious question can be whether it is a *circulus vitiosus* or a merely benign one. Even nowadays, because it is easily and often forgotten that Descartes was not only "the father of modern philosophy", but also "the child of medieval philosophy", it is not generally appreciated that and how he could simultaneously have been with respect to things epistemic so enlightened as to wonder about an answer to the question concerning the connection between evidence and truth, yet so unenlightened as to want to explain this connection by calling — quite literally — for the *deus ex machina* in appealing to God as the one who would guarantee that whatever one perceives clearly and distinctly must necessarily be true and cannot possibly be false.

Yet again, maybe a very good way — but still one which has never yet been tried — to articulate the acuteness of "the Cartesian circle" would be to use the judicial case that Kant employs in order to point out where the "Zirkel" ("circle") in one version of the correspondence theory of truth lies (he is *not* talking about Descartes here): ". . . es verhalte sich mit jener

Erklärung der Wahrheit eben so, wie wenn jemand vor Gericht
eine Aussage tue und sich dabei auf einen Zeugen berufe, den
niemand kenne, der sich aber dadurch glaubwürdig machen
wolle, daß er behaupte, der, welcher ihn zum Zeugen auf-
gerufen, sei ein ehrlicher Mann." (*Immanuel Kant's Logik. Ein
Handbuch zu Vorlesungen* [*Akademie-Ausgabe*, Vol. IX], p.
50) In other words, it is as if someone would give testimony
in court and in doing so would appeal to a witness whom no-
body would know but who would want to make himself credible by asserting that the one who called him to witness were
an honest man. *Mutatis mutandis*, Descartes would be the one
testifying and his God would be the witness. Wryly remarking
that "the accusation was indeed founded", Kant says that it is
"impossible" for any "human being" to solve the problem
represented here (*ibid.*). One reason why the example illustrates
the difficulty so nicely is that — and this is a fact which is not
generally recognized — there are certain profound things which
evidence as a legal phenomenon and evidence as an epistemic
phenomenon have in common.

   Finally, quite regardless of an answer to the question as to
whether the Cartesian circle is a vicious one or not, there can
be no doubt that, in letting the connection between evidence,
on the one hand, and truth, on the other hand, hang by the
threateningly thin thread of the *veracitas Dei*, the Cartesian kind
of foundationalism commits the epistemically countersensical
mistake of trying to found the validity of evidence on or to
ground it in something — or, better, someone — other than
evidence itself while the whole time not adequately attending
to the fact that, whatever — or, again, whoever — else this might
be, he, she or it would himself, herself or itself have to be given,
respectively, had in evidence. In other words, the Cartesian foundationalist's self-imposed dilemma is to find a foundation for
evidence, which foundation would not itself be evidence — and
to be sure, in the face of the critique which might argue that
there neither is nor can be any other way to validate evidence
except by appealing to other, more and better evidence.

In any case, a considerable difference between the epistemic position of the *Regulae* and that of the *Discours* lies in the fact that, whereas in the former clarity and distinctness as members of a pair of evidence concepts play no systematic role in the truth problematic, in the latter clarity and distinctness function as criteria of truth in connection with the *veracitas Dei*. Still, even in the *Discours* Descartes — despite his acute awareness of the necessity of providing a justification for the general rule of evidence and truth — does not (certainly not *expressis verbis*) claim to try "to demonstrate", that is, "to prove", the validity of that rule.

Descartes' Family

From 1638 to 1640 Descartes lived mainly in the countryside of northern Holland (near Santpoort), primarily because he could better pursue "the search for truth in the sciences" there than in, for example, "the air of Paris" with its "innumerable distractions" ("Letter to Mersenne" [May 17, 1638]). But although he preferred a philosophical life of solitude, Descartes did not always remain absolutely alone in his personal life. For while living in the city of Amsterdam he had entered into a relationship with his servant, Hélène, and together they had had a baby daughter, Francine (conceived on October 15, 1634 [according to a note of her father], born on July 19, 1635, and baptized [in the Reformed Church] on August 7 of that year); they now came to live with him. It appears that Descartes intended to let his daughter be educated in France, but the girl fell ill and then died of a fever on September 7, 1640. Again according to his biographer, this represented the heaviest loss of Descartes' entire life (cf. *Baillet, La vie de Descartes*, II, pp. 89 f.; his father died on October 17 of the same year [his mother had died while he was still an infant {on May 13, 1597}]). On the other hand, there is no evidence that this experience caused any significant interruption of his philosophizing — something easier to understand when seen in the light of one (an obvious-

ly Stoic one) of the principles of practical reason set down in the "Third Part" of the *Discours* (§ 4): "Ma troisième maxime était de tâcher toujours plutôt à me vaincre que la fortune, et à changer mes désirs que l'ordre du monde; et généralement, de m'accoutumer à croire qu'il n'y a rien qui soit entièrement en notre pouvoir, que nos pensées, en sorte qu'après que nous avons fait notre mieux, touchant les choses qui nous sont extérieures, tout ce qui manque de nous réussir est, au regard de nous, absolument impossible." In other words, one ought to accustom oneself to the fact that only one's own thoughts, but never, however, the vagaries of fortune, are under one's own control.

The *Meditationes de prima philosophia*

It was just in these years, from 1638 to 1640, that Descartes wrote what turned out to be both his *magnum opus* and — arguably — the most celebrated work of early modern philosophy, namely, the *Meditationes de prima philosophia* or *Meditations on First Philosophy* (completed by April, 1640).

As far as one can tell, the *Meditationes* trace their beginnings back to a small "Traité de métaphysique", now lost, which dealt with the acquisition of the knowledge of God and of the self as the only way to discover the foundations of physics and on which Descartes worked during the first nine months of his stay in Holland in 1629 ("Letter to Mersenne" [April 15, 1630]; cf. "Letter to Mersenne" [November 25, 1630]). One might take the "Fourth Part" of the *Discours* of 1637 to represent a report on the content of the "Traité". Then, from before November, 1639, to March, 1640, Descartes was writing an "Essai de métaphysique" (cf., e.g., "Letter to Mersenne" [November 13, 1639] and "Letter to Mersenne" [March 11, 1640]) expanding on this part of the *Discours* (cf. *Meditationes*, "Praefatio ad lectorem", § 1), which gradually became much closer in size to the *Meditationes* than to that section of that work. Originally Descartes had even referred to the new composition as

the "Metaphysics", but it was eventually decided that "the most fitting title is '*Meditations on First Philosophy*', because the discussion is not restricted to God and the soul, but rather treats of all those first things in general which are to be discovered by philosophizing." ("Letter to Mersenne" [November 11, 1640]) Indeed, the revisions of the titles of the individual "Meditationes" which were sent by Descartes to Mersenne (cf. "Letter to Mersenne" [January 28, 1641]) indicate that the 'original' headings patently displayed the character of the *Meditationes* as a work *both* on metaphysics or "first philosophy" *and* on mathematics and physics (cf. Aristotle, *Metaphysics*, 1004 a 1 ff., 1026 a 20 ff., etc.).

In 1641 the first edition of the *Meditationes de prima philosophia* (*Oeuvres de Descartes*, Vol. VII, pp. 1–90), together with the first six sets of *Objectiones et responsiones* or *Objections and Responses* (*ibid.*, pp. 91–447), was published in Paris by Michael Soly (August 28). This edition carried the subtitle "In qua Dei existentia et animae immortalitas demonstratur" ("In which the Existence of God and the Immortality of the Soul are Demonstrated" [formally-grammatically, "qua" {"qui, quae, quod"} is here feminine, singular and ablative, so it refers unambiguously not to "Meditationes" {plural}, but rather to "prima philosophia" {singular}]). Due to some disappointment on Descartes' part with the original publisher the second edition of the *Meditationes*, together with all seven sets of the *Objectiones et responsiones* (*ibid.*, pp. 91–561) and the *Epistola ad P. Dinet* or *Letter to Father Dinet* (*ibid.*, pp. 563–603), was published in 1642 in Amsterdam by Louis Elzevir (containing some minor corrections of the text of the first edition, so that the text of the second edition has established itself as the standard one). This edition bore the more accurate subtitle "In quibus Dei existentia, et animae humanae à corpore distinctio, demonstrantur" ("In which the Existence of God and the Distinction of the Human Soul from the Body are Demonstrated" [here the "which" is plural {"quibus"}, so it refers, again unambiguously, not to "prima philosophia", but rather to "Medita-

tiones"]). On the relationship between the real distinction of the soul and of the mind from the body, on the one hand, and the immortality of the soul and of the mind, on the other hand, the reader should consult especially what Descartes says about Meditations II and VI in the "Synopsis sex sequentium Meditationum" ("Synopsis of the following six Meditations") — which precedes the actual *Meditationes* themselves and which contains philosophically valuable overviews of what is mainly supposed to happen in each one of them. The *Meditationes* proper were introduced by, in addition, both a so called 'Dedicatory Epistle' addressed (to) "Sapientissimis Clarissimisque Viris Sacrae Facultatis Theologiae Parisiensis Decano & Doctoribus . . ." ("To those Most Wise and Distinguished Men, the Dean and Doctors of the Sacred Faculty of Theology at Paris"), in which Descartes almost obsequiously solicited their care, patronage and defence for his teachings by doing his best to let the work seem to be first and foremost one by a "Christian philosopher" (§ 3 [". . . Christianis Philosophis . . ."]) and, thus, of a Christian apologetic nature (without, however, ever receiving the so eagerly sought "Approbation of the Doctors" after all [compare the title-pages of the editions with each other]), and a "Praefatio ad Lectorem" ("Preface to the Reader"), in which he spoke principally to certain objections that had been raised against his position on the nature or essence of the human mind as consisting only in its being a thinking thing (§ 3) and against his primary argument for the existence of God (§ 4), both of which had been topics of "Part Four" of the *Discours*.

Partially due to the fact that they are nowadays one of the most commonly read philosophical texts of all, it is often ignored that the *Meditationes* were simply not addressed to everyone, or even, for that matter, to very many readers. On the contrary, they were meant to be read by, because they can be understood by, only a very few readers, that is, by those who would be ready, willing and able to fulfill certain hermeneutical presuppositions: ". . . sed ita ut nullum vulgi plausum, nullamque Lectorum frequentiam expectem: quin etiam nullis

author sum ut haec legant, nisi tantùm iis qui serió mecum meditari, mentemque a sensibus, simulque ab omnibus praejudiciis, abducere poterunt ac volent, quales non nisi admodum paucos reperiri satis scio." ("Praefatio", § 6) In a word, the author of the *Meditationes* demanded unconditionally that the readers "seriously meditate" along with him.

Indeed, as far as philosophical literature is concerned, the *Meditationes* are in terms of both form and content *sui generis*, and this makes it all the more difficult to find an answer to the question about how to understand them adequately.

The *Meditationes* proper consist of six intimately related sets of cogitations, each one of which sets is itself designated as a "Meditatio" ("Meditation"), entitled (I) "De iis quae in dubium revocari possunt" ("On the things that can be called into doubt"), (II) "De natura mentis humanae: quòd ipsa sit notior quàm corpus" ("On the nature of the human mind: that it be more known than [the] body"), (III) "De Deo, quòd existat" ("On God, that he exist"), (IV) "De vero et falso" ("On the true and the false"), (V) "De essentiâ rerum materialium; & iterum de Deo, quòd existat" ("On the essence of material things; and again on God, that he exist") and (VI) "De rerum materialium existentiâ, & reali mentis a corpore distinctione" ("On the existence of material things, and on the real distinction of the mind from the body"). Just a glance at this 'table of contents' would suffice to convince one that the *Meditationes* represent the execution of a meditative-methodological, internalist and foundationalist project aimed at determining whether, after everything that can possibly be doubted for "reasons valid and meditated upon" (Meditatio I, § 10 ["propter validas & meditatas rationes"]) has been, there is anything at all that may be regarded as certain and indubitable, and if so, what it as well as the evidence for it might be (cf., e.g., "Synopsis", § 1, etc.). Briefly, what is being sought is — to employ the metaphor of the Archimedean fulcrum by which Descartes seemed to be so charmed — a "punctum . . . firmum & immobile" (Meditatio II, § 1), or better, what are being sought are 'fundamen-

ta . . . certa & inconcussa' (cf. "Synopsis", § 1, Meditatio I, §§ 1–2, II, §§ 1 and 4, etc.). *Prima facie*, the most fundamental foundation of all turns out to be ". . . *Ego sum, ego existo* . . ." (Meditatio II, § 3 [cf. *ibid.*, § 6: ". . . Ego sum, ego existo . . ."]), which according to Descartes is something that follows from ". . . cogito . . ." (cf. *ibid.*, Meditatio III, §§ 2, 9, etc.). Still, the "seriously meditating" reader will not overlook the fact that the "lumen naturale" or "natural light [of reason]" is considered to be more epistemically basic than even the "cogito" (see again Meditatio III, § 9). Yet having thus established, in spite of the hyperbolic destruction of his beliefs in all other things, the existence of his own self (Meditatio II, § 3), Descartes proceeds with the process of reconstruction by doing the same for the existence of God (III, § 22) and for that of the material things of the external world (VI, § 10), so that as a result the reader is treated to a Cartesian epistemic epic, that is, a different version, marred merely by some cosmetic inadequacies, of the account of the creation of the world and of everything in it according to *Genesis* — this reason for there being exactly six meditations seems to be as good as any and better than most (but, unlike God, Descartes had on the seventh day to entertain questions about whether what he had so creatively written was "good" or not).

The Attempt to Demonstrate
the Connection between Evidence and Truth

Epistemically speaking, then, the core concern of the *Meditationes* is more or less identical to that of the "Fourth Part" of the *Discours*, namely, it is the universality and necessity of the connection between the clarity and distinctness or evidence of perceptions, on the one hand, and the certainty and truth of them, on the other hand — a topic which now gets systematically raised to the level of a 'quod est demonstrandum' at the beginning and a 'quod erat demonstrandum' ('Q.E.D.') at the end. As a matter of fact, any and every attempt to evaluate the

success or failure of Descartes' epistemic foundationalism is necessarily inadequate if it does not recognize that the first and foremost thesis of it is that the general rule of truth, namely, that all those things which one clearly and distinctly perceives are true in that mode in which one clearly and distinctly perceives them, gets "demonstrated" or "proved". (In passing, it is worth noting that perhaps the main reason why Descartes is never — i.e., either in the *Meditationes* or anywhere else — able to take the contrary modes of evidence, namely, vagueness and obscurity, even nearly as seriously as he does clarity and distinctness is that, while the latter appear to contribute to the preservation of the relationship between evidence and truth, the former seem to jeopardize this connection.) For whereas the author of the *Discours* had, indeed, tried to establish clarity and distinctness as criteria of truth by offering at least a kind of argument for the claim that, given the truthfulness of God as well as God's relationship to human beings as the creator of their nature, all those things which one (very) clearly and (very) distinctly perceives must necessarily be true and cannot possibly be false, the author of the *Meditationes* boldly announces from the very start that he intends rigorously "to prove" ("Synopsis", § 2 [*"Praeterea verò requiri etiam ut sciamus ea omnia quae clare & distincte intelligimus, eo ipso modo quo illa intelligimus, esse vera: quod ante quartam Meditationem probari non potuit . . ."*] and § 4 [*"In quartâ, probatur ea omnia quae clare & distincte percipimus, esse vera . . ."*]) or "to demonstrate" (Meditatio V, § 6 [". . . & jam fuse demonstravi illa omnia quae clare cognosco esse vera."]) precisely the validity of this claim, one which is now formulated, and *expressis verbis* described, as "the general rule of truth" (cf. Meditatio III, § 2 [". . . pro *regulâ generali* . . ., illud omne esse verum, quod valde clare & distincte percipio." {emphasis added}], and V, § 15 ["Atqui nulla ex iis clare & distincte perceperam, sed *hujus regulae veritatis* ignarus ob alias causas forte credideram, quas postea minus firmas esse detexi." {emphasis added}]). Obviously part of what all of this means

is that — note the extreme caution that is exercised by Descartes in this matter at the beginning of Meditatio III (". . . ac proinde jam *videor* . . . posse statuere . . ." [emphasis added because, at this point, not yet having "demonstrated" or "proved" it, he is not justified in saying anything more than that ". . . and so I now *seem* to be able to establish, as a general rule, that all that which I very clearly and distinctly perceive is true."]) — the actual 'demonstration' of or 'proof' for the validity of "the general rule of truth" must be regarded as having been completed sometime and somewhere in the course of Meditatio IV (which represents an application of Augustine's [354–430] theory of evil [cf., e.g., *Confessiones*, Bk. VII {"Unde est malum?" or "Wherefrom is evil?"}] to the problem of error and falsity [cf. "Synopsis", § 4]). And that is just the way it happens, for in the final paragraph (17) of that Meditatio Descartes writes the following about the "causa erroris & falsitatis": "Et sane nulla alia esse potest ab eâ quam explicui; nam quoties voluntatem in judiciis ferendis ita contineo, ut ad ea tantùm se extendat quae illi clare & distincte ab intellectu exhibentur, fieri plane non potest ut errem, quia omnis clara & distincta perceptio proculdubio est aliquid, ac proinde a nihilo esse non potest, sed necessariò Deum authorem habet, Deum, inquam, illum summe perfectum, quem fallacem esse repugnat; ideoque proculdubio est vera." In other words: Every clear and distinct perception is something (that *is*). But something (that *is*) cannot come from nothing (which *is not*), but rather only from God, who is the author of everything (that *is*). Yet God is a perfect being, whom it contradicts to be deceptive (more exactly, God *could* be, but does not *want* to be, a deceiver [cf. Meditatio IV, §§ 2–3 {"posse fallere" versus "velle fallere"}]). Therefore, every clear and distinct perception is true (cf. Meditatio V, § 15). (This argument presupposes familiarity with, and acceptance of, the Scholastic theory of the *transcendentia* ["transcendentals"]: *Ens et bonum convertuntur. Ens et verum convertuntur.* "Being and the good are convertible." "Being and the true are convertible." Every clear and distinct perception

is something; therefore, every clear and distinct perception is also something good and true. Etc. [Cf., e.g., Meditatio V, § 6.])

Thus, using essentially only six *loci* from the ninety (*Oeuvres de Descartes*) pages of the *Meditationes*, the preceding paragraph has summarized the main stations along the way to the 'demonstration' of or 'proof' for the validity of Descartes' "general rule of truth". Once again, for purely hermeneutical reasons it is difficult to understand how anyone could even want to try to regard anything but the supposed *demonstratio* of the validity of this rule as being the most basic aspect of Descartes' account of the foundations of the theory of epistemic rationality. On the contrary, judged according to the criteria of things epistemic, the *Meditationes* succeed or fail depending on whether Descartes does or does not "demonstrate" or "prove" that there is a universal and necessary connection between the evidence of perceptions, on the one hand, and the certainty of them, on the other hand, that is, that there exists such a relationship between their clarity and distinctness, on the one hand, and their truth, on the other hand.

An Epistemic Theodicy
and a Theological Theory of Evidence

Now for an attempt at an answer to the question as to whether the main epistemic argument of the *Meditationes* is circular or not: That is, one can know that whatever one clearly and distinctly perceives is true, if, and only if, one is certain that God exists and that he is not a deceiver. And one can know that God exists and that he is not a deceiver, if, and only if, one is certain that whatever one clearly and distinctly perceives is true. (Here it is well worth remembering that the purported 'demonstration' of or 'proof' for the validity of "the general rule of truth" is supposed to occur in Meditatio IV, i.e., right between the first proof for the existence of God in Meditatio III and the second proof for the existence of God in Meditatio V.

The alleged proof for the claim that God cannot be a deceiver is to be found in Meditatio I, § 10, III, § 38, IV, §§ 2, 8 and 15.)

Not only is this argument circular, but Descartes himself appears to say implicitly that it just might be such (of course, whether he "intended" to do so or not is, hermeneutically regarded, another issue), and to be sure, on the very first page of the book itself. The reason lies in the fact that more than a few of the roots of the *Meditationes* are to be found in the *Bible*. More exactly, the opinion that all of those things which God creates — including both human beings and their cognitive faculties — must necessarily be good and cannot possibly be bad is taken right out of *Genesis* (Ch. I, *passim* ["And God saw that it {i.e., what God had just created} was good."]; cf. Meditatio I, § 9: "Verumtamen infixa quaedam est meae menti vetus opinio, Deum esse qui potest omnia, & a quo talis, qualis existo, sum creatus. . . . At . . . Deus . . . dicitur enim summe bonus . . ."). This means that God, as the source of all those things which are good, is supposed to be good too. Indeed, the lapse of the first human beings consists precisely in the fact that they dare *to doubt* whether God were really good in the sense that God would truly *know* what is good, better or best for them, for, confronted with God's account of what will then happen to them if they eat of the forbidden fruit of the tree of knowledge of the distinction between good and evil, on the one hand, and the serpent's account, on the other hand, there being a conflict between the two, they prefer to believe the latter, not the former (*Genesis*, Chs. II–III [there is surely a difference between the fall of the first human beings and their first sin]). Of course, in the *Meditationes* it is precisely the perfection and, therefore, the goodness of God that Descartes needs in order to make his 'demonstration' of or 'proof' for the truth of all clear and distinct human perceptions function. The point is that, just as for the human being to be deceived implies imperfection for that being (Meditatio I, § 10, and IV, § 8), so too for God to be a deceiver would entail imperfection on God's part (Meditatio IV, §§ 2 and 15). So while one cannot expect him to doubt seri-

ously either the divine perfection or goodness, since this is supposed to be a book not in theology, but rather in philosophy
(cf. 'Dedicatory Epistle', §§ 2, 6, etc.), it is legitimate to ask
where the argument for the perfection or goodness of God is
supposed to be found in it. A close look reveals, however, that
here there isn't even any *indisputable* argument for God's goodness (on the "bonitas Dei" cf. Meditatio I, § 9, VI, §§ 16, 18
and 22–23), let alone for God's perfection (cf. *ibid.*, "Synopsis", § 3, Meditatio III, §§ 25, 29, IV, §§ 4, 17, and V, §§ 7–8)
— on the contrary. As a matter of fact, to concentrate on the
weaker of the two, the goodness of God is something that Descartes takes as an article of faith from the *Bible* — and for granted (indeed, at least partially out of fear of the charge of *asebeia*
he shrinks back from the epistemic scenario of the worst of all
impossible worlds in Meditatio I by substituting the "genius
malignus" [commonly called "the *evil* genius", but more accurately described as "the *deceitful* genius" — after all, this figure
has an epistemic, not a{n im}moral, role to play in the argument; on the other hand, {s}he does remind one of Iago] for a
'Deus deceptor' [§§ 9–12 {cf. II, §§ 3, 6 and 9, III, § 4, VI, §
7, etc.}]). Now there is only a single place in the *Meditationes*
where the word "circulus" is used in the logical sense ('Epistle',
§ 1), and that is in connection with the apologetic problem of
how best to demonstrate to unbelievers that God exists. In that
place, Descartes says: "Et quamvis omnino verum sit, Dei existentiam credendam esse, quoniam in sacris scripturis docetur,
& vice versâ credendas sacras scripturas, quoniam habentur
a Deo; quia nempe, cùm fides sit donum Dei, ille idem qui dat
gratiam ad reliqua credenda, potest etiam dare, ut ipsum existere credamus; non tamen hoc infidelibus proponi potest, quia
circulum esse judicarent." In other words, one cannot argue
to unbelievers that the existence of God is to be believed in because it is taught in Sacred Scripture and, *vice versa*, that Sacred
Scripture is to be believed in because it is from God, since they
would judge it to be a circle. Obviously they would not be the
only ones, for this is a circle for anyone, believer as well as un-

believer, who makes use of the natural light of reason (a point which Descartes, who is here trying to present an argument for the interpretation that the *Meditationes* represent an exercise in Christian apologetics, is careful not to mention explicitly, let alone to emphasize). But would it not also, by the same token, be a circle if someone were to believe that God is good because (s)he had read it in the *Bible* and, *vice versa*, that the *Bible* is good (e.g., reliable as a source of knowledge about God) because it is from God? One might think that it very well would be a circle. (Surely it does not change anything essential here to say that this has been the traditional way to look at these things.) Nonetheless, in lieu of any apt argument for the goodness of God, this is exactly what the "Christian Philosopher" Descartes (see again 'Epistle', § 3) believes in his capacity as the author of the *Meditationes*. Therefore, in so far as the 'demonstration' of or 'proof' for "the general rule of truth" in the *Meditationes* depends on Descartes' belief in the goodness — to bracket the perfection (the latter, for which, again, there is no *cogent* argument either, entails the former) — of God, for which belief, in turn, there is no argument that is not patently circular, the justification of the rule itself must be judged to be correspondingly circular. Or to put it somewhat differently: The main epistemic argument of the *Meditationes* is circular at worst, and at best it rests on a tenet of faith (naturally, both of these things are possible). Throughout this objection to the procedure in the *Meditationes*, the question has never been whether it is true that God is good and perfect, but rather only whether or not Descartes has shown that and how the belief that God is good or perfect can be justified rationally in the context of the quest for a foundation of knowledge so fundamental that it would not make any sense to demand something more epistemically basic than it. In a word, the main topic of the whole *Meditationes* is — and here is where Meditatio VI with the systematic distinction between the "lumen naturale" and the 'doctrina naturae' or 'teaching of nature' as two radically different (therein lies the *epistemic* "Cartesian dualism" [the existence

of the external world cannot be demonstrated or proved, either, without presupposing the epistemic reliability of God {cf. the syllogism in § 10}]) sources of knowledge about things comes into play (cf., e.g., §§ 6–7 and 11–15) — the relationship between the human being with his or her cognitive capacities and functions, on the one hand, and the God who created that being with those capacities and functions (from the beginning, God is the creator of the human being: I, § 9), on the other hand. And as a solution to this philosophical problem of an epistemic theodicy (i.e., how to reconcile the apparent contradiction between the goodness and perfection of the creator God with respect to cognitive matters and the weakness and imperfection of the created human being in the same respect [cf. again Meditatio I, § 9, and VI, §§ 16, 18 and 22–23 {the book ends with a very strong statement to the effect that human life is prone to errors and that human nature is weak: ". . . fatendum est humanam vitam . . . saepe erroribus esse obnoxiam, & naturae nostrae infirmitas est agnoscenda."}]) Descartes presents what is substantially "a theological theory of evidence" — amazingly, "Deus" is mentioned a total of 170 times in the book (once even in the plural [Meditatio V, § 11]).

The *Objectiones et responsiones*

Importantly, the last remark of the "Preface to the Reader" is to the effect that the reader should not pass judgment on the *Meditationes* until (s)he would have read carefully all of the "Objections and Responses". In fact, during the time between the completion of the manuscript and the publication of the *Meditationes* Descartes let his *opus* circulate among his friends, requesting comments, criticisms and suggestions for improvements. Also, Descartes sent a copy of the manuscript to Mersenne and asked him to get even further reactions, preferably of distinguished theologians and philosophers. Indeed, the author wanted the critics to make as many and as strong objections as possible, for he hoped "that, as a result, the truth

will stand out all the better" ("Letter to Mersenne" [January 28, 1641]).

The "First Objections" were done by a Catholic theologian, Johannes Caterus, who was also at the same time the pastor of the church of St. Laurens at Alkmaar (Holland). Asked by fellow priests who were, in turn, friends of Descartes to take on the task, Caterus obliged, but preferred to remain anonymous ("Letter [from Descartes] to Mersenne" [December 24, 1640]), so the "Objections" as well as the "Replies" were addressed to the priests as agents.

Despite the fact that in the first edition the "Second Objections" were attributed to "theologians and philosophers", they were mainly the work of Mersenne himself.

The "Third Objections" were submitted by the English philosopher Thomas Hobbes (1588–1679 [from 1640 to 1651 in Paris for daring to try "to teach political philosophy to speak English"]), whose materialism made his theism suspect. Unfortunately, Descartes does not seem to have taken Hobbes' criticisms very seriously.

The "Fourth Objections", in the case of which the objector and the respondent communicated with each other *via* Mersenne, were put together by the French theologian and logician Antoine Arnauld (1612–1694), who had just (1641) become *Doctor theologiae* at the Sorbonne and who would go on to such achievements as the *Grammaire générale et raisonnée* (1660 [with Claude Lancelot]) and *La logique ou l'art de penser* (1662 [with Pierre Nicole]).

The "Fifth Objections", which are approximately exactly as long as the *Meditationes* themselves and which consist virtually of a textual commentary on them, came from the philosopher Pierre Gassendi (1592–1655). What made Gassendi such a sharp critic was that, quite independently of his role in this connection, he was trying to defend a moderate empiricism and scepticism by appropriating ancient Greek, especially Epicurean, sensualism and atomism (cf. *Syntagma philosophicum* [1658]). It may be common nowadays to classify modern philosophers

as "Continental rationalists" (Descartes, Leibniz and Spinoza), on the one hand, and as "British empiricists" (Locke, Berkeley and Hume), on the other hand, but Gassendi defies stereotyping. In so far as these designations mean anything at all, he would be a "Continental empiricist". In 1644 Gassendi himself published the *Disquisitio metaphysica seu dubitationes et instantiae adversus Renati Cartesii metaphysicam et responsa*, in other words, his objections (1641) to the *Meditationes*, Descartes' responses and his, Gassendi's, responses to the responses (1642). It is too bad that Descartes declared the latter to be unworthy of a detailed reply ("Letter to Clerselier" [January 12, 1646]).

The "Sixth Objections" were, like the second set, from Mersenne, but, unlike them, they were apparently merely collected by him.

The "Seventh Objections" were drawn up by the mathematician Pierre Bourdin (1595–1653), a Jesuit, and represented, given Descartes' hope to win the support of the Society for his teachings, a big disappointment for him in terms of both charitable interpretation and philosophical quality: "I have never seen a piece of writing so full of faults" ("Letter to Mersenne" [March, 1642]).

In the "Letter to Father Dinet" Descartes related his reaction to Bourdin's objections. The Jesuit Dinet was connected to Bourdin as well as to Descartes, for he was both the former's superior in the Society and had been one of the latter's professors at La Flèche.

As far as the circularity of the foundationalist argumentation of the *Meditationes* goes, the objectors do not seem to have been able to convince Descartes of anything important (cf., e.g., "Second Objections" [*Oeuvres de Descartes*, Vol. VII], pp. 124–125 and 126, versus "Second Responses" [*ibid.*], pp. 140–141 and 143–146, and "Fourth Objections" [*ibid.*], p. 214, versus "Fourth Responses" [*ibid.*], pp. 245–246). In this respect, there is unfortunately a noticeable tendency both in the "Objections" and in the "Responses" to prefer to discuss subordinate

issues, for example, the temporal problem of how it is that one can still be sure of the certainty of a perception even when one no longer enjoys the 'live' clarity and distinctness of it, instead of concentrating on the real, logical difficulty, namely, what it is that guarantees the relationship between the evidence and the truth of perceptions. For these are obviously two different things.

The Condemnation of the Cartesian Philosophy

By the early years of the decade 1640–1650, when he was living first near Leiden and then near Alkmaar, it had become adequately transparent to everyone who had taken the time and made the effort to read his writings that Descartes' philosophy, with its emphasis on the primacy and ultimacy of experience over authority, represented something not only untraditional, but also antitraditional — in a word, "antischolastic".

One of his opponents was Gisbertus Voetius (1589–1676), an influential minister and a professor of theology at the University of Utrecht as well as, at that time, the rector of the school, who in writings from 1642 to 1643 attacked the Cartesian philosophy for its alleged atheistic and sceptical tendencies. As a result, on March 16, 1642, the Cartesian philosophy was condemned and forbidden to be taught in the following pronouncement issued by the Academic Senate of the University of Utrecht: ". . . se [i.e., the professors] rejicere novam istam Philosophiam: primò, quia veteri Philosophiae, quam Academiae toto orbe terrarum hactenus optimo consilio docuere, adversatur, ejusque fundamenta subvertit; deinde, quia juventutem a vetere & sanâ Philosophiâ avertit, impeditque quominus ad culmen eruditionis provehatur: eo quòd, istius praesumptae Philosophiae adminiculo, technologemata, in auctorum libris professorumque lectionibus & disputationibus usitata, percipere nequit; postremò, quòd ex eâdem variae, falsae & absurdae opiniones partim consequantur, partim ab improvidâ juventute deduci possint, pugnantes cum caeteris disciplinis &

facultatibus, atque inprimis cum orthodoxâ Theolo-
giâ. . . . Censere igitur ac statuere, omnes philosophiam in
hac Academiâ docentes in posterum a tali instituto atque in-
cepto abstinere debere, contentos modicâ libertate dissentien-
di in singularibus nonnullis opinionibus, ad aliarum celebri-
um Academiarum exemplum, hîc usitatâ: ita ut veteris &
receptae philosophiae fundamenta non labefactent, & in eo
etiam atque etiam laborent, ut Academiae tranquillitas in omnibus sarta tecta conservetur." (*Oeuvres de Descartes*, Vol. VII,
pp. 592–593) In other words, Descartes' philosophy was condemned for three reasons: (1) It was supposed to be opposed
to the traditional philosophy and to undermine its foundations;
(2) it was supposed to lead the youth away from the traditional philosophy ("corrupting the youth" [cf. Plato's *Apology of
Socrates*]?), and even to render it incomprehensible to them;
and (3) it was supposed to lead to false and absurd opinions,
meaning, apparently, 'opinions conflicting with "orthodox Theology [i.e., Philosophy]" '.

But what is at issue here is precisely the relative truthfulness
or falsity of the traditional versus the new philosophy, that is,
whether it makes any sense at all to adhere blindly to the traditional philosophy regardless of its scientific value compared with
that of the new philosophy. Thus, in the statement issued, academic tranquility was judged to be a higher good than the truth.
In this respect, those who formulated the condemnation profoundly missed the point.

In 1643 Descartes did write an "Epistola ad Voetium" or
"Letter to Voetius" (*Oeuvres de Descartes*, Vol. VIII/2, pp.
1–194 [cf. his "Lettre apologétique aux Magistrats d'Utrecht"
or "Defense Letter to the Magistrates of Utrecht" {June 16, 1645},
ibid., pp. 283–317]) in which he responded that the attacks
on his teachings were untenable, but this was — of course —
in vain. For at about the same time the Magistrates of Utrecht
issued an edict (June 12, 1645) prohibiting anything to be published *pro* or *contra* Descartes' philosophy. Thus did one try
to silence him.

Correspondence with Elizabeth: *Les passions de l'âme*

In 1643 Descartes began a lengthy and famous correspondence with the young Princess Elizabeth of Bohemia (who was the daughter of King Frederick of Bohemia ["The Winter King"] and who had gone with her family into exile in Holland after the Battle of the White Mountain on November 8, 1620 [her dates are 1618–1680]). It was by wondering how the soul can be ruled by the body in the light of the fact that they seem to have nothing in common that Elizabeth got interested in the passions. So she asked Descartes to explain "the manner of [the soul's] actions and passions in the body" ("Letter to Descartes" [June 20, 1643]). In her questions the Princess articulated some major difficulties with his position on the relationship between the mind and the body — she was not satisfied with his vague and obscure initial 'explanation' that the body causes the soul to have feelings and passions, and the soul causes the body to move (by means of an inexplicable "union" between the body and the soul) — , and in his detailed answers Descartes provided much valuable information about his philosophy of mind. Another topic of the correspondence was the explanation of the relation between reason and the passions. Elizabeth ultimately demanded that Descartes give "a definition of the passions, in order to make them well known" ("Letter to Descartes" [September 13, 1645]). It was then that Descartes wrote a short "treatise on the passions", which he presented to Elizabeth in 1646. Some of Descartes' thoughts on this subject were later included in the final work of his to be published in his own lifetime, *Les passions de l'âme* or *The Passions of the Soul* (1649 [*Oeuvres de Descartes*, Vol. XI, pp. 291–497]), a sweeping treatise on physiology, psychology, ethics and much more.

The *Principia philosophiae*

In 1644 Descartes published the *Principia philosophiae* or *Principles of Philosophy* (*Oeuvres de Descartes*, Vol. VIII/1,

pp. 1–329), a comprehensive presentation of his philosophical and scientific system that he planned as a university text-
book which would rival the traditional scholastic manuals based
on the writings of Aristotle and Thomas Aquinas (originally
it was to be entitled the "*Summa philosophiae*" ["Letter to Con-
stantijn Huygens" {January 31, 1642}]) and which would, he
hoped, eventually even render them superfluous and obsolete.
The work contains four parts (divided into altogether 504 articles), namely, "On the Principles of Human Knowledge", "On
the Principles of Material Things", "On the Visible World" and
"On the Earth". Originally two more parts were planned, namely, on plants and animals and on the human being, but these
were never finished. Interestingly, there is a lot of material in
the *Principia* that represents a publication, after all, of stuff
which Descartes had once written for the unpublished, because
unpublishable, *Le monde*.

From an epistemic standpoint, the "First Part" of the *Principia* ("De principiis cognitionis humanae"), which sets out "les
principes de la connaissance" — that is, "la première philosophie
ou . . . la métaphysique" ("Letter of the Author"/'Preface to
the French Edition' [*Oeuvres de Descartes*, Vol. IX/2, pp.
1–20], p. 16) — according to Descartes in a manner very different from that of the *Meditationes*, exhibits all of the peculiarly
characteristic features of his major work on the same topic, and
then some. In regard to the connection between the evidence
of "les principes" of the *Principia*, on the one hand, and their
truth, on the other hand, in particular Descartes writes:
". . . qu'il y a un Dieu, qui est auteur de tout ce qui est au
monde, et qui, étant la source de toute vérité, n'a point créé
notre entendement de telle nature qu'il se puisse tromper au juge-
ment qu'il fait des choses dont il a une perception fort claire
et fort distincte." ("Letter of the Author"/'Preface to the French
Edition', p. 10) In regard to the connection between evidence
and truth in general he says: "Primum Dei attributum quod hîc
venit in considerationem, est, quòd sit summè verax, & dator
omnis luminis: adeò ut planè repugnet ut nos fallat, sive ut

propriè ac positivè sit causa errorum, quibus nos obnoxios esse experimur. Nam quamvis fortè posse fallere nonnullum ingenii argumentum apud nos homines esse videatur, nunquam certè fallendi voluntas nisi ex malitiâ vel metu & imbecillitate procedit, nec proinde in Deum cadere potest. . . . Atque hinc sequitur, lumen naturae, sive cognoscendi facultatem à Deo nobis datam, nullum unquam objectum posse attingere, quod non sit verum, quatenus ab ipsâ attingitur, hoc est, quatenus clarè & distinctè percipitur. Meritò enim deceptor esset dicendus, si perversam illam ac falsum pro vero sumentem nobis dedisset. Ita tollitur summa illa dubitatio, quae ex eo petebatur, quòd nesciremus an fortè talis essemus naturae, ut falleremur etiam in iis quae nobis evidentissima esse videntur. Quin & aliae omnes dubitandi causae, priùs recensitae, facilè ex hoc principio tollentur. . . . Certum autem est, nihil nos unquam falsum pro vero admissuros, si tantùm iis assensum praebeamus quae clarè & distinctè percipiemus. Certum, inquam, quia, cùm Deus non sit fallax, facultas percipiendi quam nobis dedit, non potest tendere in falsum; ut neque etiam facultas assentiendi, cùm tantùm ad ea quae clarè percipiuntur se extendit. Et quamvis hoc nullâ ratione probaretur, ita omnium animis à naturâ impressum est, ut quoties aliquid clarè percipimus, ei sponte assentiamur, & nullo modo possimus dubitare quin sit verum." (*Principia philosophiae*, I, §§ XXIX ["Deum non esse errorum causam."], XXX ["Hinc sequi omnia quae clarè percipimus, vera esse, ac tolli dubitationes antè recensitas."] and XLIII ["Nos nunquam falli, cùm solis clarè & distinctè perceptis assentimur."]) In other words, just as in the *Discours* (in a very rudimentary fashion) as well as in the *Meditationes* (in a highly developed form), the argument of the *Principia* for the position that all those things which one clearly and distinctly perceives must necessarily be true and cannot possibly be false would look something like this: It is God who has given the human being those cognitive faculties which are by nature so constituted that, if (s)he clearly and distinctly perceives something, then (s)he must, that is, cannot do otherwise than to,

judge that it be true (cf. *Meditationes*, IV, § 10, and V, §§ 6 and 14). But God is not, and cannot possibly be, a deceiver (cf. again *ibid.*, IV, §§ 2–3). Therefore, whatever the human being clearly and distinctly perceives is also true, and to be sure, in that mode in which (s)he clearly and distinctly perceives it. (Although this argument might or might not be sound, it most certainly is not — as some critics, who do not believe that Descartes' account of evidence and truth should be taken seriously, would have it — patently absurd; on the contrary, there is a profound affinity between the kind of thinking about the relationship between God as the creator and the human being as one of God's creatures — God being the maker of the human being, including that being's cognitive faculties — which lies at the basis of it and some positions in contemporary cognitive theory, e.g., "proper functionalism".) So this is what must be recognized as remaining constant both in the transition from the *Discours* to the *Meditationes* and in the transition from the *Meditationes* to the *Principia*.

The Definition of "Clear Perception" and of "Distinct Perception"

Of course, in order to find out what has changed in the transitions from the ones to the others, one has to notice that what the author of the *Discours* and the *Meditationes* had neglected to do, and precisely what the author of the *Principia* tries to do, is to define the concepts "clear perception" and "distinct perception": "Quin & permulti homines nihil planè in totâ vitâ percipiunt satis rectè, ad certum de eo judicium ferendum. Etenim ad perceptionem, cui certum & indubitatum judicium possit inniti, non modò requiritur ut sit clara, sed etiam ut sit distincta. Claram voco illam, quae menti attendenti praesens & aperta est: sicut ea clarè à nobis videri dicimus, quae, oculo intuenti praesentia, satis fortiter & apertè illum movent. Distinctam autem illam, quae, cùm clara sit, ab omnibus aliis ita sejuncta est & praecisa, ut nihil planè aliud, quàm quod clarum est, in

se contineat. . . . Atque ita potest esse clara perceptio, quae non sit distincta; non autem ulla distincta, nisi sit clara." (*Principia*, I, §§ XLV ["Quid sit perceptio clara, quid distincta."] and XLVI [". . . ostenditur, claram esse posse perceptionem, etsi non sit distincta; non autem distinctam, nisi sit clara."]) In other words, the criteria of clarity are "presence" and "openness", and the criteria of distinctness are "separateness" and "precision". Thus it is possible for a perception to be clear without being distinct, but impossible for a perception to be distinct without being clear (a good example is pain: see *ibid.*, §§ XLVI and LXVII–LXIX [cf. *Meditationes*, VI, § 7 {". . . nam quid dolore intimius esse potest?"}]).

Yet the careful and cautious reader will recognize almost at first sight that what is provided here amounts at the very most, on a loose construction, to definitions of the modes of evidence "clarity" ("praesens & aperta") and "distinctness" ("sejuncta . . . & praecisa"). Once again, one might, as a matter of fact, even want to argue — with promising prospects of success — that, on a strict construction, Descartes is here not at all defining "clarity" and "distinctness" *per se*, but rather only the concepts "clear *perception*" and "distinct *perception*". Yet for the present purposes one does not have to make anything out of this.

More importantly, what is certain and indubitable is that one does not find any definition of the concept of "evidence" itself in these paragraphs of the *Principia*; nor does one find anything of the sort in any of the other paragraphs of this work. At this point, it almost goes without saying that to define the modes of evidence "clarity" and "distinctness" is not the same thing as to define the concept of "evidence" itself, no more than to define the modes of evidence "vagueness" and "obscurity" would be to do so. Therefore, Descartes has no definition — and, for that matter, no definite description — of "evidence" itself at all here.

The Development of Descartes' Position
on the Relationship between Evidence and Truth

So to judge on the basis of the evidence presented by a co-
herent and contextualizing reading of the *Regulae ad directionem ingenii*, the *Discours de la méthode*, the *Meditationes de
prima philosophia* and the *Principia philosophiae*, one may say
that the mature Cartesian position on the epistemic relationship between evidence, on the one hand, and truth, on the other
hand, involves the following, relatively straightforward *Ent-
stehungsgeschichte*: First of all, in the *Regulae* of 1628–1629
all knowledge is understood to be certain and "evident" cognition, while the concepts of evidence "clarity" and "distinctness",
as members of an explicitly and thematically paired dyad, play
no really significant role in the truth problematic; then, in the
Discours of 1637 clarity and distinctness are systematically
paired off as being — with, of course, indispensable help from
the *veracitas Dei* — the criteria of truth, while no claim is made,
expressis verbis, to the effect that a justification in the sense of
a 'demonstration' or 'proof' is being proposed of or for the
universality and necessity of the rule-governed connection between evidence and truth; next, in the *Meditationes* of
1641–1642 it is explicitly and thematically asserted at a number of places that the general rule of truth, namely, that all those
things which one clearly and distinctly perceives are also true,
and to be sure, in that mode in which one clearly and distinctly
perceives them, will be, respectively, has been "demonstrated"
or "proved" — once again by appealing to *Deus* as the author
of all clear and distinct perceptions and thus as the guarantor
of the validity of the said rule —, while, nonetheless, no definitions of the basic concepts of evidence, namely, "clarity" and
"distinctness" themselves, are proposed; finally, in the *Principia*
of 1644 clarity and distinctness are laid down as supposed criteria of truth, it is allegedly shown — yet again with reference to
God — that whatever is clearly and distinctly perceived is also
true, and — at best — the modes of evidence "clarity" and "dis-

tinctness" or — at least — "clear perception" and "distinct perception" are defined, while even here no definition of "evidence" itself is ever given.

What Is Missing: A Definition of "Evidence"

Therefore, one result of all of this is the insight that that philosopher who has somehow managed to persuade almost everyone to associate his name with the discussion about the connection between clarity and distinctness, on the one hand, and certainty, on the other hand, and, therefore — *mutatis mutandis* — , with the attempt to find an answer to the question concerning the relationship between evidence, on the one hand, and truth, on the other hand, simply does not seem to have recognized the importance of at least proposing a definition of the concept of "evidence" itself. Philosophically, then, one is just plain left wondering about what exactly *evidence* itself is supposed to be in all of this — again, the word "evidentia" does not occur even once in the *Meditationes* proper.

Obviously there is an intimate connection between the project of grounding evidence in, or of founding it on, something or someone supposedly more epistemically basic than—and, therefore, other than—it itself, on the one hand, and the failure to take evidence seriously enough philosophically to define it itself at all, on the other hand. Somehow evidence was just not held to be sufficiently primary or ultimate to warrant working out conceptually what it may properly be taken to be. One got interested in establishing a basis for knowledge, a basis-more-basic-than-which-none-can-be-based—and that basis was supposed to be not evidence, but rather something or someone different from evidence. Of course, the question is whether, epistemically speaking, such an enterprise makes any sense at all, or whether it does not, in fact, represent something totally and countersensically circular. The answer that one gives to this question will, in turn, pretty much determine what one thinks of the *Meditationes de prima philosophia* as an essay in epistemic foundationalism.

The French Translation of the *Principia*
and of the *Meditationes*

In the same year as the appearance of the *Principia* Descartes visited his *patrie* France after an absence of more than fifteen years. There he met the Abbé Claude Picot, an old friend who now undertook, with Descartes' approval, to render the *Principia* into French. The translation appeared in 1647 (*Oeuvres de Descartes*, Vol. IX/2, pp. 1–325), and Descartes even wrote an important philosophical introduction ("Lettre de l'auteur" or "Préface") to accompany it upon publication.

There one finds, among other things, a now famous description of the relationship between philosophy ("Or ce souverain bien, consideré par la raison naturelle sans la lumière de la foi, n'est autre chose que la connaissance de la vérité par ses premières causes, c'est-à-dire la Sagesse, dont la Philosophie est l'étude." [p. 4]) and its constituent disciplines (p. 14): "Ainsi toute la philosophie est comme un arbre, dont les racines sont la métaphysique, le tronc est la physique, et les branches qui sortent de ce tronc sont toutes les autres sciences, qui se réduisent à trois principales, à savoir la médecine, la méchanique et la morale, j'entends la plus haute et la plus parfaite morale, qui, présupposant une entière connaissance des autres sciences, est le dernier degré de la sagesse." In other words, philosophy, that is, the study of, or the striving after, wisdom, is like a tree, whose roots are metaphysics, whose trunk is physics and whose branches are all the other sciences, which may be reduced to three principal ones, namely, medicine, mechanics and morality. The end of the metaphor vividly recalls both the beginning of the "Sixth Part" of the *Discours* and *Genesis*, I–III. Medicine may contribute to 'the preservation of health, that is, the highest good and the foundation of all of the other goods in this life' (*Discours*, VI, § 2: ". . . la conservation de la santé, laquelle est sans doute le premier bien et le fondement de tous les autres biens de cette vie . . ."), and mechanics might even

promise to make human beings "the masters and possessors of nature" (*ibid.*: ". . . et ainsi nous rendre comme maîtres et possesseurs de la nature."), but will the science of morality really provide human beings with the fruits of the tree of philosophy in the form of genuine knowledge of the distinction between good and evil?

In addition, Descartes approved a French translation of the *Meditationes de prima philosophia* which had been prepared by Louis-Charles d'Albert, Duc de Luynes (1620–1690). In 1647 it was published as the *Méditations métaphysiques touchant la première philosophie . . .* (*Oeuvres de Descartes*, Vol. IX / 1, pp. 1–72), together with a French version of the first six sets of "Objectiones et responsiones" (*ibid.*, pp. 73–244) done by Descartes' disciple Claude Clerselier (1618–1684).

In 1644 a Latin version of the *Discours de la méthode* (*Oeuvres*, Vol. VI, pp. 540–583) and the first two *Essais* (*ibid.*, pp. 584–720), translated by Étienne de Courcelles, had been published in Amsterdam.

Just as much as he wanted there to be French translations of his Latin works, Descartes wanted there to be Latin translations of his French ones. Like all of his seventeenth-century scholarly contemporaries — for example, Thomas Hobbes (who published the Latin *De cive* in 1642, the English *Leviathan* in 1651, the English *Philosophical Rudiments concerning Government and Society* [= "On the Citizen"] in that same year, the Latin *Leviathan* in 1668, etc.) — , Descartes realized that Latin was unquestionably the principal language of the *mundus doctorum* and that publication in this medium was the best way to insure the universal accessibility of one's writings.

The *Comments on a certain Broadsheet*

On September 6, 1647, Descartes was awarded a pension by Louis XIV, the King of France. In December of that same year Descartes wrote *Comments on a certain Broadsheet* ("Notae in programma quoddam"; published in January, 1648 [*Oeuvres*

de Descartes, Vol. VIII/2, pp. 335–369]), directed against certain — less innatist-idealist and more empiricist-materialist — interpretations of his positions on the nature of thought and on the relationship between it and sensation by his former follower Henricus Regius (cf. *Explicatio mentis humanae* [December, 1647]: '. . . all thought is derived from sensation . . .'). In fact, it was Regius who, in his capacity as a professor of medicine at the University of Utrecht, had undertaken to teach Descartes' philosophy there, and in provocatively doing so had apparently helped — *nolens volens* — to provide the occasion for the condemnation of Descartes' philosophy by that school.

During the winter of 1647–1648 Descartes was working on a treatise on physiology. Although it was never completed, it did get published posthumously — by Clerselier with his edition of the *Traité de l'homme* in 1664 — under the title "*Description du corps humain*" or "*Description of the Human Body*" (*Oeuvres de Descartes*, Vol. XI, pp. 223 ff.).

The "Conversation with Burman"

From November 1644 to the summer of 1649 — except for one other visit to France in 1647 — Descartes lived at Egmond-Binnen in Holland. It was there that on April 16, 1648, Descartes was interviewed by the young Dutchman and student of theology Frans Burman (1628–1679 [in 1662 ff. professor of theology at the University of Utrecht]), who put to him very many questions concerning the *Discours, Meditationes* and *Principia*. The interviewer took detailed notes on Descartes' answers, and the result was the "Responsiones Renati Des Cartes ad quasdam difficultates ex Meditationibus ejus, etc. ab ipso haustae" or "Conversation with Burman" (*Oeuvres de Descartes*, Vol. V, pp. 144–179). This piece of writing represents a valuable source for ascertaining what Descartes thought about his own scientific and philosophical achievements at this point in his life,

and it is especially important for the interpretation of the *Meditationes*.

Descartes' Death in Stockholm

In February of 1649 Descartes received an invitation to the royal court at Stockholm from Queen Christina of Sweden (1626–1689), who, having both corresponded with him and read the *Principia* as well as other things by him, was so impressed by his work as to ask him to come to her country in order to instruct her in philosophy. After long hesitation and with much reluctance — he thought of Sweden as being, among other things, "a country of bears among the rocks and the ice" ("Letter to Brasset" [April 23, 1649]) — Descartes finally got under way in September of that year. Having arrived in Stockholm on October 1, however, Descartes ended up spending a miserable autumn during which he was engaged in mostly unphilosophical activities, for example, writing a pastoral comedy (lost) and — disputably — verse to celebrate the Queen's birthday (December 18) and the Peace of Westphalia (treaties for which had been signed on October 24, 1648) — the ballet *La naissance de la paix* was danced on December 19 of that year and rediscovered in 1920 —, etc. Thus it was only in January of the following year that Descartes was at last able to take up the task of instructing the Queen in philosophy. Unfortunately for him, she required him to attend to her regularly at five o'clock in the morning, thereby profoundly disturbing his lifelong established sleeping patterns (as an adult still adhering to the habits formed in his youth at La Flèche, he usually rose at about eleven o'clock — a preference which he regarded as being very conducive to philosophizing). Descartes presented the Queen with the statutes of an *Académie des Sciences* (February 1), very quickly contracted pneumonia (February 2), and died at Stockholm on February 11, 1650.

In a way, it was an ironic, but fitting fate for a man who had once tried to excuse what he considered to be the superficiality of his treatment of the argument(s) for the existence

of God in the "Fourth Part" of the *Discours* by saying that it was meant to be "a book where I had wanted that even the women would be able to understand something" ("un livre, où j'ai voulu que les femmes mêmes puissent entendre quelque chose" ["Letter to Vatier" {February 22, 1638}]).

Today, Descartes' body lies in the church of Saint-Germain-des-Prés, Paris.

La recherche de la vérité

La recherche de la vérité par la lumière naturelle or *The Search for Truth by means of the Natural Light* (*Oeuvres de Descartes*, Vol. X, pp. 495–527) — whose date of composition is quite uncertain — remained an incomplete work which was not published during Descartes' lifetime. The main idea of the piece is that "this light alone, without any help from religion or philosophy, determines what opinions a good man should hold on any matter that may occupy his thoughts, and penetrates into the secrets of the most recondite sciences" (*ibid.*, p. 495).

Light being both for the epistemic tradition of Western philosophy in general and for him in particular a metaphor for evidence, René Descartes was certainly a philosopher, in so far as his whole life lets itself be characterized as the as pure as humanly possible pursuit of clarity and distinctness — and no other work represents his kind of life more typically than do the *Meditationes de prima philosophia*.

On the Present Edition

The present edition of the *Meditationes de prima philosophia/Meditations on First Philosophy* derives its justification first and foremost from the fact that it is the first bilingual Latin-English edition ever to be published. Next, the aim in translating has been to achieve a version which would be both as literal as possible and as liberal as necessary. Then, there

was need of an index which would be far more comprehensive, in terms of breadth as well as of depth, than any other index in any other edition of the work. Finally, there had to be an introduction that would offer philosophically more and better contextualization of the text of the *Meditationes*.

The two models for this edition have been: René Descartes, *Meditationes de prima philosophia. Meditationen über die Grundlagen der Philosophie* (Philosophische Bibliothek Band 250 a). Auf Grund der Ausgaben von Artur Buchenau neu herausgegeben von Lüder Gäbe. Durchgesehen von Hans Günter Zekl. Hamburg: Felix Meiner, 1977. And: René Descartes, *Meditationes de Prima Philosophia. Meditationen über die Erste Philosophie*. Lateinisch/Deutsch (Universal-Bibliothek Nr. 2888). Übersetzt und herausgegeben von Gerhart Schmidt. Stuttgart: Philipp Reclam jun., 1986.

The edition and the translation are of: René Descartes, *Meditationes de prima philosophia, Oeuvres de Descartes*, Vol. VII, pp. 1–90. Ed. Charles Adam and Paul Tannery. Paris: Librairie Philosophique J. Vrin, 1983 (First Edition: 1904). The new, revised edition of the original series (13 volumes), which appeared at the turn of the century (Paris: L. Cerf, 1897–1913), is: *Oeuvres de Descartes*. Publiées par Charles Adam & Paul Tannery. Paris: Librairie Philosophique J. Vrin and Le Centre National de la Recherche Scientifique, 1964–1976 (13 Volumes: 1–11 contain Descartes' writings, 12 contains Adam's *Vie et oeuvres de Descartes*, and 13 contains biographical material, correspondence and indices). This edition has been reprinted.

Some slight improvements on this text had to be made — for example, in the middle of p. 23 (l. 12) "quum" should be "cum", at the top of p. 28 (ll. 1–2) "imanatione" should be "imaginatione", at the bottom of p. 43 (l. 28) "posset" should be "posse", etc. Whenever and wherever it was necessary, such changes have been marked by the use of square brackets ("[. . .]"). The regular numbers in, again, the same kind of brackets that have been inserted into the Latin text refer to the pagination of the Adam and Tannery edition. The regular num-

bers in, yet again, the same kind of brackets that stand at the beginning of every paragraph of the English text are not in the Latin text; they have been added for the assistance of those who prefer to cite and to quote the *Meditations* according to Meditation and paragraph ("§"). Compared with doing so by giving the pages of the Adam and Tannery edition, this is in most cases the much more exact way to refer to Descartes' text. In addition, a minimal amount of other material aimed at filling in some of the gaps left by the conservative translating has been added in the English translation by means of still another, final, use of the square brackets.

It hardly needs to be mentioned that the present edition of the text of the *Meditationes de prima philosophia* does not represent a critical one, which remains a *desideratum*.

If the translation has any merit at all, it will probably be due to all that the translator has learned from the following versions of the *Meditationes*: René Descartes, *Meditations on First Philosophy, The Philosophical Works of Descartes*. Rendered into English by Elizabeth S. Haldane and G. R. T. Ross. In Two Volumes. Cambridge: Cambridge University Press, 1911 (ff.). Vol. I, pp. 131–199 (Translator of the *Meditationes*: E. S. H.); René Descartes, *Meditations on First Philosophy In Which The Existence of God And The Distinction of the Soul from the Body Are Demonstrated*. Translated from the Latin by Donald A. Cress. Indianapolis, Indiana: Hackett Publishing Company, Inc., 1979; and René Descartes, *Meditations on First Philosophy, The Philosophical Writings of Descartes*. Translated by John Cottingham, Robert Stoothoff and Dugald Murdoch. Volumes I–II. Cambridge: Cambridge University Press, 1984 (Vol. II)–1985 (Vol. I). Vol. II, pp. 1–62 (Translator of the *Meditationes*: Cottingham). Here the translations of Buchenau (*et al.*) and Schmidt too should not only be mentioned, but also emphasized strongly. As for the English versions: Haldane's translation has served the purpose for which it was done, that is, to make the work of Adam and Tannery's editions available in some scholarly form to English readers at

the beginning of this century; Cress' translation appears to be the most straightforward of the three; on the other hand, Cottingham's translation might just be the most elegant — his Descartes' *Meditations* read as if they had been written for a recent number of a philosophical journal, and a first-class one at that.

Throughout, the translator of this translation has tried to translate that which Descartes does appear to have *written* in the *Meditationes*, and — whenever and wherever there happens to be a significant difference between the two things — *not* that which he might seem to have *meant*. In fact, because one of the main goals of a bilingual edition should be to present the translation as an aid to a better understanding of the original than would be possible in a monolingual edition, the present English text attempts to translate not only the sense, but also the grammar itself of the original, for example, by adhering rather rigorously to even the very punctuation of the Latin text — at least *as far as possible*. Of course, it does not really matter very much to the present reader whether that punctuation was Descartes' own — that is something for the philologists and palaeographers to determine. The point is that it is the punctuation that (s)he will be looking at in trying to decide whether the translator has left "the same thing" standing in the English version as there was in the Latin original. In other words, although the Latin colons and semicolons, for example, do not have precisely the same grammatical functions as the English ones, holding the units of sense demarcated by the former constant *as far as possible* makes it much easier for the student of the text to find the way back from the English translation to the Latin original — discrete philosophical statement by discrete philosophical statement. Thus retaining the punctuation of the Latin text *as far as possible* also bestows a remarkable meditative fluency on the philosophical argument of the English version which would be simply unachievable if the "normal" grammatical rules were followed. Besides, Descartes' sentences just don't run on *that much*. In general, then, the passive

has been translated as passive, the subjunctive as subjunctive, the logical connectives as logical connectives, etc., except when and where to do so would have become altogether too clumsy. Naturally this goes very much against the *Zeitgeist*, for the democratization and the universalization of the English language seem to entail that fewer and fewer forms assume more and more meanings. So everything is put into the active, the indicative, etc. — more and more senses being indicated by fewer and fewer signs peculiar to them. Thus it is a commonplace to pick up even *The New York Times* and to read such things as: "If Ronald Reagan still *was* the President of the United States of America . . .". The fewer people there are who, while they do speak English, have taken the trouble to learn Latin or German or other languages that appreciate the difference, say, between the *oratio recta* and the *oratio obliqua*, the worse this situation is going to get. So *caveat lector*: It has not been one of the aims of the present translation to attempt to convey the impression that Descartes' *Meditationes* would — or even should — have been written in English; rather, on the contrary, one goal has been to make an extended effort at awakening in the reader something very much like the feeling which a Latin speaking reader would have had upon studying the edition of the *Meditationes* that Adam and Tannery published in 1904 — to the extent, of course, that this is, hermeneutically speaking, still possible at all in the present time and under the present circumstances. It will not be easy reading, and it will not be to the taste of many. Thus, depending on the many and different criteria that can be set up for making judgments about such things, this translation does not necessarily claim to be a very "good" one, even less a "better" one than any others, and most certainly not "the best" — whatever "the best" is supposed to mean here — translation of Descartes' *Meditationes*. It is, however, guaranteed to be accurate in a way *different* from the ways in which any of the other translations of this work are. Throughout, higher value has consistently been placed on the *Nachvollziehbarkeit* — that is, 'the followability with understanding' —

of the original than on the elegance of the translation. Naturally this is also quite a dangerous thing to have done, for while one strives to achieve the standards of William of Moerbeke, one very much dreads having a translation judged by such high criteria.

The present translator has followed the lead of Buchenau (*et al.*) — with very few exceptions — and Cress in translating only the classic Latin text of the *Meditationes*. On the other hand, Cottingham and Schmidt also give numerous selections indicating some of the differences between the Latin and the French versions. (Haldane's version is a truly polyglot one, with no systematic attempt to let the reader know what is going on.) The French translation is, having been published with Descartes' personal approval, reasonably accurate. Although Baillet, the philosopher's biographer, thought that Descartes had taken the opportunity of the French edition "to retouch his original work", there appears to be no justification whatsoever for attributing greater authority to the French version than to the Latin original. What is decisive is that it is certain that Descartes personally composed the Latin text of the *Meditationes*, while the answer to the question about which changes *he himself* may have made for the French text is thoroughly obscure. Besides, a glance at the French translation shows that the differences between it and the Latin original are so many and so considerable that virtually any selection would necessarily have to be very limited and arbitrary. Most likely, it would also diminish any inclination which the reader might already have to go personally and to get the other version in order to compare the one presented here with it.

Since easy to understand instructions have been placed at the head of the Index, it is not necessary to comment on it here other than to point out that it was compiled by a human being without any help at all from a computer. May it serve as an *instrumentarium* for the better understanding of Descartes' philosophical positions and arguments in the *Meditationes*.

In thanksgiving, the following institutions and individuals should be mentioned (affiliations are, unless noted otherwise, with The Department of Philosophy of The University of Notre Dame): Prof. Dr. Karl Ameriks helped in his usual manner, that is, by knowing just plain everything. Jon Beane put the Latin text into the computer. The Department of Philosophy of The University of Bonn very generously permitted the editor-and-translator to work there as a Visiting Teacher and Researcher, with all privileges, during the summer semesters of 1988 and 1989: Dr. Hubertus Busche, Dr. Eduard Gerresheim and Dr. Dieter Lohmar were especially accommodating. Prof. Dr. Cornelius F. Delaney read the translation and convinced the translator to translate in such a way that the text would not have to be "re-translated" into English after having been "translated" out of Latin. Prof. Dr. JoAnn Della Neva of The Department of Romance Languages and Literatures of The University of Notre Dame checked the modernization of the orthography of the French quotations in the Introduction. Prof. Dr. Mic Detlefsen provided constant moral support by arguing persuasively that it is indeed a fallen world — although he was never able to explain in any convincing way why it insists so much on dragging others down with it. John Ehmann, Administrative Director of The University of Notre Dame Press, was patient and encouraging beyond the bounds of reasonable expectation. Prof. Dr. Richard Foley recognized, independently of how the present finished product has turned out, the importance of there being an edition of the *Meditationes* of this kind when he peer-reviewed the original proposal submitted to The University of Notre Dame Press. Prof. Dr. Alfred J. Freddoso was always there to say how he would (have) translate(d) it. The Office of Advanced Studies at The University of Notre Dame, under the direction of Prof. Dr. Robert E. Gordon, provided a Jesse H. Jones Faculty Research Travel Award for the summer of 1988. The Institute for Scholarship in the Liberal Arts at The University of Notre Dame, under the direction of Prof. Dr. Nathan

O. Hatch, offered a Summer Stipend for the summer of 1987. Margaret Jasiewicz of the stenopool of The College of Arts and Letters at The University of Notre Dame put the English translation and the Index into the computer. Prof. Dr. Lynn S. Joy read, and commented on, the Introduction. Dr. Michael Kremer had interesting ideas on the problem of logical circularity in Descartes' argument. Karen Kuss assisted Jon Beane. It was very enlightening to talk with Dr. Tad Schmaltz of The Department of Philosophy of Duke University about many of the philosophical matters discussed in the Introduction. The Index was compiled in July, 1989, in Cambrils, Spain, at the home of Herr Rudolf and Frau Teresa Schmickler of Cologne, Germany; their daughter, Dr. med. Mireya Schmickler of The University of Cologne, helped out in many different ways. Throughout the entire project Prof. Dr. Gerhart Schmidt of The Department of Philosophy of The University of Bonn was of invaluable assistance in the solution of all kinds of technical and philosophical problems: His edition of the *Meditationes* and the present one enjoyed a common conception during the editor-and-translator's time as his *Wissenschaftlicher Mitarbeiter* (1983–86). Eric Watkins assisted in the same way as Tad Schmaltz.

I alone am responsible for any errors that might remain. May the readers be kind enough to point them out to me, thereby making their own contribution to the improvement of the edition.

The book is dedicated to my colleagues, the members of The Department of Philosophy of The University of Notre Dame. They and I both know why.

Université de Notre Dame du Lac   George Heffernan
March 1990

RENATI
DES-CARTES,
MEDITATIONES
DE PRIMA
PHILOSOPHIA,
IN QUA DEI EXISTENTIA
ET ANIMAE IMMORTALITAS
DEMONSTRATUR.

PARISIIS,

Apud MICHAELEM SOLY, viâ Iacobeâ, sub
signo Phoenicis.

M. DC. XLI.

Cum Privilegio, & Approbatione Doctorum.

RENÉ
DESCARTES,
MEDITATIONS
ON FIRST
PHILOSOPHY,
IN WHICH THE EXISTENCE OF GOD
AND THE IMMORTALITY OF THE SOUL
ARE DEMONSTRATED.

PARIS,
By MICHAEL SOLY, James Street, under
the sign of the Phoenix.
1641.

*With the Privilege, & the Approbation
of the Doctors.*

RENATI

DES-CARTES,

MEDITATIONES

De Prima

PHILOSOPHIA,

*In quibus Dei existentia, & animae
humanae à corpore distinctio,
demonstrantur.*

His adjunctae sunt variae objectiones doctorum virorum in istas de Deo & anima
demonstrationes;

Cum Responsionibus Authoris.

Secunda editio septimis objectionibus antehac
non visis aucta.

Amstelodami,

Apud Ludovicum Elzevirium. 1642.

RENÉ
DESCARTES,
MEDITATIONS
On First
PHILOSOPHY,

In which the existence of God,
& the distinction of the human soul from the body,
are demonstrated.

To which have been added various objections of
learned men against these demonstrations
concerning God and the soul;

With the Responses of the Author.

Second edition, enlarged by the previously
unpublished seventh objections.

Amsterdam,
By Ludwig Elzevir. 1642.

SACRAE FACULTATIS THEOLOGIAE PARISIENSIS
DECANO & DOCTORIBUS
RENATUS DES CARTES S. D.

Tam justa causa me impellit ad hoc scriptum vobis offeren-
dum, & tam justam etiam vos habituros esse confido ad ejus
deffensionem suscipiendam, postquam instituti mei rationem
intelligetis, ut nullâ re melius illud hîc possim commendare,
quàm si quid in eo sequutus sim paucis dicam.

Semper existimavi duas quaestiones, de Deo & de Animâ,
praecipuas esse ex iis quae Philosophiae potius quàm Theologiae ope sunt demonstrandae: nam quamvis nobis fidelibus animam humanam cum corpore non [2] interire, Deumque existere,
fide credere sufficiat, certe infidelibus nulla religio, nec fere etiam
ulla moralis virtus, videtur posse persuaderi, nisi prius illis ista
duo ratione naturali probentur: cùmque saepe in hac vitâ majora
vitiis quàm virtutibus praemia proponantur, pauci rectum uti-
li praeferrent, si nec Deum timerent, nec aliam vitam expec-
tarent. Et quamvis omnino verum sit, Dei existentiam credendam esse, quoniam in sacris scripturis docetur, & vice versâ
credendas sacras scripturas, quoniam habentur a Deo; quia
nempe, cùm fides sit donum Dei, ille idem qui dat gratiam ad

60

TO THOSE MOST WISE AND DISTINGUISHED MEN,

THE DEAN AND THE DOCTORS

OF THE SACRED FACULTY OF THEOLOGY AT PARIS,

RENÉ DESCARTES SAYS "GREETINGS".

[1.] So just a cause impels me to offer this writing to you, and I trust that you too are going to have such a just one for taking up its defence after you will have understood the reason for my undertaking, that I could here commend it by no better means than if I were to say with a few words what I have pursued in it.

[2.] Of the questions that need to be demonstrated by philosophy rather than theology I have always thought that two, about God and about the soul, are foremost. For although it might suffice for us faithful to believe by faith that the human soul does not perish with the body and that God exists, it certainly seems that no religion — nor almost even any moral virtue — can persuade unbelievers unless these two things were first proved to them by natural reason. And since in this life greater rewards often be offered to vices than to virtues, few people would prefer what is right to what is useful if they did not fear God or expect another life. And although it might be quite true that the existence of God is to be believed in because it is taught in the Holy Scriptures and — vice versa — that the Holy Scriptures are to be believed in because they are had from God — because since faith be a gift of God, he, the same one who gives the grace to believe the other things, can of course also give

reliqua credenda, potest etiam dare, ut ipsum existere credamus; non tamen hoc infidelibus proponi potest, quia circulum
esse judicarent. Et quidem animadverti non modo vos omnes
aliosque Theologos affirmare Dei existentiam naturali ratione
posse probari, sed & ex sacrâ Scripturâ inferri, ejus cognitionem multis, quae de rebus creatis habentur, esse faciliorem, atque omnino esse tam facilem, ut qui illam non habent sint cul-
pandi. Patet enim Sap. 13 ex his verbis: *Nec his debet ignosci.*
Si enim tantum potuerunt scire, ut possent aestimare saeculum,
quomodo hujus dominum non facilius invenerunt? Et ad Rom.
cap. I, dicitur illos esse *inexcusabiles.* Atque ibidem etiam per
haec verba: *Quod notum est Dei, manifestum est in illis*, videmur
admoneri ea omnia quae de Deo sciri possunt, rationibus non
aliunde petitis quàm ab ipsâmet nostrâ mente posse ostendi.
Quod idcirco quomodo fiat, & quâ viâ Deus facilius & certius
quàm res saeculi cognoscatur, non putavi a me esse alienum
inquirere.

Atque quantum ad animam, etsi multi ejus naturam [3] non
facile investigari posse judicarint, & nonnulli etiam dicere ausi
sint rationes humanas persuadere illam simul cum corpore interire, solâque fide contrarium teneri, quia tamen hos condemnat
Concilium Lateranense sub Leone 10 habitum, sessione 8, &
expresse mandat Christianis Philosophis ut eorum argumenta
dissolvant, & veritatem pro viribus probent, hoc etiam aggre-
di non dubitavi.

Praeterea, quoniam scio plerosque impios non aliam ob causam nolle credere Deum esse, mentemque humanam a corpore
distingui, quàm quia dicunt haec duo a nemine hactenus potuisse
demonstrari: etsi nullo modo iis assentiar, sed contrà rationes

it to us in order that we might believe that he exists — , this still cannot be proposed to unbelievers because they would judge that it is a circle. And I have surely noticed not only that you and all the other theologians affirm that the existence of God can be proved by natural reason, but also that it is inferred from the Holy Scriptures that the cognition of him is easier than many cognitions which are had of created things, and that it is indeed so easy that those people who do not have it be at fault. For this is obvious from these words in *Wisdom*, chapter 13: *"Nor should it be forgiven them. For if they have been able to know so much that they could value the world, why have they not more easily found its Lord?"* And in *To the Romans*, chapter 1, it is said that these people are *"inexcusable"*. And in the same place, by these words, ". . . *what is known of God is manifest in them* . . .", we also seem to be warned that all the things that can be known about God can be shown by reasoning drawn from nowhere else than from our mind itself. Therefore I have not thought it to be alien to me to inquire into how this might be done, and by which way God might be cognized more easily and more certainly than the things of the world.

[3.] And as for the soul, even if many people may have judged that its nature cannot easily be investigated, and even if some people may have even dared to say that human reasoning persuades us that it perishes together with the body and that the contrary is held by faith alone, because the Lateran Council held under Pope Leo X in Session 8 condemns these people and expressly mandates to Christian philosophers that they should dissolve the arguments of them and prove the truth according to their abilities, I have still not hesitated to attempt this too.

[4.] Moreover, because I know that most impious people do not want to believe that there is a God and that the human mind is distinguished from the body for any other reason than because, they say, these two things have hitherto been able to be demonstrated by no one — even if I would in no way assent to them, but rather would I — on the contrary — think that almost

fere omnes, quae pro his quaestionibus a magnis viris allatae sunt, cùm satis intelliguntur, vim demonstrationis habere putem, vixque ullas dari posse mihi persuadeam, quae non prius ab aliquibus aliis fuerint inventae: nihil tamen utilius in Philosophiâ praestare posse existimo, quàm si semel omnium optimae studiose quaerantur, tamque accurate & perspicue exponantur, ut apud omnes constet in posterum eas esse demonstrationes. Ac denique, quoniam nonnulli quibus notum est me quandam excoluisse Methodum ad quaslibet difficultates in scientiis resolvendas, non quidem novam, quia nihil est veritate antiquius, sed quâ me saepe in aliis non infoeliciter uti viderunt, hoc a me summopere flagitarunt: ideoque officii mei esse putavi nonnihil hac in re conari. [4]

Quicquid autem praestare potui, totum in hoc Tractatu continetur. Non quod in eo diversas omnes rationes, quae ad eadem probanda afferri possent, colligere conatus sim, neque enim hoc videtur operae pretium esse, nisi ubi nulla habetur satis certa; sed primas tantùm & praecipuas ita prosecutus sum, ut jam pro certissimis & evidentissimis demonstrationibus illas ausim proponere. Addamque etiam tales esse, ut non putem ullam viam humano ingenio patere, per quam meliores inveniri unquam possint: cogit enim me causae necessitas, & gloria Dei, ad quam totum hoc refertur, ut hîc aliquanto liberius de meis loquar quàm mea fert consuetudo. Atqui quantumvis certas & evidentes illas putem, non tamen ideo mihi persuadeo ad omnium captum esse accommodatas: sed, quemadmodum in Geometriâ multae sunt ab Archimede, Apollonio, Pappo, aliisve

all the arguments that have been brought forward for these questions by great men then have the force of demonstration when they are satisfactorily understood, and I might hardly persuade myself that any arguments can be given which had not been found earlier by some others—, I still think that nothing more useful can have priority in philosophy than if once and for all the best of all the arguments be inquired into studiously and be set out so accurately and perspicuously that in posterity it might be a constant for all people that they are demonstrations. And finally, because some people to whom it is known that I have developed a certain method for resolving whatever difficulties there are in the sciences—surely not a new method, for nothing is older than the truth, but one which they have seen me often use not infelicitously in other things—strongly urged this of me, therefore I have thought it to be my duty to attempt to accomplish something in this matter.

[5.] Furthermore, whatever I have been able to achieve is all contained in this treatise. Not that I had attempted to collect in it all the different arguments which could be put forward to prove the same things, for except where none is held to be certain enough this does not seem to be worth the effort. Rather have I prosecuted only the first and foremost arguments, so that I would now dare to propose these as very certain and very evident demonstrations. And I would even add that these demonstrations are such that I would not think that there is any way open to the human mind by which better ones could ever be found. For the necessity of the cause and the glory of God—to which this whole thing is referred—here force me to speak about the things that pertain to me somewhat more freely than my custom brings me to do. Yet however much certain and evident that you will I might think these demonstrations to be, I still cannot therefore persuade myself that they have been accommodated to the capacity of all people. Rather, just as in geometry many demonstrations have been written by Archimedes, Apollonius, Pappus and others which, even if they be held by all people to be evident and also certain because they

scriptae, quae, etsi pro evidentibus etiam ac certis ab omnibus habeantur, quia nempe nihil plane continent quod seorsim spectatum non sit cognitu facillimum, nihilque in quo sequentia cum antecedentibus non accurate cohaereant, quia tamen longiusculae sunt, & valde attentum lectorem desiderant, non nisi ab admodum paucis intelliguntur: ita, quamvis eas quibus hîc utor, certitudine & evidentiâ Geometricas aequare, vel etiam superare, existimem, vereor tamen ne a multis satis percipi non possint, tum quia etiam longiusculae sunt, & aliae ab aliis pendent, tum praecipue quia requirunt mentem a praejudiciis plane liberam, & quae se ipsam a sensuum consortio facile subducat. Nec certe plures in mundo Metaphysicis studiis quàm Geometricis apti reperiuntur. Ac [5] praeterea in eo differentia est, quod in Geometriâ, cùm omnibus sit persuasum nihil scribi solere, de quo certa demonstratio non habeatur, saepius in eo peccant imperiti, quod falsa approbent, dum ea videri volunt intelligere, quàm quod vera refutent: contrà verò in Philosophiâ, cùm credatur nihil esse de quo non possit in utramque partem disputari, pauci veritatem investigant, & multo plures, ex eo quod ausint optima quaeque impugnare, famam ingenii aucupantur.

Atque ideo, qualescunque meae rationes esse possint, quia tamen ad Philosophiam spectant, non spero me illarum ope magnum operae pretium esse facturum, nisi me patrocinio vestro adjuvetis. Sed cùm tanta inhaereat omnium mentibus de vestrâ Facultate opinio, tantaeque sit authoritatis SORBONAE nomen, ut non modo in rebus fidei nulli unquam Societati post sacra Concilia tantum creditum sit quàm vestrae, sed etiam in humanâ Philosophiâ nullibi major perspicacia & soliditas, nec ad ferenda judicia major integritas & sapientia esse existimetur; non dubito quin, si tantam hujus scripti curam suscipere dig-

indeed contain nothing at all which—regarded with respect to itself—would not be very easy to cognize and nothing in which consequent things would not accurately cohere with antecedent ones, because they are somewhat long and require a very attentive reader, are still understood by only very few people: so also, even if I would consider the demonstrations that I use here to equal or even to surpass geometrical ones with respect to certitude and evidence, I still fear that they could not satisfactorily be perceived by many people, both because they too are somewhat long and some depend on others and above all because they require a mind fully free from prejudices and one that might easily withdraw itself from the company of the senses. Certainly not more people are found in the world fit for metaphysical studies than for geometrical ones. And moreover, there is a difference in that in geometry, since all people have been persuaded that usually nothing is written of which a certain demonstration not be had, the inexperienced people err more often in that they would accept false things while they want to seem to understand them than in that they would reject true things: but in philosophy, on the contrary, since it is believed that there is nothing that could not be disputed on either side, few people investigate the truth and many more pursue fame of mind from thence that they would dare to attack whatever optimal things there are.

[6.] And therefore whatever the quality of my arguments might be, because they have to do with philosophy I still do not expect that I am going to accomplish very valuable work by means of them unless you would support me by your patronage. But since there is so great an opinion of your Faculty in the minds of all people and the name of the "SORBONNE" is of so great authority that not only in matters of faith no society after the Sacred Councils has ever been believed so much as yours, but also in human philosophy there is nowhere else thought to be more perspicacity and solidity nor more integrity and wisdom in rendering judgment, I do not doubt that if you would deign to give so much care to this writing — name-

nemini, *primo* quidem, ut a vobis corrigatur: memor enim, non modo humanitatis, sed maxime etiam inscitiae meae, non affirmo nullos in eo esse errores; *deinde*, ut quae vel desunt, vel non satis absoluta sunt, vel majorem explicationem desiderant, addantur, perficiantur, illustrentur, aut a vobis ipsis, aut saltem a me, postquam a vobis ero admonitus; ac *denique*, ut postquam rationes in eo contentae, quibus Deum esse, mentemque a corpore aliam esse probatur, ad eam perspicuitatem erunt perductae, ad quam ipsas perduci posse confido, ita [6] nempe ut pro accuratissimis demonstrationibus habendae sint, hoc ipsum declarare & publice testari velitis: non dubito, inquam, quin, si hoc fiat, omnes errores, qui de his quaestionibus unquam fuerunt, brevi ex hominum mentibus deleantur. Veritas enim ipsa facile efficiet ut reliqui ingeniosi & docti vestro judicio subscribant; & authoritas, ut Athei, qui scioli magis quàm ingeniosi aut docti esse solent, contradicendi animum deponant, atque etiam ut forte rationes, quas ab omnibus ingenio praeditis pro demonstrationibus haberi scient, ipsi propugnent, ne non intelligere videantur. Ac denique caeteri omnes tot testimoniis facile credent, nemoque amplius erit in mundo, qui vel Dei existentiam, vel realem humanae animae a corpore distinctionem ausit in dubium revocare. Cujus rei quanta esset utilitas, vos ipsi, pro vestrâ singulari sapientiâ, omnium optime aestimare potestis; nec deceret me vobis, qui maximum Ecclesiae Catholicae columen semper fuistis, Dei & Religionis causam pluribus hîc commendare. [7]

ly, *first*, in order that it might be corrected by you, for, remembering not only my humanity, but also, maximally, my ignorance, I do not affirm that there are no errors in it, *then*, in order that the things that are lacking or are not satisfactorily absolute or require more explication might be added, perfected or illustrated either by you yourselves or at least by me, after I will have been warned by you, and *finally*, in order that, after the arguments contained in it, by means of which it is proved that there is a God and that the mind is other than the body, will have been led through to that perspicuity through to which, I am confident, they can be led, so that thus they might of course be held to be very accurate demonstrations, you might want to declare and to attest publicly to this very thing —, I do not doubt, I say, that if this were to happen, then all the errors which there have ever been on these questions would soon be deleted from the minds of human beings. For the truth itself will easily effect that the other ingenious and learned people would subscribe to your judgment, and authority will easily effect that the atheists, who are usually more pretenders than ingenious or learned, would lay down the spirit of contradiction and also that they themselves would perhaps fight for these arguments, which they will know to be held to be demonstrations by all people gifted of mind, so that they might not seem not to understand the arguments. And finally, all the other people will easily believe so many testimonies and there will be no one in the world any longer who would dare to call into doubt the existence of God or the real distinction of the human soul from the body. By virtue of your singular wisdom you can estimate best of all yourselves how great be the utility of this matter. Nor would it become me to commend to you, who have always been the greatest pillar of the Catholic Church, the cause of God and religion with any more words here.

PRAEFATIO AD LECTOREM

Quaestiones de Deo & mente humanâ jam ante paucis attigi in *Dissertatione de Methodo recte regendae rationis & veritatis in scientiis investigandae*, gallice editâ anno 1637, non quidem ut ipsas ibi accurate tractarem, sed tantùm ut delibarem, & ex lectorum judiciis addiscerem quâ ratione postea essent tractandae. Tanti enim momenti mihi visae sunt, ut plus unâ vice de ipsis agendum esse judicarem; viamque sequor ad eas explicandas tam parum tritam, atque ab usu communi tam remotam, ut non utile putarim ipsam in gallico & passim ab omnibus legendo scripto fusiùs docere, ne debiliora etiam ingenia credere possent eam sibi esse ingrediendam.

Cùm autem ibi rogassem omnes quibus aliquid in meis scriptis reprehensione dignum occurreret, ut ejus me monere dignarentur, nulla in ea quae de his quaestionibus attigeram notatu digna objecta sunt, praeter duo, ad quae hîc paucis, priusquam earumdem accuratiorem explicationem aggrediar, respondebo.

Primum est, ex eo quod mens humana in se con[8]versa non percipiat aliud se esse quàm rem cogitantem, non sequi ejus naturam sive *essentiam* in eo tantùm consistere, quod sit res cogitans, ita ut vox *tantùm* caetera omnia excludat quae forte etiam dici possent ad animae naturam pertinere. Cui objectio-

PREFACE TO THE READER

[1.] I have already a few years ago touched on the questions of God and the human mind in the *Discourse on the Method of correctly Conducting the Reason and of Investigating the Truth in the Sciences*, published in French in the year 1637, surely not in order that I might there treat of them accurately, but only in order that I might offer a sampling of my views and discern from the judgments of the readers how they were to be treated of later on. For these questions have seemed to me to be of such importance that I would judge that with them is to be dealt more than one time, and I follow a way of explicating them so little trodden and so remote from the common usage that I had thought it to be not useful to teach it in more detail in a writing in French and in one to be read by all people without distinction, so that the weaker minds could not believe that it is to be taken by them too.

[2.] But although I have there requested of all those people to whom there would occur something in my writings worthy of reprehension that they might deign to warn me of it, nothing worthy of notice has been objected to the things on which I had touched of these questions except for two matters, to which I shall here respond with a few words before I go on to a more accurate explication of the same things.

[3.] The first thing is that from thence that the human mind — turned towards itself — were not to perceive itself to be anything other than a cogitating thing, it does not follow that its nature or *essence* consists only therein that it be a cogitating thing, so that the word "*only*" would exclude all the other things which could perhaps also be said to pertain to the nature of

ni respondeo me etiam ibi noluisse illa excludere in ordine ad ipsam rei veritatem (de quâ scilicet tunc non agebam), sed dumtaxat in ordine ad meam perceptionem, adeo ut sensus esset me nihil plane cognoscere quod ad essentiam meam scirem pertinere, praeterquam quod essem res cogitans, sive res habens in se facultatem cogitandi. In sequentibus autem ostendam quo pacto, ex eo quod nihil aliud ad essentiam meam pertinere cognoscam, sequatur nihil etiam aliud revera ad illam pertinere.

Alterum est, ex eo quod ideam rei me perfectioris in me habeam, non sequi ipsam ideam esse me perfectiorem, & multo minùs illud quod per istam ideam repraesentatur existere. Sed respondeo hîc subesse aequivocationem in voce ideae: sumi enim potest vel materialiter, pro operatione intellectûs, quo sensu me perfectior dici nequit, vel objective, pro re per istam operationem repraesentatâ, quae res, etsi non supponatur extra intellectum existere, potest tamen me esse perfectior ratione suae essentiae. Quomodo verò, ex hoc solo quod rei me perfectioris idea in me sit, sequatur illam rem revera existere, fuse in sequentibus exponetur.

Vidi quidem praeterea duo quaedam scripta satis longa, sed quibus non tam meae his de rebus rationes quàm conclusiones argumentis ex Atheorum locis [9] communibus mutuatis impugnabantur. Et quoniam istiusmodi argumenta nullam vim habere possunt apud eos, qui rationes meas intelligent, adeoque praepostera & imbecillia sunt multorum judicia, ut magis a primum acceptis opinionibus, quantumvis falsis & a ratione alienis, persuadeantur, quàm a verâ & firmâ, sed posterius auditâ, ipsarum refutatione, nolo hîc ad illa respondere, ne mihi sint prius referenda. Tantùmque generaliter dicam ea omnia,

the soul. To which objection I respond that there I too have not wanted to exclude these things in the order of the truth itself of the matter (with which, scil., I was not then dealing), but rather only in the order of my perception, so that the sense were that I cognized nothing at all that I were to know to pertain to my essence except that I were a cogitating thing, or a thing having in itself the faculty of cogitating. However, in the following meditations I shall show how from thence that I were to cognize that nothing else pertains to my essence, it would also follow that nothing else really and truly pertains to it.

[4.] The other thing is that from thence that I were to have in me an idea of a thing more perfect than me, it does not follow that this idea itself is more perfect than me, and much less that that which is represented by this idea exists. But I respond that here there is an equivocation hidden in the word "idea": for it can be taken materially, as an operation of the intellect, in which sense it cannot be called "more perfect than me"; or it can be taken objectively, as the thing represented by this operation, which thing — even if it were not to be supposed to exist outside the intellect — can still be more perfect than me by reason of its essence. Yet in the following meditations it will be set forth in detail how from thence alone that the idea of a thing more perfect than me be in me, it would follow that this thing really and truly exists.

[5.] Moreover, I have indeed seen two rather long writings, by which, however, not so much my reasoning concerning these matters as rather my conclusions were attacked with arguments borrowed from the common places in the texts of the atheists. And because arguments of this kind can have no force for those people who will understand my reasoning, and because the judgments of many people are so preposterous and weak that they be persuaded more by opinions at first accepted — however much that you will false and alien to reason — than by a refutation of them true and firm — but heard later on — , I do not want to respond to these arguments here, so that they not first be referred to by me. And I would only generally say that all the things

quae vulgo jactantur ab Atheis ad existentiam Dei impugnandam, semper ex eo pendere, quod vel humani affectus Deo affingantur, vel mentibus nostris tanta vis & sapientia arrogetur, ut quidnam Deus facere possit ac debeat, determinare & comprehendere conemur; adeo ut, modò tantùm memores simus mentes nostras considerandas esse ut finitas, Deum autem ut incomprehensibilem & infinitum, nullam ista difficultatem sint nobis paritura.

Jam verò, postquam hominum judicia semel utcunque sum expertus, iterum hîc aggredior easdem de Deo & mente humanâ quaestiones, simulque totius primae Philosophiae initia tractare; sed ita ut nullum vulgi plausum, nullamque Lectorum frequentiam expectem: quin etiam nullis author sum ut haec legant, nisi tantùm iis qui seriò mecum meditari, mentemque a sensibus, simulque ab omnibus praejudiciis, abducere poterunt ac volent, quales non nisi admodum paucos reperiri satis scio. Quantum autem ad illos, qui, rationum mearum seriem & nexum comprehendere non curantes, in singulas tantùm clausulas, ut [10] multis in more est, argutari studebunt, non magnum ex hujus scripti lectione fructum sunt percepturi; & quamvis forte in multis cavillandi occasionem inveniant, non facile tamen aliquid quod urgeat aut responsione dignum sit objicient.

Quia verò nequidem etiam aliis spondeo me in omnibus primâ fronte satisfacturum, nec tantum mihi arrogo ut confidam me omnia posse praevidere quae alicui difficilia videbuntur, primò quidem in Meditationibus illas ipsas cogitationes exponam, quarum ope ad certam & evidentem cognitionem veritatis mihi videor pervenisse, ut experiar an fortè iisdem rationibus, qui-

that are commonly thrown about by the atheists to attack the existence of God always depend thereupon that human emotions be feigned of God or thereupon that so much power and wisdom be arrogated to our minds that we would try to determine and to comprehend what God could and should do. So long as we would only just remember that our minds are to be considered as finite, but that God is to be considered as incomprehensible and infinite, these things are going to cause us no difficulty.

[6.] But after I have now gotten to know by experience to a certain extent the judgments of human beings, I here go on once again to the same questions about God and the human mind and simultaneously to treat of the initial things of the whole of First Philosophy. Yet I do so in such a way that I would expect no applause of the common people and no frequency of readers. Rather am I an author to none who might read these things except only to those people who will be able and willing to meditate seriously with me and to lead the mind simultaneously away from the senses and away from all prejudices: whom I satisfactorily know to be very few. But as for those people who — not caring to comprehend the order and the connection of my arguments — will attempt to argue only against individual formulations — as it is in fashion for many — , they are not going to find the reading of this writing very fruitful. And although these people might perhaps find occasion to cavil against many things, they will still not easily object something that would be urgent or worthy of a response.

[7.] But because I also do not even promise that I am going to satisfy the other readers in all matters from the very first page, nor do I arrogate so much wisdom to myself that I would be confident that I can foresee all the things that will seem difficult to anyone, first I shall at least set out in the *Meditations* those cogitations themselves with the help of which I seem to me to have arrived at a certain and evident cognition of the truth, so that I might know by experience whether I could perhaps persuade other people too by the same arguments by which *I* have

bus ego persuasus sum, alios etiam possim persuadere. Postea vero respondebo ad objectiones virorum aliquot ingenio & doctrinâ excellentium, ad quos hae Meditationes, antequam typis mandarentur, examinandae missae sunt. Satis enim multa & varia ab illis fuerunt objecta, ut ausim sperare non facile quicquam aliis, saltem alicujus momenti, venturum in mentem, quod ii nondum attigerint. Ideoque rogo etiam atque etiam Lectores, ut non prius de Meditationibus judicium ferant, quàm objectiones istas earumque solutiones omnes perlegere dignati sint. [11/12]

been persuaded. But I shall afterwards respond to the objections of some men, excellent with respect to mind and learning, to whom these *Meditations* have been sent to be examined before they were submitted to print. For the things objected to by these men have been many and varied enough that I would dare to hope it not to be easy that anything — at least anything of any importance — on which they had not already touched is going to come to mind for others. And therefore I also request of even the readers too that they would not render judgment on the *Meditations* before they had been kind enough to read through all these objections and their solutions.

SYNOPSIS

SEX SEQUENTIUM MEDITATIONUM

In primâ, causae exponuntur propter quas de rebus omnibus, praesertim materialibus, possumus dubitare; quandiu scilicet non habemus alia scientiarum fundamenta, quàm ea quae antehac habuimus. Etsi autem istius tantae dubitationis utilitas primâ fronte non appareat, est tamen in eo maxima quòd ab omnibus praejudiciis nos liberet, viamque facillimam sternat ad mentem a sensibus abducendam; ac denique efficiat, ut de iis, quae posteà vera esse comperiemus, non amplius dubitare possimus.

In secundâ, mens quae, propriâ libertate utens, supponit ea omnia non existere de quorum existentiâ vel minimum potest dubitare, animadvertit fieri non posse quin ipsa interim existat. Quod etiam summae est utilitatis, quoniam hoc pacto facile distinguit quaenam ad se, hoc est, ad naturam intellectualem, & quaenam ad corpus pertineant. Sed quia forte nonnulli rationes de animae immortalitate illo in loco expectabunt, eos hîc monendos [13] puto me conatum esse nihil scribere quod non accurate demonstrarem; ideoque non alium ordinem sequi potuisse, quàm illum qui est apud Geometras usitatus, ut nempe omnia praemitterem ex quibus quaesita propositio dependet, antequam de ipsâ quidquam concluderem. Primum autem & praecipu-

SYNOPSIS

OF THE FOLLOWING SIX MEDITATIONS

[1.] *In the first Meditation the reasons are set out due to which we can doubt all things, especially material ones — so long as, scil., we do not have foundations of the sciences other than the ones that we have had up until now. But even if the utility of such great doubt would not be apparent at first sight, it is still maximal, in that it might free us from all prejudices and prepare a very easy way for leading the mind away from the senses; and finally, it might effect that we could no longer doubt the things that we will afterwards find out to be true.*

[2.] *In the second Meditation the mind, which — using its own freedom — supposes that all those things whose existence it can even at a minimum doubt do not exist, notices that it cannot happen that it itself would not exist during this time. Which is also of the greatest utility, because by this means the mind easily distinguishes between which things would pertain to it, that is, to an intellectual nature, and which things would pertain to the body. But because some people will perhaps expect arguments for the immortality of the soul in this place, I think that they are to be warned here that I have tried to write nothing that I would not accurately demonstrate, and therefore that I could have followed no other order than that which is usual with the geometers, so that I would of course set forth all the things on which the questioned proposition depends before I would conclude anything about it. Moreover, I think that they are to be warned here that the first and foremost thing which*

80   *Synopsis*

um quod praerequiritur ad cognoscendam animae immortalitatem, esse ut quàm maxime perspicuum de eâ conceptum, & ab omni conceptu corporis plane distinctum, formemus; quod ibi factum est. Praeterea verò requiri etiam ut sciamus ea omnia quae clare & distincte intelligimus, eo ipso modo quo illa intelligimus, esse vera: quod ante quartam Meditationem probari non potuit; & habendum esse distinctum naturae corporeae conceptum, qui partim in ipsâ secundâ, partim etiam in quintâ & sextâ formatur; atque ex his debere concludi ea omnia quae clare & distincte concipiuntur ut substantiae diversae, sicuti concipiuntur mens & corpus, esse revera substantias realiter a se mutuò distinctas; hocque in sextâ concludi. Idemque etiam in ipsâ confirmari ex eo quòd nullum corpus nisi divisibile intelligamus, contrà autem nullam mentem nisi indivisibilem: neque enim possumus ullius mentis mediam partem concipere, ut possumus cujuslibet quantamvis exigui corporis; adeo ut eorum naturae non modo diversae, sed etiam quodammodo contrariae agnoscantur. Non autem ulteriùs eâ de re in hoc scripto me egisse; tum quia haec sufficiunt ad ostendendum ex corporis corruptione mentis interitum non sequi, atque sic ad alterius vitae spem mortalibus faciendam; tum etiam quia praemissae, ex quibus ipsa mentis immortalitas concludi potest, ex totius Physicae explicatione dependent: primo [14] ut sciatur omnes omnino substantias, sive res quae a Deo creari debent ut existant, ex naturâ suâ esse incorruptibiles, nec posse unquam desinere esse, nisi ab eodem Deo concursum suum iis denegante ad nihilum reducantur; ac deinde ut advertatur corpus quidem in genere sumptum esse substantiam, ideoque nunquam etiam perire. Sed corpus humanum, quatenus a reli-

is prerequisite for cognizing the immortality of the soul is that we were to form a concept of it maximally perspicuous and plainly distinct from every concept of body, which has been done here. But in addition, I think that they are to be warned here that it is also required that we were to know that all the things that we clearly and distinctly understand are true in that mode itself in which we understand them, which has not been able to be proved before the fourth Meditation; and that a distinct concept of corporeal nature is to be had, which is formed partly in the second Meditation itself and partly in the fifth and sixth Meditation; and that from these things it should be concluded that all the things that are clearly and distinctly conceived as different substances, as mind and body are conceived, really and truly are substances really mutually distinct from each other; and that this is concluded in the sixth Meditation. And I think that they are to be warned here that in the sixth Meditation the same thing is also confirmed from thence that we might understand no body except as being divisible, but—on the contrary—no mind except as being indivisible, for we cannot conceive of a half-part of any mind as we can conceive of a half-part of any body, however small that you will—so much so that the natures of mind and body be recognized not only as being different, but also as being in a certain manner contrary. But I think that they are to be warned here that I have not further dealt with this matter in this writing, first, because these things suffice to show that from the corruption of the body the perishing of the mind does not follow—and thus to make hope to mortals of another life—, then too, because the premisses from which the immortality itself of the mind can be concluded depend on the explication of the whole of physics: first, that it be known that absolutely all substances—or things which must be created by God in order that they may exist—are by their nature incorruptible, nor can they ever cease to be unless they be reduced to nothing by the same God's denying his concurrence to them, and then, that it be noticed that body—at least taken in general—is a substance and therefore that it too never perishes. But I think that they are to be warned here that the

quis differt corporibus, non nisi ex certâ membrorum configuratione aliisque ejusmodi accidentibus esse conflatum; mentem verò humanam non ita ex ullis accidentibus constare, sed puram esse substantiam: etsi enim omnia ejus accidentia mutentur, ut quòd alias res intelligat, alias velit, alias sentiat, &c, non idcirco ipsa mens alia evadit; humanum autem corpus aliud fit ex hoc solo quòd figura quarumdam ejus partium mutetur: ex quibus sequitur corpus quidem perfacile interire, mentem autem ex naturâ suâ esse immortalem.

In tertiâ Meditatione, meum praecipuum argumentum ad probandum Dei existentiam satis fusè, ut mihi videtur, explicui. Verumtamen, quia, ut Lectorum animos quàm maxime a sensibus abducerem, nullis ibi comparationibus a rebus corporeis petitis volui uti, multae fortasse obscuritates remanserunt, sed quae, ut spero, postea in responsionibus ad objectiones plane tollentur; ut, inter caeteras, quomodo idea entis summe perfecti, quae in nobis est, tantum habeat realitatis objectivae, ut non possit non esse a causâ summe perfectâ, quod ibi illustratur comparatione machinae valde perfectae, cujus idea est in mente alicujus artificis; ut enim artificium objectivum hujus ideae debet habere aliquam causam, nempe scientiam hujus artificis, vel alicujus alterius a quo illam accepit, ita [15] *idea Dei, quae in nobis est, non potest non habere Deum ipsum pro causâ.*

In quartâ, probatur ea omnia quae clare & distincte percipimus, esse vera, simulque in quo ratio falsitatis consistat explicatur: quae necessariò sciri debent tam ad praecedentia firmanda, quàm ad reliqua intelligenda. (Sed ibi interim est advertendum nullo modo agi de peccato, vel errore qui committitur in persecutione boni & mali, sed de eo tantùm qui con-

human body, in so far as it differs from other bodies, is not made up of anything except of a certain configuration of members and other accidents of this kind, yet that the human mind does not thus consist of any accidents, but rather is it a pure substance. For even if all its accidents would change, so that it would understand other things, want other things, sense other things, etc., the mind itself does not therefore become another mind. But the human body becomes another body from thence alone that the figure of some of its parts were to change. From which things it follows that the body very easily indeed perishes, but that the mind is by its nature immortal.

[3.] In the third Meditation I have explicated in satisfactory detail—as it seems to me—my foremost argument for proving the existence of God. But because there I have wanted to use no comparisons taken from corporeal things in order that I might maximally lead the minds of the readers away from the senses, many obscurities have perhaps still remained, which will, however, as I hope, fully be eliminated afterwards in the responses to the objections, obscurities such as, among others, how the idea of a most highly perfect being, which is in us, may have so much objective reality that it could not not be from a most highly perfect cause—which is there illustrated by the comparison with a very perfect machine of which the idea is in the mind of some artificer. For just as the objective artifice must have some cause of the idea of it, namely, the scientific knowledge of its artificer—or of someone else from whom he has received it—, so the idea of God which is in us cannot not have God himself as its cause.

[4.] In the fourth Meditation it is proved that all the things that we clearly and distinctly perceive are true and it is simultaneously explicated wherein the nature of falsity were to consist: which things should necessarily be known, as much to render firm the things that precede as to understand the others. (But it is to be noticed, however, that sin—or error that is committed in the pursuit of good and evil—is in no way dealt with there; rather is that error only which occurs in the judging of

tingit in dijudicatione veri & falsi. Nec ea spectari quae ad fidem pertinent, vel ad vitam agendam, sed tantùm speculativas & solius luminis naturalis ope cognitas veritates.)

In quintâ, praeterquam quòd natura corporea in genere sumpta explicatur, novâ etiam ratione Dei existentia demonstratur: sed in quâ rursus nonnullae fortè occurrent difficultates, quae postea in responsione ad objectiones resolventur: ac denique ostenditur quo pacto verum sit, ipsarum Geometricarum demonstrationum certitudinem a cognitione Dei pendere.

In sextâ denique, intellectio ab imaginatione secernitur; distinctionum signa describuntur; mentem realiter a corpore distingui probatur; eandem nihilominus tam arctè illi esse conjunctam, ut unum quid cum ipsâ componat, ostenditur; omnes errores qui a sensibus oriri solent recensentur; modi quibus vitari possint exponuntur; & denique rationes omnes ex quibus rerum materialium existentia possit concludi, afferuntur: non quòd eas valde utiles esse putarim ad probandum id ipsum quod [16] probant, nempe revera esse aliquem mundum, & homines habere corpora, & similia, de quibus nemo unquam sanae mentis serò dubitavit; sed quia, illas considerando, agnoscitur non esse tam firmas nec tam perspicuas quàm sunt eae, per quas in mentis nostrae & Dei cognitionem devenimus; adeo ut hae sint omnium certissimae & evidentissimae quae ab humano ingenio sciri possint. Cujus unius rei probationem in his Meditationibus mihi pro scopo proposui. Nec idcirco hîc recenseo varias illas quaestiones de quibus etiam in ipsis ex occasione tractatur. [17]

the true and the false dealt with there. Nor are the things regard-
ed that pertain to faith or to the conduct of life, but rather are
regarded only the truths that are speculative and cognized with
the help of the natural light alone.)

[5.] *In the fifth Meditation, in addition thereto that corporeal*
nature — taken in general — is explicated, the existence of God
is also demonstrated by a new argument. But again perhaps
there occur in it some difficulties, which will later be resolved
in the response to the objections. And finally, it is shown how
it be true that the certitude of geometrical demonstrations them-
selves depends on the cognition of God.

[6.] *In the sixth Meditation, finally, intellection is distin-*
guished from imagination; the criteria of the distinctions are
described; it is proved that the mind is really to be distinguished
from the body; the mind is shown to be nonetheless so closely
joined to the body that it might compose one thing with it; all
the errors that usually arise from the senses are reviewed; the
means by which these errors could be avoided are set out; and
finally, all the arguments from which the existence of material
things could be concluded are brought forward: not that I would
think these arguments to be very useful for proving that itself
which they do prove, namely, that there really and truly is a
world and that human beings have bodies and similar things —
which no one of sane mind has ever seriously doubted —, but
rather because by considering these arguments it is recognized
that they are not as firm nor as perspicuous as are those argu-
ments by which we arrive at the cognition of our own mind
and of God — so much so that these latter arguments be the most
certain and the most evident of all the arguments that could
be known by the human mind. Of which one thing I have pro-
posed the proof as my goal in these Meditations. Nor there-
fore do I here review those various other questions of which
are also occasionally treated in these Meditations.

MEDITATIONUM
DE PRIMA
PHILOSOPHIA

IN QUIBUS DEI EXISTENTIA & ANIMAE A CORPORE DISTINCTIO DEMONSTRANTUR

PRIMA

De iis quae in dubium revocari possunt.

Animadverti jam ante aliquot annos quàm multa, ineunte aetate, falsa pro veris admiserim, & quàm dubia sint quaecunque istis postea superextruxi, ac proinde funditus omnia semel in vitâ esse evertenda, atque a primis fundamentis denuo inchoandum, si quid aliquando firmum & mansurum cupiam in scientiis stabilire; sed ingens opus esse videbatur, eamque aetatem expectabam, quae foret tam matura, ut capessendis disciplinis aptior nulla sequeretur. Quare tamdiu cunctatus sum ut deinceps essem in culpâ, si quod temporis superest ad agendum, deliberando consumerem. Opportune igitur hodie mentem curis [18] omnibus exsolvi, securum mihi otium procuravi, solus secedo, seriò tandem & libere generali huic mearum opinionum eversioni vacabo.

Ad hoc autem non erit necesse, ut omnes esse falsas ostendam, quod nunquam fortassis assequi possem; sed quia jam

OF THE MEDITATIONS
ON FIRST
PHILOSOPHY

IN WHICH THE EXISTENCE OF GOD &
THE DISTINCTION OF THE SOUL FROM THE BODY
ARE DEMONSTRATED

THE FIRST

Concerning the things that can be called into doubt.

[1.] Already some years ago I have noticed how many false things I, going into my youth, had admitted as true and how dubious were whatever things I have afterwards built upon them, and therefore that once in my life all things are fundamentally to be demolished and that I have to begin again from the first foundations if I were to desire ever to stabilize something firm and lasting in the sciences. But the task seemed to be a huge one, and I waited for that age which would be so mature that none more fit for the disciplines to be pursued would follow. Thus I have delayed so long that I would now be at fault if by deliberating I were to consume that time which remains for what is to be done. Today then I have opportunely rid the mind of all cares and I have procured for myself secure leisure, I am withdrawing alone and I shall at last devote myself seriously and freely to this general demolition of my opinions.

[2.] Yet to do this it will not be necessary that I would show that all my opinions are false, which I could perhaps never

ratio persuadet, non minus accurate ab iis quae non plane certa sunt atque indubitata, quàm ab aperte falsis assensionem esse
cohibendam, satis erit ad omnes rejiciendas, si aliquam rationem dubitandi in unâquâque reperero. Nec ideo etiam singulae erunt percurrendae, quod operis esset infiniti; sed quia,
suffossis fundamentis, quidquid iis superaedificatum est sponte
collabitur, aggrediar statim ipsa principia, quibus illud omne
quod olim credidi nitebatur.

Nempe quidquid hactenus ut maxime verum admisi, vel a
sensibus, vel per sensus accepi; hos autem interdum fallere deprehendi, ac prudentiae est nunquam illis plane confidere qui nos
vel semel deceperunt.

Sed forte, quamvis interdum sensus circa minuta quaedam
& remotiora nos fallant, pleraque tamen alia sunt de quibus
dubitari plane non potest, quamvis ab iisdem hauriantur: ut
jam me hîc esse, foco assidere, hyemali togâ esse indutum, chartam istam manibus contrectare, & similia. Manus verò has ipsas, totumque hoc corpus meum esse, quâ ratione posset negari?
nisi me forte comparem nescio quibus insanis, [19] quorum cere-
bella tam contumax vapor ex atrâ bile labefactat, ut constanter
asseverent vel se esse reges, cùm sunt pauperrimi, vel purpurâ
indutos, cùm sunt nudi, vel caput habere fictile, vel se totos esse
cucurbitas, vel ex vitro conflatos; sed amentes sunt isti, nec minùs ipse demens viderer, si quod ab iis exemplum ad me trans-
ferrem.

Praeclare sane, tanquam non sim homo qui soleam noctu
dormire, & eadem omnia in somnis pati, vel etiam interdum
minùs verisimilia, quàm quae isti vigilantes. Quàm frequenter

achieve anyway. Because reason already persuades me that assent is to be withheld no less accurately from the opinions that are not fully certain and indubitable than from the ones that are overtly false, rather will it suffice to reject all my opinions if I shall have found any reason for doubting in each one. And therefore nor will these opinions have to be gone through individually, which would be an infinite task. But because—the foundations having been undermined—whatever has been built upon them will collapse spontaneously, I will go right for those principles upon which rested all that which I have once believed.

[3.] Namely, whatever I have admitted up until now as maximally true I have accepted from the senses or through the senses. Yet I have found that these senses sometimes deceive me, and it is a matter of prudence never to confide completely in those who have deceived us even once.

[4.] But even if the senses would perhaps sometimes deceive us about certain minute and more remote things, there are still many other things that plainly cannot be doubted, although they be derived from the same senses: such as that I am now here, that I am sitting by the fire, that I am clothed in a winter robe, that I am holding this piece of paper with the hands, and similar things. Truly, by means of what reason could it be denied that these hands themselves and this whole body are mine? Unless I were perhaps to compare myself with—I know not which—insane people, whose brains the stubborn vapor of black bile so weakens that they might constantly assert that they are kings when they are very poor, or that they are clothed in purple when they are nude, or that they have an earthenware head, or that they are—as wholes—pumpkins or made of glass. But these people are without minds, nor would I myself seem less demented if I were to transfer something as an example from them to me.

[5.] Brilliantly soundly argued, as if I were not a human being who would be accustomed to sleep at night and to undergo passively in dreams all the same things as—or even sometimes things less verisimilar than—those which these insane people

verò usitata ista, me hîc esse, togâ vestiri, foco assidere, quies nocturna persuadet, cùm tamen positis vestibus jaceo inter strata! Atqui nunc certe vigilantibus oculis intueor hanc chartam, non sopitum est hoc caput quod commoveo, manum istam prudens & sciens extendo & sentio; non tam distincta contingerent dormienti. Quasi scilicet non recorder a similibus etiam cogitationibus me aliàs in somnis fuisse delusum; quae dum cogito attentius, tam plane video nunquam certis indiciis vigiliam a somno posse distingui, ut obstupescam, & fere hic ipse stupor mihi opinionem somni confirmet.

Age ergo somniemus, nec particularia ista vera sint, nos oculos aperire, caput movere, manus extendere, nec forte etiam nos habere tales manus, nec tale totum corpus; tamen profecto fatendum est visa per quietem esse veluti quasdam pictas imagines, quae non nisi ad similitudinem rerum verarum fingi potuerunt; ideoque saltem generalia haec, oculos, caput, manus, totumque corpus, res quasdam non imaginarias, sed veras existere. Nam sane pictores ipsi, ne tum qui[20]dem, cùm Sirenas & Satyriscos maxime inusitatis formis fingere student, naturas omni ex parte novas iis possunt assignare, sed tantummodo diversorum animalium membra permiscent; vel si forte aliquid excogitent adeo novum, ut nihil omnino ei simile fuerit visum, atque ita plane fictitium sit & falsum, certe tamen ad minimum veri colores esse debent, ex quibus illud componant. Nec dispari ratione, quamvis etiam generalia haec, oculi, caput, manus, & similia, imaginaria esse possent, necessario tamen saltem alia quaedam adhuc magis simplicia & universalia vera esse fatendum est, ex quibus tanquam coloribus veris omnes

then do when they are awake. Truly, how frequently noctur-
nal rest persuades me of such usual things—that I am here, that
I am dressed in a robe, that I am sitting by the fire—, when,
however, the clothes having been taken off, I am lying between
the sheets! And yet now I certainly intuit this piece of paper
with waking eyes. This head which I move is not asleep. As
one who is prudent and knowing I extend this hand and I sense.
Things so distinct would not happen to someone sleeping. As
if, scil., I did not remember that on other occasions I have also
been deluded in dreams by similar cogitations. While I cogitate these things more attentively, I see so plainly that being
awake can never be distinguished from sleep by certain criteria
that I be stupefied, and this stupor itself would almost confirm
for me the opinion of being asleep.

[6.] So therefore we be dreaming. Neither would these particular things be true—that we open the eyes, move the head,
extend the hands—, nor perhaps would it even be true that we
have such hands or such a whole body. It is in fact still to be
conceded that the things that are seen during sleep are like a
kind of pictured images which cannot have been feigned except according to the similitude of true things. And hence it is
in fact to be conceded that at least these general things—eyes,
head, hands and the whole body—exist as a kind of things that
are not imaginary, but rather true. For indeed painters themselves, even when they try to feign sirens and satyrs with maximally unusual forms, cannot then assign to them natures new
with respect to every part, but rather can they only mix together
the members of different animals. Or if these painters were
perhaps to excogitate something so very new that nothing at
all similar to it had ever been seen—and it would thus be completely fictitious and false—, at a minimum the colors out of
which they would compose it must certainly still be true. By
not dissimilar reasoning, although these general things too—
eyes, head, hands and similar things—could be imaginary, it
is still necessarily to be conceded that at least certain other things
even more simple and universal are true: things even more simple

istae, seu verae, seu falsae, quae in cogitatione nostrâ sunt, rerum imagines effinguntur.

Cujus generis esse videntur natura corporea in communi, ejusque extensio; item figura rerum extensarum; item quantitas, sive earumdem magnitudo & numerus; item locus in quo existant, tempusque per quod durent, & similia.

Quapropter ex his forsan non male concludemus Physicam, Astronomiam, Medicinam, disciplinasque alias omnes, quae a rerum compositarum consideratione dependent, dubias quidem esse; atqui Arithmeticam, Geometriam, aliasque ejusmodi, quae nonnisi de simplicissimis & maxime generalibus rebus tractant, atque utrum eae sint in rerum naturâ necne, parum curant, aliquid certi atque indubitati continere. Nam sive vigilem, sive dormiam, duo & tria simul juncta sunt quinque, quadratumque non plura habet latera quàm quatuor; nec fieri posse videtur ut tam perspicuae veritates in suspicionem falsitatis incurrant. [21]

Verumtamen infixa quaedam est meae menti vetus opinio, Deum esse qui potest omnia, & a quo talis, qualis existo, sum creatus. Unde autem scio illum non fecisse ut nulla plane sit terra, nullum coelum, nulla res extensa, nulla figura, nulla magnitudo, nullus locus, & tamen haec omnia non aliter quàm nunc mihi videantur existere? Imò etiam, quemadmodum judico interdum alios errare circa ea quae se perfectissime scire arbitrantur, ita ego ut fallar quoties duo & tria simul addo, vel numero quadrati latera, vel si quid aliud facilius fingi potest? At forte noluit Deus ita me decipi, dicitur enim summe bonus; sed si hoc ejus bonitati repugnaret, talem me creasse ut semper fallar, ab eâdem etiam videretur esse alienum permittere ut interdum fallar; quod ultimum tamen non potest dici.

and universal out of which—as from true colors—are feigned all those images of things which, whether true or false, are in our cogitation.

[7.] Of which kind seem to be corporeal nature in general, and its extension; also, the figure of extended things; also, the quantity, or the magnitude and the number of the same things; also, the place in which they may exist, and the time through which they may endure, and similar things.

[8.] Therefore we will perhaps well conclude from these things that physics, astronomy, medicine and all the other disciplines that depend on the consideration of composite things are indeed dubious, but that arithmetic, geometry and the others of this kind—which treat only of the simplest and maximally general things and which care little about whether these would be in the nature of things or not—contain something certain and indubitable. For whether I would be awake or sleeping, two and three added together are five, and a square has no more than four sides. Nor does it seem that it can happen that truths so perspicuous would incur the suspicion of falsity.

[9.] And yet there is fixed in my mind a certain old opinion that there is a God who can do all things and by whom I, as such as I exist, have been created. But how do I know that he has not made it so that there would be no earth at all, no heavens, no extended thing, no figure, no magnitude, no place, and yet that all these things would seem to me to exist not otherwise than they seem to now? And how do I even know that he has not made it so that I—just as I sometimes judge that other people err about the things that they think that they know perfectly, so too I—would be deceived whenever I add two and three together or count the sides of a square, or something else easier, if it can be imagined? But perhaps God has not willed to deceive me thus, for he is called "the most highly good". Yet if this—to have created me such that I were always to be deceived—would contradict his goodness, it would also seem to be alien to the same goodness to permit that I were sometimes to be deceived: which last thing, however, cannot be said.

Essent verò fortasse nonnulli qui tam potentem aliquem Deum mallent negare, quàm res alias omnes credere esse incertas. Sed iis non repugnemus, totumque hoc de Deo demus esse fictitium; at seu fato, seu casu, seu continuatâ rerum serie, seu quovis alio modo me ad id quod sum pervenisse supponant; quoniam falli & errare imperfectio quaedam esse videtur, quo minùs potentem originis meae authorem assignabunt, eo probabilius erit me tam imperfectum esse ut semper fallar. Quibus sane argumentis non habeo quod respondeam, sed tandem cogor fateri nihil esse ex iis quae olim vera putabam, de quo non liceat dubitare, idque non per inconsiderantiam vel levitatem, sed propter validas & meditatas rationes; ideoque etiam ab iisdem, non minùs quàm ab aperte falsis, [22] accurate deinceps assensionem esse cohibendam, si quid certi velim invenire.

Sed nondum sufficit haec advertisse, curandum est ut recorder; assidue enim recurrunt consuetae opiniones, occupantque credulitatem meam tanquam longo usu & familiaritatis jure sibi devinctam, fere etiam me invito; nec unquam iis assentiri & confidere desuescam, quamdiu tales esse supponam quales sunt revera, nempe aliquo quidem modo dubias, ut jam jam ostensum est, sed nihilominus valde probabiles, & quas multo magis rationi consentaneum sit credere quàm negare. Quapropter, ut opinor, non male agam, si, voluntate plane in contrarium versâ, me ipsum fallam, illasque aliquandiu omnino falsas imaginariasque esse fingam, donec tandem, velut aequatis utrimque praejudiciorum ponderibus, nulla amplius prava consuetudo judicium meum a rectâ rerum perceptione detorqueat. Etenim

[10.] But there might perhaps be some people who would prefer to deny the existence of a God so powerful than to believe that all other things are uncertain. Yet let us not contradict them, and let us grant that all this about God is fictitious. On the other hand, these people might suppose that I have come by fate, or by chance, or by a continuous series of things, or by whatever other means that you will, to be that which I am. Because to be deceived and to err seem to be certain imperfections, the less powerful an author of my origin these people will assign, the more probable will it be that I am so imperfect that I would always be deceived. To which arguments I do not have anything that I might soundly respond, but rather am I forced, finally, to concede that of the things which I once held to be true there is none that it would not be permitted to doubt—and this is so not through lack of consideration or levity, but because of reasons valid and meditated on. And therefore I am forced to concede that from now on assent is accurately to be withheld from the same things too no less than from the overtly false ones, if I would want to find something certain.

[11.] But to have noticed these things does not yet suffice. Care is to be taken that I might remember them. For accustomed opinions assiduously recur, and almost even involuntarily for me do they occupy my credulity, which is bound to them as though by long use and the right of familiarity. Nor shall I ever break the habit of assenting to and confiding in these opinions, so long as I were to suppose that they are such as they really and truly are, namely, at least in a certain mode dubious, as has just been shown, but nonetheless very probable, and opinions that it would be much more consentaneous to reason to believe than to deny. Therefore I am of the opinion that I would not do badly if—the will having been turned completely to the contrary—I were to deceive myself, and if I were to feign for a time that these opinions are entirely false and imaginary, until finally, the weights of prejudices having been—as it were—balanced on both sides, no depraved custom would any longer detour my judgment from the correct perception of things. For

scio nihil inde periculi vel erroris interim sequuturum, & me plus aequo diffidentiae indulgere non posse, quandoquidem nunc non rebus agendis, sed cognoscendis tantùm incumbo. Supponam igitur non optimum Deum, fontem veritatis, sed genium aliquem malignum, eundemque summe potentem & callidum, omnem suam industriam in eo posuisse, ut me falleret: putabo coelum, aërem, terram, colores, figuras, sonos, cunctaque externa nihil aliud esse quàm ludificationes somniorum, quibus insidias credulitati meae tetendit: considerabo [23] meipsum tanquam manus non habentem, non oculos, non carnem, non sanguinem, non aliquem sensum, sed haec omnia me habere falsò opinantem: manebo obstinate in hac meditatione defixus, atque ita, siquidem non in potestate meâ sit aliquid veri cognoscere, at certe hoc quod in me est, ne falsis assentiar, nec mihi quidquam iste deceptor, quantumvis potens, quantumvis callidus, possit imponere, obfirmatâ mente cavebo. Sed laboriosum est hoc institutum, & desidia quaedam ad consuetudinem vitae me reducit. Nec aliter quàm captivus, qui forte imaginariâ libertate fruebatur in somnis, cùm postea suspicari incipit se dormire, timet excitari, blandisque illusionibus lente connivet: sic sponte relabor in veteres opiniones, vereorque expergisci, ne placidae quieti laboriosa vigilia succedens, non in aliquâ luce, sed inter inextricabiles jam motarum difficultatum tenebras, in posterum sit degenda.

I know that in the meantime no danger or error is going to follow therefrom, and that I cannot indulge in too much diffidence, since I am now occupied not with things to be done, but rather only with things to be cognized.

[12.] I shall, then, suppose that not the optimal God — the font of truth — , but rather some malign genius — and the same one most highly powerful and most highly cunning — , has put all his industriousness therein that he might deceive me: I shall think that the heavens, the air, the earth, colors, figures, sounds and all external things are nothing other than the playful deceptions of dreams by means of which he has set traps for my credulity; I shall consider myself as not having hands, not eyes, not flesh, not blood, not any senses, but rather as falsely opining that I have all these things; I shall obstinately remain as one fixed in this meditation, and even if it would thus not be in my power to cognize something true, yet that which is in me is certainly that I shall with a firm mind be cautious that I were not to assent to false things, and that the deceiver — however powerful that you will, however cunning that you will — could not impose anything on me. But this undertaking is laborious, and a certain slothfulness reduces me to the custom of life. Not otherwise than a prisoner who perhaps enjoyed an imaginary freedom in a dream, and who, when he begins after a while to suspect that he is sleeping, then is afraid to be awakened and languidly connives with the agreeable illusions: thus do I spontaneously fall back into old opinions and fear waking up, lest the laborious wakefulness following the placid rest would in the future have to be spent not in some light, but rather among the inextricable shadows of the difficulties already raised.

MEDITATIO II.

De natura mentis humanae:
quòd ipsa sit notior quàm corpus.

In tantas dubitationes hesternâ meditatione conjectus sum, ut nequeam ampliùs earum oblivisci, nec videam tamen quâ ratione solvendae sint; sed, tanquam [24] in profundum gurgitem ex improviso delapsus, ita turbatus sum, ut nec possim in imo pedem figere, nec enatare ad summum. Enitar tamen & tentabo rursus eandem viam quam heri fueram ingressus, removendo scilicet illud omne quod vel minimum dubitationis admittit, nihilo secius quàm si omnino falsum esse comperissem; pergamque porro donec aliquid certi, vel, si nihil aliud, saltem hoc ipsum pro certo, nihil esse certi, cognoscam. Nihil nisi punctum petebat Archimedes, quod esset firmum & immobile, ut integram terram loco dimoveret; magna quoque speranda sunt, si vel minimum quid invenero quod certum sit & inconcussum.

Suppono igitur omnia quae video falsa esse; credo nihil unquam extitisse eorum quae mendax memoria repraesentat; nullos plane habeo sensus; corpus, figura, extensio, motus, locusque sunt chimerae. Quid igitur erit verum? Fortassis hoc unum, nihil esse certi.

Sed unde scio nihil esse diversum ab iis omnibus quae jam jam recensui, de quo ne minima quidem occasio sit dubitandi?

MEDITATION II.

Concerning the nature of the human mind:
that it be more known than [the] body.

[1.] I have been thrown into so great doubts by yesterday's meditation that I could no longer forget them, nor would I yet see by means of what reasoning they were to be resolved. Like one who has improvidently fallen into a deep whirlpool, rather am I so perturbed that I could neither fix a foot on the bottom nor swim to the top. However, I shall make an effort, and I shall once again attempt to go the way that I have gone yesterday, scil., by removing all that which admits of doubt even at a minimum no less than if I had found it to be completely false. And I shall proceed further in this direction until I might cognize something certain, or — if nothing else — at least this itself for certain: that there is nothing certain. Archimedes demanded nothing but a point that be firm and immovable in order that he might move the entire earth from its place: great things are also to be hoped for if I shall have found even something minimal that be certain and unshakeable.

[2.] I am supposing, then, that all the things that I see are false. I believe that none of the things that the mendacious memory represents has ever existed. I have no senses at all. Body, figure, extension, movement and place are chimeras. What will, then, be true? Perhaps just this one thing: that there is nothing certain.

[3.] But from whence do I know that there is nothing which is different from all the things that I have already reviewed, and concerning which there were not even a minimal occasion of

Nunquid est aliquis Deus, vel quocunque nomine illum vocem, qui mihi has ipsas cogitationes immittit? Quare verò hoc putem, cùm forsan ipsemet illarum author esse possim? Nunquid ergo saltem ego aliquid sum? Sed jam negavi me habere ullos sensus, & ullum corpus. Haereo tamen; nam quid [25] inde? Sumne ita corpori sensibusque alligatus, ut sine illis esse non possim? Sed mihi persuasi nihil plane esse in mundo, nullum coelum, nullam terram, nullas mentes, nulla corpora; nonne igitur etiam me non esse? Imo certe ego eram, si quid mihi persuasi. Sed est deceptor nescio quis, summe potens, summe callidus, qui de industriâ me semper fallit. Haud dubie igitur ego etiam sum, si me fallit; & fallat quantum potest, nunquam tamen efficiet, ut nihil sim quamdiu me aliquid esse cogitabo. Adeo ut, omnibus satis superque pensitatis, denique statuendum sit hoc pronuntiatum, *Ego sum, ego existo*, quoties a me profertur, vel mente concipitur, necessario esse verum.

Nondum verò satis intelligo, quisnam sim ego ille, qui jam necessario sum; deincepsque cavendum est ne forte quid aliud imprudenter assumam in locum meî, sicque aberrem etiam in eâ cognitione, quam omnium certissimam evidentissimamque esse contendo. Quare jam denuo meditabor quidnam me olim esse crediderim, priusquam in has cogitationes incidissem; ex quo deinde subducam quidquid allatis rationibus vel minimum potuit infirmari, ut ita tandem praecise remaneat illud tantùm quod certum est & inconcussum.

Quidnam igitur antehac me esse putavi? Hominem scilicet. Sed quid est homo? Dicamne animal rationale? Non, quia postea quaerendum foret quidnam animal sit, & quid rationale, atque ita ex unâ quaestione in plures difficilioresque delaberer;

doubting? Is there not a "God"—or by whatever other name I would call him—who immits these cogitations themselves into me? But why would I think this, since I myself could perhaps be the author of them? Am *I* not therefore at least something? Yet I have already denied that I have any senses and any body. I pause, however. For what follows from thence? Am I not so bound to the body and to the senses that I could not be without them? But I have persuaded myself that there is nothing at all in the world, no heavens, no earth, no minds, no bodies: also, then, that I am not? No, if I was persuading myself of something, then certainly *I* was. Yet there is a deceiver—I know not who he is—, most highly powerful and most highly cunning, who always industriously deceives me. If he is deceiving me, then without doubt *I* also am. And he might deceive me as much as he can, he will still never effect that I would be nothing, so long as I shall cogitate that I am something. So that—all things having been weighed enough, and more—this statement were, finally, to be established: "*I am, I exist*" is necessarily true, so often as it is uttered by me or conceived by the mind.

[4.] But I do not yet satisfactorily understand who I be, as that *I* who I now necessarily am. And from the start it is to be cautioned that I would not perhaps imprudently assume something else in place of me and thus err off even in that cognition which I contend to be the most certain and the most evident one of all. Which is why I shall now meditate anew on what I had once believed myself to be before I have gone into these cogitations, from which I shall then subtract whatever could have been weakened even at a minimum by the reasons brought forth, so that thus, finally, precisely only that which is certain and unshakeable might remain.

[5.] What, then, have I formerly thought myself to be? Scil., a human being. But what is a human being? Shall I say "a rational animal"? No, because then it would have to be asked what an animal be, and what rational be, and thus from one question I would slide down into many and more difficult ones. Nor do I now have so much leisure that I would want to abuse

nec jam mihi tantum otii est, ut illo velim inter istiusmodi sub-
tilitates abuti. Sed hîc potius attendam, quid sponte [26] &
naturâ duce cogitationi meae antehac occurrebat, quoties quid
essem considerabam. Nempe occurrebat primo, me habere vul-
tum, manus, brachia, totamque hanc membrorum machinam,
qualis etiam in cadavere cernitur, & quam corporis nomine
designabam. Occurrebat praeterea me nutriri, incedere, sentire, & cogitare: quas quidem actiones ad animam referebam.
Sed quid esset haec anima, vel non advertebam, vel exiguum
nescio quid imaginabar, instar venti, vel ignis, vel aetheris, quod
crassioribus meî partibus esset infusum. De corpore verò ne
dubitabam quidem, sed distincte me nosse arbitrabar ejus
naturam, quam si forte, qualem mente concipiebam, describere
tentassem, sic explicuissem: per corpus intelligo illud omne quod
aptum est figurâ aliquâ terminari, loco circumscribi, spatium
sic replere, ut ex eo aliud omne corpus excludat; tactu, visu,
auditu, gustu, vel odoratu percipi, necnon moveri pluribus modis, non quidem a seipso, sed ab alio quopiam a quo tangatur:
namque habere vim seipsum movendi, item sentiendi, vel
cogitandi, nullo pacto ad naturam corporis pertinere judicabam; quinimo mirabar potius tales facultates in quibusdam corporibus reperiri.

Quid autem nunc, ubi suppono deceptorem aliquem potent-
issimum, &, si fas est dicere, malignum, datâ operâ in omnibus, quantum potuit, me delusisse? Possumne affirmare me habere vel minimum quid ex iis omnibus, quae jam dixi ad naturam
corporis perti[27]nere? Attendo, cogito, revolvo, nihil occurrit; fatigor eadem frustrà repetere. Quid verò ex iis quae animae tribuebam? Nutriri vel incedere? Quandoquidem jam corpus non habeo, haec quoque nihil sunt nisi figmenta. Sentire?

it on subtleties of this sort. Rather shall I here pay attention to what formerly occurred to my cogitation spontaneously and with nature as a guide whenever I considered what I might be. Namely, it occurred to me, first, that I had a face, hands, arms and this whole machine of members such as it also shows itself in a corpse and which I designated by the term "body". It occurred to me, in addition, that I was nourished, that I walked about, that I sensed and that I cogitated: which actions I referred of course to the soul. But what this soul might be, I did not notice, or else I imagined it as something—I know not what—exiguous, like a wind or a fire or an ether, which had been infused into the coarser parts of me. Yet I did not even doubt about the body, but rather did I think that I distinctly knew its nature, which—if I had perhaps attempted to describe it as such as I conceived it with the mind—I would have explicated thus: By "body" I understand all that which is fit to be determined by some figure, to be circumscribed by place, to fill up space in such a way as that all other body be excluded from it, to be perceived by touch, sight, hearing, taste or smell, and to be moved in many ways, surely not by itself, but by whatever else by which it be touched. For I also judged that to have the power of moving itself, as well as the power of sensing or of cogitating, in no way pertains to the nature of a body. Rather was I indeed surprised that such faculties are found in certain bodies.

[6.] But what am I then now: when I suppose that some very powerful and, if it is permitted to say so, malign deceiver has—the effort having been made in all things—deluded me as much as he could have? Can I affirm that I have even some minimum of all the things that I have just said to pertain to the nature of the body? I am paying attention to them. I cogitate about them. I return to them. Nothing else occurs to me. I get tired of repeating the same things in a frustrating way. But what about the things that I attributed to the soul? To be nourished or to walk about? Since I do not now have a body, these things too are nothing but figments. To sense? Of course this too does not

Nempe etiam hoc non fit sine corpore, & permulta sentire visus sum in somnis quae deinde animadverti me non sensisse. Cogitare? Hîc invenio: cogitatio est; haec sola a me divelli nequit. Ego sum, ego existo; certum est. Quandiu autem? Nempe quandiu cogito; nam forte etiam fieri posset, si cessarem ab omni cogitatione, ut illico totus esse desinerem. Nihil nunc admitto nisi quod necessario sit verum; sum igitur praecise tantùm res cogitans, id est, mens, sive animus, sive intellectus, sive ratio, voces mihi priùs significationis ignotae. Sum autem res vera, & vere existens; sed qualis res? Dixi, cogitans.

Quid praeterea? Imaginabor: non sum compages illa membrorum, quae corpus humanum appellatur; non sum etiam tenuis aliquis aër istis membris infusus, non ventus, non ignis, non vapor, non halitus, non quidquid mihi fingo: supposui enim ista nihil esse. Manet positio: nihilominus tamen ego aliquid sum. Fortassis verò contingit, ut haec ipsa, quae suppono nihil esse, quia mihi sunt ignota, tamen in rei veritate non differant ab eo me quem novi? Nescio, de hac re jam non disputo; de iis tantùm quae mihi nota sunt, judicium ferre possum. Novi me existere; quaero quis sim ego ille quem novi. Certissimum est hujus sic praecise sumpti notitiam non pendere ab iis quae exi[28]stere nondum novi; non igitur ab iis ullis, quae ima[gi]natione effingo. Atque hoc verbum, *effingo*, admonet me erroris mei: nam fingerem reverà, si quid me esse imaginarer, quia nihil aliud est imaginari quàm rei corporeae figuram, seu imaginem, contemplari. Jam autem certò scio me esse, simulque fieri posse ut omnes istae imagines, & generaliter quaecunque ad corporis naturam referuntur, nihil sint praeter insomnia. Quibus animadversis, non minus ineptire videor, dicendo: im-

happen without a body, and I have seemed to sense very many
things in dreams that I have then noticed that I have not sensed.
To cogitate? Here I find: it is cogitation; this alone cannot be
rent from me. *I* am, *I* exist; it is certain. But for how long? So
long as I am cogitating, of course. For it could perhaps also
happen that if I would cease all cogitation I as a whole would
at once cease to be. I am now admitting nothing except what
be necessarily true. I am, then, precisely only a cogitating thing,
that is, a mind, or animus, or intellect, or reason: words with
significations previously unknown to me. But I am a true thing,
and truly existing. Yet what kind of thing? A thinking thing,
I have said.

[7.] What else am I? I shall imagine: I am not that structure
of members which is called "a human body". I am also not some
tenuous air infused into these members, not a wind, not a fire,
not a vapor, not a breath, not something that I feign to myself:
for I have supposed that these things are nothing. There remains
the proposition: "*I* am nonetheless still something." But perhaps
it happens that these things themselves, which I suppose to be
nothing because they are unknown to me, would in the truth
of the matter still not differ from that me whom I know? I do
not know. I am not now disputing about this matter. I can render
judgment only on the things that are known to me. I know that
I exist. I am asking who I be, as that *I* whom I know. It is very
certain that the knowledge of it — taken thus precisely — does
not depend on the things that I do not yet know to exist. And
it does not depend, then, on any of the things that I feign with
the imagination. And these very words, "*I feign*", warn me of
my error: for I would really and truly be feigning if I were to
imagine that I am something, because to imagine is nothing other
than to contemplate the figure or image of a corporeal thing.
But now I certainly know that I am and simultaneously that
it can happen that all these images and whatever things generally are referred to the nature of the body would be nothing
but dreams. Which things having been noticed, I seem to be
no less inept in saying that I shall imagine in order that I might

aginabor, ut distinctius agnoscam quisnam sim, quàm si dicerem: jam quidem sum experrectus, videoque nonnihil veri, sed quia nondum video satis evidenter, datâ operâ obdormiam, ut hoc ipsum mihi somnia verius evidentiusque repraesentent. Itaque cognosco nihil eorum quae possum imaginationis ope comprehendere, ad hanc quam de me habeo notitiam pertinere, mentemque ab illis diligentissime esse avocandam, ut suam ipsa naturam quàm distinctissime percipiat.

Sed quid igitur sum? Res cogitans. Quid est hoc? Nempe dubitans, intelligens, affirmans, negans, volens, nolens, imaginans quoque, & sentiens.

Non pauca sanè haec sunt, si cuncta ad me pertineant. Sed quidni pertinerent? Nonne ego ipse sum qui jam dubito ferè de omnibus, qui nonnihil tamen intelligo, qui hoc unum verum esse affirmo, nego caetera, cupio plura nosse, nolo decipi, multa vel invitus imaginor, multa etiam tanquam a sensibus venientia animadverto? Quid est horum, quamvis semper dor[29]miam, quamvis etiam is qui me creavit, quantum in se est, me deludat, quod non aeque verum sit ac me esse? Quid est quod a meâ cogitatione distinguatur? Quid est quod a me ipso separatum dici possit? Nam quod ego sim qui dubitem, qui intelligam, qui velim, tam manifestum est, ut nihil occurrat per quod evidentius explicetur. Sed verò etiam ego idem sum qui imaginor; nam quamvis fortè, ut supposui, nulla prorsus res imaginata vera sit, vis tamen ipsa imaginandi revera existit, & cogitationis meae partem facit. Idem denique ego sum qui sentio, sive qui res corporeas tanquam per sensus animadverto: videlicet jam lucem video, strepitum audio, calorem sentio. Falsa haec sunt, dormio enim. At certe videre videor, audire, calescere. Hoc falsum esse non potest; hoc est proprie quod

more distinctly recognize who I might be, than if I were to say that I am indeed already awake and I see something true, but because I do not yet see it evidently enough I shall—the effort having been made—fall asleep in order that dreams might more truly and evidently represent this itself to me. Thus do I cognize that none of the things that I can comprehend with the help of the imagination pertains to that knowledge which I have of me, and that the mind is very diligently to be called away from these things in order that it might itself perceive its own nature as distinctly as possible.

[8.] But what, then, am I? A cogitating thing. What is that? A thing doubting, understanding, affirming, denying, willing, not willing, also imagining and sensing, of course.

[9.] These things are indeed many—if they would all pertain to me. But why would they not pertain to me? Is it not *I* myself who am now doubting almost all things, who still understand something, who affirm that this one thing is true, deny the other things, desire to know more things, do not want to be deceived, imagine many things even involuntarily, as well as notice many things coming as though from the senses? What is there of these things that, although I were always sleeping, although he who has created me were even to be deluding me as much as it is in him to do, would not be equally as true as that I am? What is there of these things that might be distinguished from my cogitation? What is there of these things that could be called "separate" from me myself? For that it be *I* who be doubting, who be understanding, who be willing, is so manifest that there might occur to me nothing through which it might be explicated more evidently. But truly *I* am also the same one who imagines. For although perhaps—as I have supposed—no imagined thing at all be true, the power of imagining itself still really and truly exists, and it makes up a part of my cogitation. Finally, *I* am the same one who senses or who notices corporeal things as though through the senses: viz., I am now seeing light, I am hearing noise, I am sensing warmth. These things are false, for I am sleeping. But certainly I seem to see, I seem to hear, I seem to be warmed. This cannot be

in me sentire appellatur; atque hoc praecise sic sumptum nihil aliud est quàm cogitare.

Ex quibus equidem aliquanto melius incipio nosse quisnam sim; sed adhuc tamen videtur, nec possum abstinere quin putem, res corporeas, quarum imagines cogitatione formantur, & quas ipsi sensus explorant, multo distinctius agnosci quàm istud nescio quid meî, quod sub imaginationem non venit: quanquam profecto sit mirum, res quas animadverto esse dubias, ignotas, a me alienas, distinctius quàm quod verum est, quod cognitum, quàm denique me ipsum, a me comprehendi. Sed video quid sit: gaudet aberrare mens mea, necdum se patitur intra veritatis limites cohiberi. Esto igitur, & adhuc semel laxissimas habe[30]nas ei permittamus, ut, illis paulo post opportune reductis, facilius se regi patiatur.

Consideremus res illas quae vulgo putantur omnium distinctissime comprehendi: corpora scilicet, quae tangimus, quae videmus; non quidem corpora in communi, generales enim istae perceptiones aliquantò magis confusae esse solent, sed unum in particulari. Sumamus, exempli causâ, hanc ceram: nuperrime ex favis fuit educta; nondum amisit omnem saporem sui mellis; nonnihil retinet odoris florum ex quibus collecta est; ejus color, figura, magnitudo, manifesta sunt; dura est, frigida est, facile tangitur, ac, si articulo ferias, emittet sonum; omnia denique illi adsunt quae requiri videntur, ut corpus aliquod possit quàm distinctissime cognosci. Sed ecce, dum loquor, igni admovetur: saporis reliquiae purgantur, odor expirat, color mutatur, figura tollitur, crescit magnitudo, fit liquida, fit calida, vix tangi potest, nec jam, si pulses, emittet sonum. Remanetne adhuc eadem cera? Remanere fatendum est; nemo

false. It is this which in me is properly called "to sense". And this—taken thus precisely—is nothing other than to cogitate.

[10.] From which things I am indeed beginning to know rather better who I be. But yet it still seems, and I cannot refrain from thinking, that corporeal things—of which the images are formed by cogitation and which the senses themselves explore—are much more distinctly recognized than that of me—I know not what—which does not come under the focus of the imagination. Yet it would be perfectly surprising that things that I notice to be dubious, unknown and alien to me be comprehended more distinctly by me than what is true, than what is cognized and, finally, than me myself. But I see what the problem might be: my mind likes to err off, and it does not suffer itself to be held within the limits of the truth. Let it be, then, and we may once more permit it very lax reins in order that—these having opportunely been restricted a little later on—it might suffer itself to be ruled more easily.

[11.] We might consider those things which are commonly thought to be comprehended most distinctly of all things: scil., the bodies that we touch, that we see—surely not bodies in general, for these general perceptions are usually somewhat more confused, but rather one body in particular. We might take, for example, this piece of wax here: It has very recently been taken from the honeycomb. It has not yet lost all the taste of its honey. It retains some of the odor of the flowers from which it has been gathered. Its color, figure and magnitude are manifest. It is hard. It is cold. It is easily touched. And if you were to hit it with a knuckle it will emit a sound. In short, all the things are present in it which seem to be required in order that a body might be cognized very distinctly. But voilà, while I am speaking the piece of wax is moved towards the fire: The remains of the taste are purged, the odor goes away, the color is changed, the figure is lost, the magnitude increases, the piece of wax becomes liquid, it becomes hot, it can hardly be touched, and it will no longer emit a sound if you were to strike it. Does it still remain the same piece of wax? It is to be conceded that

negat, nemo aliter putat. Quid erat igitur in eâ quod tam distincte comprehendebatur? Certe nihil eorum quae sensibus attingebam; nam quaecunque sub gustum, vel odoratum, vel visum, vel tactum, vel auditum veniebant, mutata jam sunt: remanet cera.

Fortassis illud erat quod nunc cogito: nempe ceram ipsam non quidem fuisse istam dulcedinem mellis, nec florum fragrantiam, nec istam albedinem, nec figuram, nec sonum, sed corpus quod mihi apparebat paulo ante modis istis conspicuum, nunc diversis. Quid est autem hoc praecise quod sic imaginor? Attenda[31]mus, &, remotis iis quae ad ceram non pertinent, videamus quid supersit: nempe nihil aliud quàm extensum quid, flexibile, mutabile. Quid verò est hoc flexibile, mutabile? An quod imaginor, hanc ceram ex figurâ rotundâ in quadratam, vel ex hac in triangularem verti posse? Nullo modo; nam innumerabilium ejusmodi mutationum capacem eam esse comprehendo, nec possum tamen innumerabiles imaginando percurrere; nec igitur comprehensio haec ab imaginandi facultate perficitur. Quid extensum? Nunquid etiam ipsa ejus extensio est ignota? Nam in cerâ liquescente fit major, major in ferventi, majorque rursus, si calor augeatur; nec recte judicarem quid sit cera, nisi putarem hanc etiam plures secundùm extensionem varietates admittere, quàm fuerim unquam imaginando complexus. Superest igitur ut concedam, me nequidem imaginari quid sit haec cera, sed solâ mente percipere; dico hanc in particulari, de cerâ enim in communi clarius est. Quaenam verò est haec cera, quae non nisi mente percipitur? Nempe eadem quam video, quam tango, quam imaginor, eadem denique quam ab initio esse arbitrabar. Atqui, quod notandum est, ejus per-

it does remain the same piece of wax. No one denies it. No one thinks otherwise. What was it, then, in the piece of wax that was so distinctly comprehended? Certainly none of the things to which I attained with the senses. For whatever things came under the scope of taste or smell or sight or touch or hearing have now been changed. The piece of wax remains.

[12.] Perhaps it—what was so distinctly comprehended in the piece of wax—was that which I am now cogitating: namely, that the piece of wax itself has not at all been that sweetness of the honey, nor that fragrance of the flowers, nor that whiteness, nor that figure, nor that sound, but rather has it been a body that appeared to me, looked at a little earlier in these ways, and now in different ways. But what precisely is this that I thus imagine? Let us pay attention to the matter and—the things that do not pertain to the piece of wax having been removed—let us see what would remain: obviously nothing other than something extended, flexible and changeable. But what is this: "flexible" and "changeable"? Is it what I imagine: that this piece of wax can be changed from a round figure into a quadratic one, or from it into a triangular one? In no way. For I comprehend that the piece of wax is capable of innumerable changes of this kind, and yet I cannot go through innumerable ones by imagining. And this comprehension is not achieved, then, by the faculty of imagining. What is "extended"? Is perhaps the extension itself of the piece of wax also unknown? For in the liquefying piece of wax the extension becomes greater, greater in the hot one, and greater again if the heat would be increased. And I would not be correctly judging what the piece of wax be unless I did think that it also admits of more variations with respect to extension than I might have ever encompassed by imagining. It remains, then, that I should concede that I do not at all imagine what this piece of wax here be, but rather that I perceive it by the mind alone. I say "this piece of wax here in particular", for it is clearer of wax in general. But what is this wax which is not perceived except by the mind? Of course it is the same wax that I see, that I touch and that I imagine: the same wax, in short, that I thought it to be from the very beginning.

ceptio non visio, non tactio, non imaginatio est, nec unquam fuit, quamvis prius ita videretur, sed solius mentis inspectio, quae vel imperfecta esse potest & confusa, ut prius erat, vel clara & distincta, ut nunc est, prout minus vel magis ad illa ex quibus constat attendo.

Miror verò interim quàm prona sit mea mens in errores; nam quamvis haec apud me tacitus & sine [32] voce considerem, haereo tamen in verbis ipsis, & fere decipior ab ipso usu loquendi. Dicimus enim nos videre ceram ipsammet, si adsit, non ex colore vel figurâ eam adesse judicare. Unde concluderem statim: ceram ergo visione oculi, non solius mentis inspectione, cognosci; nisi jam forte respexissem ex fenestrâ homines in plateâ transeuntes, quos etiam ipsos non minus usitate quàm ceram dico me videre. Quid autem video praeter pileos & vestes, sub quibus latere possent automata? Sed judico homines esse. Atque ita id quod putabam me videre oculis, solâ judicandi facultate, quae in mente meâ est, comprehendo.

Sed pudeat supra vulgus sapere cupientem, ex formis loquendi quas vulgus invenit dubitationem quaesivisse; pergamusque deinceps, attendendo utrùm ego perfectius evidentiusque percipiebam quid esset cera, cùm primùm aspexi, credidique me illam ipso sensu externo, vel saltem sensu communi, ut vocant, id est potentiâ imaginatrice, cognoscere? an verò potiùs nunc, postquam diligentiùs investigavi tum quid ea sit, tum quomodo cognoscatur? Certe hac de re dubitare esset ineptum; nam

And yet—which is something to be noted—the perception of the wax is not vision, not taction and not imagination, nor has it ever been—although it might previously have seemed so—, but rather is the perception of it the inspection of the mind alone, which inspection can be imperfect and confused—as it was previously—or clear and distinct—as it is now—, depending on how I pay more or less attention to those things of which the wax consists.

[13.] But meanwhile I am surprised at how prone to errors my mind might be. For although I would consider these things within me tacitly and without a word, I still hang on the words themselves and am almost deceived by the use itself of speech. For we say that we see the wax itself if it be there, and not that we judge from the color or the figure that it is there. From whence I would immediately conclude that therefore the wax is cognized by the vision of the eye, not by the inspection of the mind alone—if perhaps I had not now looked out the window at human beings going by in the street, whom themselves I also say, as a matter of the usage of language, that I see, no less than I say, as a matter of the same usage, that I see the wax. But what do I see besides hats and clothes under which automata might be concealed? Yet I judge that there are human beings there. And thus that which I thought that I saw with the eyes I comprehend with the faculty of judging alone, which faculty is in my mind.

[14.] But one desiring to know above and beyond the common people should be ashamed to have quested after doubt drawn from the forms of speech that the common people have invented. And let us continue, then, paying attention to the question as to whether *I* more perfectly and more evidently perceived what the wax be, after I have first looked at it and believed that I have cognized it by this external sense—or at least by "the common sense", as they call it, that is, by the imaginative power—, or rather now, however, after I have more diligently investigated both what it might be and how it might be cognized. Certainly it would be inept to doubt about this matter.

quid fuit in primâ perceptione distinctum? Quid quod non a
quovis animali haberi posse videretur? At verò cùm ceram ab
externis formis distinguo, & tanquam vestibus detractis nudam
considero, sic illam revera, quamvis adhuc error in judicio meo
esse possit, non possum tamen sine humanâ mente percipere.
[33]
    Quid autem dicam de hac ipsâ mente, sive de me ipso? Ni-
hildum enim aliud admitto in me esse praeter mentem. Quid,
inquam, ego qui hanc ceram videor tam distincte percipere?
Nunquid me ipsum non tantùm multo verius, multo certius,
sed etiam multo distinctius evidentiusque, cognosco? Nam, si
judico ceram existere, ex eo quod hanc videam, certe multo
evidentius efficitur me ipsum etiam existere, ex eo ipso quod
hanc videam. Fieri enim potest ut hoc quod video non vere sit
cera; fieri potest ut ne quidem oculos habeam, quibus quidquam
videatur; sed fieri plane non potest, cùm videam, sive (quod
jam non distinguo) cùm cogitem me videre, ut ego ipse cogitans non aliquid sim. Simili ratione, si judico ceram esse, ex
eo quod hanc tangam, idem rursus efficietur, videlicet me esse.
Si ex eo quod imaginer, vel quâvis aliâ ex causâ, idem plane.
Sed & hoc ipsum quod de cerâ animadverto, ad reliqua omnia, quae sunt extra me posita, licet applicare. Porro autem,
si magis distincta visa sit cerae perceptio, postquam mihi, non
ex solo visu vel tactu, sed pluribus ex causis innotuit, quanto
distinctiùs me ipsum a me nunc cognosci fatendum est, quandoquidem nullae rationes vel ad cerae, vel ad cujuspiam alterius
corporis perceptionem possint juvare, quin eaedem omnes mentis meae naturam melius probent! Sed & alia insuper tam multa sunt in ipsâ mente, ex quibus ejus notitia distinctior reddi

For what is it that has been distinct in the first perception? What is it which—it would seem—cannot be had by any animal that you will? But truly, when I distinguish the wax from the external forms and consider it—the clothes having been taken off it—as though nude, although there could then yet be error in my judgment, I still cannot thus really and truly perceive it without a human mind.

[15.] But what shall I say about this mind itself, or about me myself? For as yet I admit nothing else to be in me besides a mind. What, I say, *I* who seem to perceive this piece of wax here so distinctly? Perhaps I cognize me myself not only much more truly and much more certainly, but also much more distinctly and much more evidently? For if from thence that I were to see it, I judge that the wax exists, certainly it is much more evidently effected from thence itself that I were to see it, that I myself also exist. For it can happen that this which I see would not truly be wax. And it can happen that I would not even have eyes with which anything could be seen. But it plainly cannot happen that when I were to see or (which I do not now distinguish therefrom) when I were to cogitate that I see, *I* myself as the one who is cogitating would not then be something. For a similar reason, if from thence that I were to touch it, I judge that the wax is, the same thing will again be effected, viz., that I am. If from thence that I were to imagine it, I judge that the wax is, or for any other cause that you will, plainly the same thing will again and again be effected. But that itself which I notice about the wax may also be applied to all the other things that are posited outside me. Yet moreover, if the perception of the wax may have seemed more distinct after it had become known to me not by vision or touch alone, but rather by many causes, how much more distinctly—it is to be conceded—am I myself now cognized by me, since no reasoning could aid in the perception of the wax or of any other body that would not—as all the same reasoning —better prove the nature of my mind! But—above and beyond this—there are also so many other things in the mind itself from which the knowledge of it can

potest, ut ea, quae ex corpore ad illam emanant, vix numeranda videantur.

Atque ecce tandem sponte sum reversus eò quò [34] volebam; nam cùm mihi nunc notum sit ipsamet corpora, non proprie a sensibus, vel ab imaginandi facultate, sed a solo intellectu percipi, nec ex eo percipi quòd tangantur aut videantur, sed tantùm ex eo quòd intelligantur aperte cognosco nihil facilius aut evidentius meâ mente posse a me percipi. Sed quia tam cito deponi veteris opinionis consuetudo non potest, placet hîc consistere, ut altius haec nova cognitio memoriae meae diuturnitate meditationis infigatur.

be rendered more distinct that the things that emanate to it from a body would hardly seem to be worthy to be enumerated.

[16.] And voilà, I have, finally, spontaneously returned to there where I wanted to be. For because it now be known to me that bodies themselves are properly perceived not by the senses or by the faculty of imagining, but rather by the intellect alone, and that bodies are perceived not from thence that they would be touched or seen, but rather from thence only that they were to be understood, I cognize overtly that nothing can be perceived by me more easily or more evidently than my mind. But because the custom of an old opinion cannot be laid down so quickly, it is fitting to stop here in order that by the length of meditation this new cognition might be fixed more deeply in my memory.

MEDITATIO III.

De Deo, quòd existat.

Claudam nunc oculos, aures obturabo, avocabo omnes sensus, imagines etiam rerum corporalium omnes vel ex cogitatione meâ delebo, vel certe, quia hoc fieri vix potest, illas ut inanes & falsas nihili pendam, meque solum alloquendo & penitius inspiciendo, meipsum paulatim mihi magis notum & familiarem reddere conabor. Ego sum res cogitans, id est dubitans, affirmans, negans, pauca intelligens, multa ignorans, volens, nolens, imaginans etiam & sentiens; ut enim ante animadverti, quamvis illa quae sentio vel imaginor extra me fortasse nihil sint, illos tamen cogitandi modos, quos sensus & imaginationes [35] appello, quatenus cogitandi quidam modi tantùm sunt, in me esse sum certus.

Atque his paucis omnia recensui quae vere scio, vel saltem quae me scire hactenus animadverti. Nunc circumspiciam diligentiùs an forte adhuc apud me alia sint ad quae nondum respexi. Sum certus me esse rem cogitantem. Nunquid ergo etiam scio quid requiratur ut de aliquâ re sim certus? Nempe in hac primâ cognitione nihil aliud est, quàm clara quaedam & distincta perceptio ejus quod affirmo; quae sane non sufficeret ad me certum de rei veritate reddendum, si posset unquam contingere, ut aliquid, quod ita clare & distincte perciperem, fal-

MEDITATION III.

Concerning God, that he exist.

[1.] Now I shall close my eyes. I shall stop up my ears. I shall call away all my senses. I shall also delete all the images of corporeal things from my cogitation — or rather shall I, because this can hardly be done, certainly regard these images, as empty and false, as being nothing —, and by conversing with and more penetratingly inspecting me alone I shall attempt to render me myself gradually more known and familiar to me. *I* am a cogitating thing, that is, a thing doubting, affirming, denying, understanding a few things, being ignorant of many things, willing, not willing, as well as imagining and sensing. For as I have noticed before, although those things which I sense or imagine would perhaps be nothing outside me, I am still certain that those modes of cogitating which I call "sensations" and "imaginations", in so far as they are only certain modes of cogitating, are in me.

[2.] And with these few words I have reviewed all the things that I truly know, or at least all the things that I have hitherto noticed that I know. Now I will look around more diligently to see whether there might perhaps be still other things within me at which I have not yet looked. I am certain that I am a cogitating thing. Do I therefore also now know what would be required in order that I might be certain of anything? In this primary cognition there is, namely, nothing other than a certain clear and distinct perception of that which I affirm: which would indeed not suffice to render me certain of the truth of the matter if it could ever happen that something that I did so clearly and distinctly perceive were false. And so I now seem

119

sum esset; ac proinde jam videor pro regulâ generali posse statuere, illud omne esse verum, quod valde clare & distincte percipio.

Verumtamen multa prius ut omnino certa & manifesta admisi, quae tamen postea dubia esse deprehendi. Qualia ergo ista fuere? Nempe terra, coelum, sydera & caetera omnia quae sensibus usurpabam. Quid autem de illis clare percipiebam? Nempe ipsas talium rerum ideas, sive cogitationes, menti meae obversari. Sed ne nunc quidem illas ideas in me esse inficior. Aliud autem quiddam erat quod affirmabam, quodque etiam ob consuetudinem credendi clare me percipere arbitrabar, quod tamen revera non percipiebam: nempe res quasdam extra me esse, a quibus ideae istae procedebant, & quibus omnino similes erant. Atque hoc erat, in quo vel fallebar, vel certe, si verum judicabam, id non ex vi meae perceptionis contingebat.

Quid verò? Cùm circa res Arithmeticas vel Geome[36]tricas aliquid valde simplex & facile considerabam, ut quòd duo & tria simul juncta sint quinque, vel similia, nunquid saltem illa satis perspicue intuebar, ut vera esse affirmarem? Equidem non aliam ob causam de iis dubitandum esse postea judicavi, quàm quia veniebat in mentem forte aliquem Deum talem mihi naturam indere potuisse, ut etiam circa illa deciperer, quae manifestissima viderentur. Sed quoties haec praeconcepta de summâ Dei potentiâ opinio mihi occurrit, non possum non fateri, siquidem velit, facile illi esse efficere ut errem, etiam in iis quae me puto mentis oculis quàm evidentissime intueri. Quoties verò ad ipsas res, quas valde clare percipere arbitror, me converto, tam plane ab illis persuadeor, ut sponte erumpam in has voces: fallat me quisquis potest, nunquam tamen efficiet ut nihil sim, quandiu me aliquid esse cogitabo; vel ut

to be able to establish as a general rule that all that which I very clearly and distinctly perceive is true.

[3.] But yet I have previously admitted many things as completely certain and manifest which later I have still found to be dubious. What kinds of things therefore have these been? Obviously the earth, the heavens, the stars and all the other things that I grasped with the senses. But what concerning these things did I clearly perceive? Obviously that the ideas or cogitations themselves of such things were before my mind. Yet not even now am I denying that these ideas are in me. But there was something else that I affirmed and also that — due to the custom of believing it — I thought that I clearly perceived, yet that I did not really and truly perceive, namely, that there were certain things outside me from which those ideas proceeded and to which they were completely similar. And it was in this that I was deceived — or if I judged the true, it certainly did not happen by virtue of the power of my perception.

[4.] But then what? When I considered something very simple and easy about things arithmetical or geometrical, such as that two and three added together were five, or similar things, did I not then intuit at least these things perspicuously enough that I might affirm that they are true? I have indeed later judged that these things are to be doubted for no other reason than because it came to mind that some God could perhaps have given to me such a nature that I were to be deceived even about those things which would seem most manifest. But so often as there occurs to me this preconceived opinion about the very high power of God, I cannot not admit that — if he were only to will it — it is easy for him to effect that I would err even in the things that I think that I most evidently intuit with the eyes of the mind. Yet so often as I turn to those things which I think that I very clearly perceive, I am so fully persuaded by them that I would spontaneously erupt in these words: "Whoever can, may deceive me, he will still never effect that I would be nothing, so long as I shall be cogitating that I am something, or that it would

aliquando verum sit me nunquam fuisse, cùm jam verum sit me esse; vel forte etiam ut duo & tria simul juncta plura vel pauciora sint quàm quinque, vel similia, in quibus scilicet repugnantiam agnosco manifestam. Et certe cùm nullam occasionem habeam existimandi aliquem Deum esse deceptorem, nec quidem adhuc satis sciam utrùm sit aliquis Deus, valde tenuis &, ut ita loquar, Metaphysica dubitandi ratio est, quae tantùm ex eâ opinione dependet. Ut autem etiam illa tollatur, quamprimum occurret occasio, examinare debeo an sit Deus, &, si sit, an possit esse deceptor; hac enim re ignoratâ, non videor de ullâ aliâ plane certus esse unquam posse.

Nunc autem ordo videtur exigere, ut prius omnes [37] meas cogitationes in certa genera distribuam, & in quibusnam ex illis veritas aut falsitas proprie consistat, inquiram. Quaedam ex his tanquam rerum imagines sunt, quibus solis proprie convenit ideae nomen: ut cùm hominem, vel Chimaeram, vel Coelum, vel Angelum, vel Deum cogito. Aliae verò alias quasdam praeterea formas habent: ut, cùm volo, cùm timeo, cùm affirmo, cùm nego, semper quidem aliquam rem ut subjectum meae cogitationis apprehendo, sed aliquid etiam amplius quàm istius rei similitudinem cogitatione complector; & ex his aliae voluntates, sive affectus, aliae autem judicia appellantur.

Jam quod ad ideas attinet, si solae in se spectentur, nec ad aliud quid illas referam, falsae proprie esse non possunt; nam sive capram, sive chimaeram imaginer, non minus verum est me unam imaginari quàm alteram. Nulla etiam in ipsâ voluntate, vel affectibus, falsitas est timenda; nam, quamvis prava, quamvis etiam ea quae nusquam sunt, possim optare, non tamen ideo non verum est illa me optare. Ac proinde sola supersunt judicia, in quibus mihi cavendum est ne fallar. Praecipuus

ever be true that I have never been, since it be now true that I am, or even perhaps that two and three added together would be more or less than five, or similar things, in which, scil., I recognize a manifest contradiction." And since I would have no occasion for thinking that there is a deceiver God, and so far I would not even satisfactorily know whether there be any God at all, the reason for doubting which depends only on this opinion is certainly very tenuous and—as I would so say—metaphysical. But in order that even this reason for doubting might be removed I ought, as soon as the occasion will occur, to examine whether there be a God, and if there be, whether he could be a deceiver. For this matter being unknown, I do not seem to be able ever to be fully certain about any other matter.

[5.] But order now seems to require that I would first classify all my cogitations into certain kinds, and that I would inquire as to in which of them truth or falsity were properly to consist. Some of these cogitations are—as it were—the images of things—which ones alone the term "idea" properly fits—, such as then when I cogitate a human being, or a chimera, or heaven, or an angel, or God. But other cogitations have, in addition, some other forms, such as when I will, when I fear, when I affirm, when I deny, I surely always then apprehend something as the subject of my cogitation, but by cogitation I also encompass something more than the similitude of that thing. And of these cogitations some are called "volitions" or "emotions", but others are called "judgments".

[6.] Now as for what pertains to ideas, if they were to be regarded solely in themselves and I were not to refer them to something else, they cannot properly be false. For whether I would imagine a goat or a chimera, it is no less true that I imagine the one than the other. Moreover, no falsity is to be feared in the will itself or in the emotions. For although I could wish for depraved things, and although I could even wish for those things which nowhere are, it is still not therefore not true that I wish for them. And thus there remain judgments alone in which I have to be cautious in order that I would not be deceived. Fur-

autem error & frequentissimus qui possit in illis reperiri, consistit in eo quòd ideas, quae in me sunt, judicem rebus quibusdam extra me positis similes esse sive conformes; nam profecto, si tantùm ideas ipsas ut cogitationis meae quosdam modos
considerarem, nec ad quidquam aliud referrem, vix mihi ullam errandi materiam dare possent.

Ex his autem ideis aliae innatae, aliae adventitiae, [38] aliae
a me ipso factae mihi videntur: nam quòd intelligam quid sit
res, quid sit veritas, quid sit cogitatio, haec non aliunde habere
videor quàm ab ipsâmet meâ naturâ; quòd autem nunc strepitum audiam, solem videam, ignem sentiam, a rebus quibusdam extra me positis procedere hactenus judicavi; ac denique
Syrenes, Hippogryphes, & similia, a me ipso finguntur. Vel
forte etiam omnes esse adventitias possum putare, vel omnes
innatas, vel omnes factas: nondum enim veram illarum origi-
nem clare perspexi.

Sed hîc praecipue de iis est quaerendum, quas tanquam a
rebus extra me existentibus desumptas considero, quaenam me
moveat ratio ut illas istis rebus similes esse existimem. Nempe
ita videor doctus a naturâ. Et praeterea experior illas non a meâ
voluntate nec proinde a me ipso pendere; saepe enim vel invito
obversantur: ut jam, sive velim, sive nolim, sentio calorem, &
ideo puto sensum illum, sive ideam caloris, a re a me diversâ,
nempe ab ignis cui assideo calore, mihi advenire. Nihilque magis
obvium est, quàm ut judicem istam rem suam similitudinem
potius quàm aliud quid in me immittere.

Quae rationes, an satis firmae sint, jam videbo. Cùm hîc dico
me ita doctum esse a naturâ, intelligo tantùm spontaneo quo-

thermore, the foremost and most frequent error that could be found in judgments consists therein that I were to judge that ideas that are in me are similar to—or conform to—certain things posited outside me. For if I did in fact consider these ideas only as certain modes of my cogitation and I did not refer them to anything else, they could hardly give to me any material for erring.

[7.] Furthermore, of the ideas some seem to me to be innate, while others seem to me to be adventicious, and still others seem to me to be made by me. For that I were to understand what a thing be, what truth be and what cogitation be: these things I seem to have not from elsewhere than from my own nature itself. But that I were now to hear a noise, that I were to see the sun and that I were to sense a fire: these things I have hitherto judged to proceed from certain things posited outside me. And sirens, hippogryphs and similar things, finally, are feigned by me myself. Or perhaps I can also think that all these ideas are adventicious, or that all of them are innate, or that all of them are made. For I have not yet clearly seen through to the true origin of them.

[8.] But here it is first and foremost to be asked about the ideas that I consider as though they were derived from things existing outside me what reason would move me in such a way that I would think that those ideas are similar to these things. Obviously I seem to have been thus taught by nature. And moreover, I know by experience that these ideas do not depend on my will, and therefore that they do not depend on me myself. For often these ideas are before me even involuntarily: just as—whether I would want to or not want to—I now sense warmth, and therefore I think that this sensation or idea of warmth comes to me from a thing different from me, namely, from the warmth of the fire by which I am sitting. And nothing is more obvious than that I were to judge that that thing immits into me its similitude rather than something else.

[9.] I shall now see whether these reasons be firm enough. When I say here that "I have been thus taught by nature", then

dam impetu me ferri ad hoc credendum, non lumine aliquo naturali mihi ostendi esse verum. Quae duo multum discrepant; nam quaecumque lumine naturali mihi ostenduntur, ut quòd ex eo quòd dubitem, sequatur me esse, & similia, nullo modo dubia esse possunt, quia nulla alia facultas esse potest, cui aeque fidam ac lumini isti, quaeque illa [39] non vera esse possit docere; sed quantum ad impetus naturales, jam saepe olim judicavi me ab illis in deteriorem partem fuisse impulsum, cùm de bono eligendo ageretur, nec video cur iisdem in ullâ aliâ re magis fidam.

Deinde, quamvis ideae illae a voluntate meâ non pendeant, non ideo constat ipsas a rebus extra me positis necessario procedere. Ut enim impetus illi, de quibus mox loquebar, quamvis in me sint, a voluntate tamen meâ diversi esse videntur, ita forte etiam aliqua alia est in me facultas, nondum mihi satis cognita, istarum idearum effectrix, ut hactenus semper visum est illas, dum somnio, absque ullâ rerum externarum ope, in me formari.

Ac denique, quamvis a rebus a me diversis procederent, non inde sequitur illas rebus istis similes esse debere. Quinimo in multis saepe magnum discrimen videor deprehendisse: ut, exempli causâ, duas diversas solis ideas apud me invenio, unam tanquam a sensibus haustam, & quae maxime inter illas quas adventitias existimo est recensenda, per quam mihi valde parvus apparet, aliam verò ex rationibus Astronomiae desumptam, hoc est ex notionibus quibusdam mihi innatis elicitam, vel quocumque alio modo a me factam, per quam aliquoties major quàm terra exhibetur; utraque profecto similis eidem soli

do I understand only that I am brought to believe this by a certain spontaneous impetus, not that it is shown to me by some natural light that it is true. Which two things are very different. For whatever things are shown to me by the natural light — such as that from thence that I were to doubt, it would follow that I am, and similar things — can in no mode be dubious, because there can be no other faculty that I could trust equally to that light and that could teach me that such things are not true. But as for the natural impetuses, already I have often judged earlier that I have then been impelled by them to the worse alternative when it were a matter of choosing the good, and I do not see why I would trust the same impetuses more in any other matter.

[10.] Then again, although these ideas might not depend on my will, it is not therefore so, that they necessarily proceed from things posited outside me. For just as these impetuses of which I then spoke, although they might be in me, still seem to be different from my will, thus also is there perhaps some other faculty in me which is not yet sufficiently known to me and which is the effecter of these ideas, as it has hitherto always seemed that these ideas are formed in me while I am dreaming and without any help of external things.

[11.] And finally, although these ideas might proceed from things different from me, it does not from thence follow that those ideas must be similar to these things. Indeed, I seem to have often found a great discrepancy in many things: just as I find within me, for example, two different ideas of the sun, the one, as though derived from the senses, which is maximally to be reckoned among those ideas which I think are adventicious, and through which the sun appears to me to be very small, but the other, derived from the reasoning of astronomy, that is, elicited from certain notions innate to me or made by me in some other manner, and through which the sun is exhibited as being several times greater than the earth. Both these ideas cannot in fact be similar to the same sun existing outside me,

extra me existenti esse non potest, & ratio persuadet illam ei maxime esse dissimilem, quae quàm proxime ab ipso videtur emanasse.

Quae omnia satis demonstrant me non hactenus ex [40] certo judicio, sed tantùm ex caeco aliquo impulsu, credidisse res quasdam a me diversas existere, quae ideas sive imagines suas per organa sensuum, vel quolibet alio pacto, mihi immittant.

Sed alia quaedam adhuc via mihi occurrit ad inquirendum an res aliquae, ex iis quarum ideae in me sunt, extra me existant. Nempe, quatenus ideae istae cogitandi quidam modi tantùm sunt, non agnosco ullam inter ipsas inaequalitatem, & omnes a me eodem modo procedere videntur; sed, quatenus una unam rem, alia aliam repraesentat, patet easdem esse ab invicem valde diversas. Nam proculdubio illae quae substantias mihi exhibent, majus aliquid sunt, atque, ut ita loquar, plus realitatis objectivae in se continent, quàm illae quae tantùm modos, sive accidentia, repraesentant; & rursus illa per quam summum aliquem Deum, aeternum, infinitum, omniscium, omnipotentem, rerumque omnium, quae praeter ipsum sunt, creatorem intelligo, plus profecto realitatis objectivae in se habet, quàm illae per quas finitae substantiae exhibentur.

Jam verò lumine naturali manifestum est tantumdem ad minimum esse debere in causâ efficiente & totali, quantum in ejusdem causae effectu. Nam, quaeso, undenam posset assumere realitatem suam effectus, nisi a causâ? Et quomodo illam ei causa dare posset, nisi etiam haberet? Hinc autem sequitur, nec posse aliquid a nihilo fieri, nec etiam id quod magis perfectum est, hoc est quod plus realitatis in se con[41]tinet, ab eo quod minus. Atque hoc non modo perspicue verum est de iis effectibus, quorum realitas est actualis sive formalis, sed etiam de ideis,

and reason persuades me that that one which seems to have emanated from it most proximally is maximally dissimilar to it.

[12.] All which things satisfactorily demonstrate that I have hitherto believed not by certain judgment, but rather only by some blind impulse, that there exist certain things different from me which would immit ideas or their images into me through the organs of the senses or in some other way whatever.

[13.] But there occurs to me yet a certain other way of inquiring as to whether some of those things whose ideas are in me would exist outside me. In so far as these ideas are only certain modes of cogitating, I surely do not recognize any inequality among them, and they all seem to proceed from me in the same mode. But in so far as the one idea represents one thing, and the other idea represents another thing, it is obvious that these ideas are very different from one another. For those ideas which exhibit substances to me are without doubt something greater, and—as I would so speak—they contain more objective reality in themselves, than those ideas which represent only modes or accidents. And again, that idea through which I understand a highest God—eternal, infinite, omniscient, omnipotent and the creator of all the things that, besides him, are—has in fact more objective reality in itself than those ideas through which finite substances are exhibited.

[14.] But now it is manifest by the natural light that there must be at a minimum just as much [reality] in the efficient and total cause as there is in the effect of the same cause. For from whence, I ask, could the effect get its reality if not from the cause? And how could the cause give reality to the effect, if it did not also have it? Furthermore, from thence it follows both that something cannot come to be from nothing, and also that that which is more perfect—that is, that which contains in itself more reality—cannot come to be from that which is less perfect. And this is perspicuously true not only of those effects whose reality is actual or formal, but also of ideas, in which only objective reality

in quibus consideratur tantùm realitas objectiva. Hoc est, non modo non potest, exempli causâ, aliquis lapis, qui prius non fuit, nunc incipere esse, nisi producatur ab aliquâ re in quâ totum illud sit vel formaliter vel eminenter, quod ponitur in lapide; nec potest calor in subjectum quod priùs non calebat induci, nisi a re quae sit ordinis saltem aeque perfecti atque est calor, & sic de caeteris; sed praeterea etiam non potest in me esse idea caloris, vel lapidis, nisi in me posita sit ab aliquâ causâ, in quâ tantumdem ad minimum sit realitatis quantum esse in calore vel lapide concipio. Nam quamvis ista causa nihil de suâ realitate actuali sive formali in meam ideam transfundat, non ideo putandum est illam minus realem esse debere, sed talem esse naturam ipsius ideae, ut nullam aliam ex se realitatem formalem exigat, praeter illam quam mutuatur a cogitatione meâ, cujus est modus. Quòd autem haec idea realitatem objectivam hanc vel illam contineat potius quàm aliam, hoc profectò habere debet ab aliquâ causâ in quâ tantumdem sit ad minimum realitatis formalis quantum ipsa continet objectivae. Si enim ponamus aliquid in ideâ reperiri, quod non fuerit in ejus causâ, hoc igitur habet a nihilo; atqui quantumvis imperfectus sit iste essendi modus, quo res est objective in intellectu per ideam, non tamen profectò plane nihil est, nec proinde a nihilo esse potest.

Nec etiam debeo suspicari, cùm realitas quam considero in meis ideis sit tantùm objectiva, non opus [42] esse ut eadem realitas sit formaliter in causis istarum idearum, sed sufficere, si sit in iis etiam objective. Nam quemadmodum iste modus essendi objectivus competit ideis ex ipsarum naturâ, ita modus essendi formalis competit idearum causis, saltem primis & praecipuis, ex earum naturâ. Et quamvis forte una idea ex aliâ nasci possit, non tamen hîc datur progressus in infinitum, sed tandem ad aliquam primam debet deveniri, cujus causa sit in-

is considered. That is, for example, not only cannot a stone which has not previously been begin now to be unless it would be produced by something in which there were formally or eminently all that which is posited in the stone; and heat cannot be introduced into a subject that was not previously hot except by a thing that were of an order at least equally as perfect as is the heat, and thus of the other things; but moreover, even the idea of heat or of a stone cannot be in me unless it had been posited in me by some cause in which there were at a minimum just as much reality as I conceive there to be in the heat or in the stone. For although this cause were to transfer none of its actual or formal reality into my idea, it is not therefore to be thought that it must be less real, but rather is it to be thought that the nature of that idea is such that of itself it would require no other formal reality besides that which it borrows from my cogitation, whose mode it is. Furthermore, that this idea would contain this or that objective reality rather than some other: this it must in fact have from some cause in which there were at a minimum just as much formal reality as this idea contains objective reality. For if we were to posit that something is found in the idea that had not been in its cause, this it has, then, from nothing. And yet however imperfect that you will that mode of being might be in which the thing is objectively in the intellect through the idea, it still is in fact plainly not nothing, and therefore it cannot be from nothing.

[15.] Nor must I suspect that, because the reality that I consider in my ideas be only objective, it is not necessary that the same reality be formally in the causes of these ideas, but rather that it suffices if it were in them too objectively. For just as that objective mode of being belongs to the ideas by the nature of them, so the formal mode of being belongs to the causes of the ideas — at least to the first and foremost ones — by the nature of them. And although one idea could perhaps arise from another, an infinite regress is still not given here, but rather must it come down, finally, to a primary idea, whose cause would

star archetypi, in quo omnis realitas formaliter contineatur, quae est in ideâ tantùm objective. Adeo ut lumine naturali mihi sit perspicuum ideas in me esse veluti quasdam imagines, quae possunt quidem facile deficere a perfectione rerum a quibus sunt desumptae, non autem quicquam majus aut perfectius continere.

Atque haec omnia, quò diutius & curiosius examino, tantò clarius & distinctius vera esse cognosco. Sed quid tandem ex his concludam? Nempe si realitas objectiva alicujus ex meis ideis sit tanta ut certus sim eandem nec formaliter nec eminenter in me esse, nec proinde me ipsum ejus ideae causam esse posse, hinc necessario sequi, non me solum esse in mundo, sed aliquam aliam rem, quae istius ideae est causa, etiam existere. Si verò nulla talis in me idea reperiatur, nullum plane habebo argumentum quod me de alicujus rei a me diversae existentiâ certum reddat; omnia enim diligentissime circumspexi, & nullum aliud potui hactenus reperire.

Ex his autem meis ideis, praeter illam quae me ipsum mihi exhibet, de quâ hîc nulla difficultas esse [43] potest, alia est quae Deum, aliae quae res corporeas & inanimes, aliae quae Angelos, aliae quae animalia, ac denique aliae quae alios homines meî similes repraesentant.

Et quantum ad ideas quae alios homines, vel animalia, vel Angelos exhibent, facile intelligo illas ex iis quas habeo meî ipsius & rerum corporalium & Dei posse componi, quamvis nulli praeter me homines, nec animalia, nec Angeli, in mundo essent.

Quantum autem ad ideas rerum corporalium, nihil in illis occurrit, quod sit tantum ut non videatur a me ipso potuisse proficisci; nam si penitiùs inspiciam, & singulas examinem eo modo quo heri examinavi ideam cerae, animadverto perpauca

be like an archetype in which all the reality that is in the idea only objectively be contained formally. So that by the natural light it would be perspicuous to me that the ideas in me are like certain images which surely can easily be deficient in the perfection of the things from which they have been derived, but which cannot contain anything greater or more perfect.

[16.] And the longer and the more curiously I examine them, the more clearly and distinctly do I cognize that all these things are true. But what shall I, finally, conclude from them? Surely that if the objective reality of any one of my ideas were so great that I would be certain that the same reality is neither formally nor eminently in me, and therefore that I myself cannot be the cause of this idea, it necessarily follows therefrom that I am not alone in the world, but rather that there also exists some other thing which is the cause of that idea. But if no such idea were to be found in me, I shall plainly have no argument that might render me certain about the existence of anything different from me. For I have most diligently looked around at all things and have hitherto been able to find nothing else.

[17.] But of these my ideas, besides that one which exhibits me myself to me—about which there can be no difficulty here—, there is another one, which represents God, there are others, which represent corporeal and inanimate things, others, which represent angels, others, which represent animals, and finally others, which represent other human beings similar to me.

[18.] And as for the ideas that exhibit other human beings, or animals, or angels, I easily understand that they can be composed of the ideas that I have of me myself and of corporeal things and of God, even if there were no human beings besides me, nor animals, nor angels, in the world.

[19.] But as for the ideas of corporeal things, there occurs in them nothing that would be so great that it would not seem that it can have come from me myself. For if I were to inspect more penetratingly and were to examine these ideas individually in that manner in which I have yesterday examined the idea of the wax, I notice that there are only very few things in them

tantùm esse quae in illis clare & distincte percipio: nempe magnitudinem, sive extensionem in longum, latum, & profundum;
figuram, quae ex terminatione istius extensionis exsurgit; si-
tum, quem diversa figurata inter se obtinent; & motum, sive
mutationem istius sitûs; quibus addi possunt substantia, dura-
tio, & numerus: caetera autem, ut lumen & colores, soni,
odores, sapores, calor & frigus, aliaeque tactiles qualitates, nonnisi valde confuse & obscure a me cogitantur, adeo ut etiam
ignorem an sint verae, vel falsae, hoc est, an ideae, quas de illis
habeo, sint rerum quarundam ideae, an non rerum. Quamvis
enim falsitatem proprie dictam, sive formalem, nonnisi in judiciis
posse reperiri paulo ante notaverim, est tamen profecto quaedam alia falsitas materialis in ideis, cùm non rem tanquam rem
repraesentant: ita, exempli causâ, ideae quas habeo caloris &
frigoris, tam parum clarae [44] & distinctae sunt, ut ab iis dis-
cere non possim, an frigus sit tantùm privatio caloris, vel calor
privatio frigoris, vel utrumque sit realis qualitas, vel neutrum.
Et quia nullae ideae nisi tanquam rerum esse possunt, siquidem verum sit frigus nihil aliud esse quàm privationem caloris,
idea quae mihi illud tanquam reale quid & positivum repraesentat, non immerito falsa dicetur, & sic de caeteris.

　　Quibus profecto non est necesse ut aliquem authorem a me
diversum assignem; nam, si quidem sint falsae, hoc est nullas
res repraesentent, lumine naturali notum mihi est illas a nihilo
procedere, hoc est, non aliam ob causam in me esse quàm quia
deest aliquid naturae meae, nec est plane perfecta; si autem sint
verae, quia tamen tam parum realitatis mihi exhibent, ut ne
quidem illud a non re possim distinguere, non video cur a me
ipso esse non possint.

　　Ex iis verò quae in ideis rerum corporalium clara & distincta sunt, quaedam ab ideâ meî ipsius videor mutuari potuisse,
nempe substantiam, durationem, numerum, & si quae alia sint

that I clearly and distinctly perceive: namely, magnitude, or extension in length, breadth and depth; figure, which arises from the determination of this extension; position, which different shaped things obtain among themselves; and movement, or the change of this position; to which can be added substance, duration and number. But the other things, such as light, and colors, sounds, odors, tastes, heat and cold, and other tactile qualities, are not cogitated by me except very confusedly and obscurely—so much so that I even be ignorant as to whether they would be true or false, that is, as to whether the ideas that I have of them would be ideas of certain things, or not of things. For although shortly previously I might have noted that falsity —properly said, or formal falsity—cannot be found except in judgments, there still is in fact a certain other—material—falsity in ideas, then when they represent a non-thing as if it were a thing: just as, for example, the ideas that I have of heat and cold are so little clear and distinct that I could not discern from them whether cold would be only the privation of heat or heat would be only the privation of cold, or whether both of them would be real qualities, or neither would be. And because there can be no ideas except—as it were—ideas of things, if it would indeed be true that cold is nothing other than the privation of heat, the idea that represents it to me as if it were something real and positive will not without merit be called "false". And thus of the other ideas.

[20.] To which ideas it is in fact not necessary that I would assign an author different from me. For if they would indeed be false, that is, would represent no things, it is known to me by the natural light that they proceed from nothing, that is, that they are in me not for another reason than because something is lacking in my nature and this nature is plainly not perfect. But if they would be true, because they still exhibit to me so little reality that I could not even distinguish it from a non-thing, I do not see why they could not be from me myself.

[21.] But some of the things that are clear and distinct in the ideas of corporeal things I seem to have been able to borrow from the idea of me myself, namely, substance, duration, num-

ejusmodi; nam cùm cogito lapidem esse substantiam, sive esse rem quae per se apta est existere, itemque me esse substantiam, quamvis concipiam me esse rem cogitantem & non extensam, lapidem verò esse rem extensam & non cogitantem, ac proinde maxima inter utrumque conceptum sit diversitas, in ratione tamen substantiae videntur convenire; itemque, cùm percipio me nunc esse, & priùs etiam aliquamdiu fuisse recordor, cùmque varias habeo cogitationes quarum numerum intelligo, acquiro [45] ideas durationis & numeri, quas deinde ad quascunque alias res possum transferre. Caetera autem omnia ex quibus rerum corporearum ideae conflantur, nempe extensio, figura, situs, & motus, in me quidem, cùm nihil aliud sim quàm res cogitans, formaliter non continentur; sed quia sunt tantùm modi quidam substantiae, ego autem substantia, videntur in me contineri posse eminenter.

Itaque sola restat idea Dei, in quâ considerandum est an aliquid sit quod a me ipso non potuerit proficisci. Dei nomine intelligo substantiam quandam infinitam, independentem, summe intelligentem, summe potentem, & a quâ tum ego ipse, tum aliud omne, si quid aliud extat, quodcumque extat, est creatum. Quae sane omnia talia sunt ut, quo diligentius attendo, tanto minus a me solo profecta esse posse videantur. Ideoque ex antedictis, Deum necessario existere, est concludendum.

Nam quamvis substantiae quidem idea in me sit ex hoc ipso quòd sim substantia, non tamen idcirco esset idea substantiae infinitae, cùm sim finitus, nisi ab aliquâ substantiâ, quae revera esset infinita, procederet.

Nec putare debeo me non percipere infinitum per veram ideam, sed tantùm per negationem finiti, ut percipio quietem

ber and whatever other things there might be of this kind. For when I cogitate that a stone is a substance — or that it is a thing that is fit to exist through itself — and also that I am a substance, although I were then to conceive that I am a cogitating and not an extended thing, but that a stone is an extended and not a cogitating thing, and therefore that the difference between both these concepts were maximal, by reason thereof that they both represent a substance they still seem to agree with each other. And when I also perceive that I now am and remember that I have also previously been for some time, and when I have various cogitations whose number I understand, I then acquire the ideas of duration and number, which ideas I can then transfer to whatever other things. But all the other things of which the ideas of corporeal things are made up, namely, extension, figure, position and movement, are surely not contained in me formally, since I be nothing other than a cogitating thing. Yet because they are only certain modes of a substance — whereas *I* am a substance — , they seem to be able to be contained in me eminently.

[22.] And thus there remains solely the idea of God in which it is to be considered whether there would be something that could not have come from me myself. By the term "God" I understand a substance: a substance infinite, independent, most highly intelligent, most highly powerful, and by which both *I* myself and everything else that is extant — if something else is extant — have been created. All which things are indeed such that, the more diligently I pay attention to them, so much the less would they seem to be able to have come from me alone. And from those things which have been said before it is to be concluded that therefore God necessarily exists.

[23.] For although the idea of substance would surely be in me from thence itself that I be a substance, since I be finite, this idea would therefore still not be the idea of an infinite substance unless it did proceed from some other substance which really and truly were infinite.

[24.] And I must not think that I perceive the infinite not through a true idea, but rather only through the negation of

& tenebras per negationem motûs & lucis; nam contrà manifeste intelligo plus realitatis esse in substantiâ infinitâ quàm in finitâ, ac proinde priorem quodammodo in me esse perceptionem infiniti quàm finiti, hoc est Dei quàm meî ipsius. Quâ enim ratione intelligerem me dubitare, me [46] cupere, hoc est, aliquid mihi deesse, & me non esse omnino perfectum, si nulla idea entis perfectioris in me esset, ex cujus comparatione defectus meos agnoscerem?

Nec dici potest hanc forte ideam Dei materialiter falsam esse, ideoque a nihilo esse posse, ut paulo ante de ideis caloris & frigoris, & similium, animadverti; nam contrà, cùm maxime clara & distincta sit, & plus realitatis objectivae quàm ulla alia contineat, nulla est per se magis vera, nec in quâ minor falsitatis suspicio reperiatur. Est, inquam, haec idea entis summe perfecti & infiniti maxime vera; nam quamvis forte fingi possit tale ens non existere, non tamen fingi potest ejus ideam nihil reale mihi exhibere, ut de ideâ frigoris ante dixi. Est etiam maxime clara & distincta; nam quidquid clare & distincte percipio, quod est reale & verum, & quod perfectionem aliquam importat, totum in eâ continetur. Nec obstat quod non comprehendam infinitum, vel quod alia innumera in Deo sint, quae nec comprehendere, nec forte etiam attingere cogitatione, ullo modo possum; est enim de ratione infiniti, ut a me, qui sum finitus, non comprehendatur; & sufficit me hoc ipsum intelligere, ac judicare, illa omnia quae clare percipio, & perfectionem aliquam importare scio, atque etiam forte alia innumera quae ignoro, vel formaliter vel eminenter in Deo esse, ut idea quam de illo habeo sit omnium quae in me sunt maxime vera, & maxime clara & distincta.

the finite, just as I perceive rest and shadows through the negation of movement and of light. For—on the contrary—I manifestly understand that there is more reality in an infinite substance than there is in a finite one, and therefore that the perception of the infinite is in me in some mode prior to the perception of the finite, that is, that the perception of God is in me in some mode prior to the perception of me myself. For how would I understand that I doubt and that I desire, that is, that something is lacking in me and that I am not completely perfect, if there were no idea of a more perfect being in me from whose comparison I might recognize my defects?

[25.] And it cannot be said that this idea of God is perhaps materially false and therefore that it can be from nothing, just as I have shortly previously noted concerning the ideas of heat and cold and similar things. For—on the contrary—because this idea of God be maximally clear and distinct, and because it contain more objective reality than any other idea, there is no idea more true through itself, nor is there any idea in which less suspicion of falsity would be found. This idea of a most highly perfect and infinite being is, I say, maximally true. For although it could perhaps be feigned that such a being does not exist, it still cannot be feigned that the idea of it exhibits nothing real to me, just as I have said before of the idea of cold. Moreover, this idea is maximally clear and distinct. For whatever I clearly and distinctly perceive that is real and true and that implies some perfection is totally contained in that idea. And it is not an obstacle to this that I would not comprehend the infinite, or that there would be innumerable other things in God that I can in no way either comprehend or even perhaps attain to by cogitation. For it is of the nature of the infinite that it not be comprehended by me, who am finite. And it suffices that I understand this itself, and that I judge that all those things which I clearly perceive and which I know to imply some perfection—and also perhaps innumerable other things of which I am ignorant— are formally or eminently in God, in order that the idea that I have of him might be the maximally true and the maximally clear and distinct idea of all the ideas that are in me.

Sed forte majus aliquid sum quàm ipse intelligam, omnesque illae perfectiones quas Deo tribuo, potentiâ quodammodo in me sunt, etiamsi nondum sese exe[47]rant, neque ad actum reducantur. Experior enim jam cognitionem meam paulatim augeri; nec video quid obstet quominus ita magis & magis augeatur in infinitum, nec etiam cur, cognitione sic auctâ, non possim ejus ope reliquas omnes Dei perfectiones adipisci; nec denique cur potentia ad istas perfectiones, si jam in me est, non sufficiat ad illarum ideam producendam.

Imo nihil horum esse potest. Nam primo, ut verum sit cognitionem meam gradatim augeri, & multa in me esse potentiâ quae actu nondum sunt, nihil tamen horum ad ideam Dei pertinet, in quâ nempe nihil omnino est potentiale; namque hoc ipsum, gradatim augeri, certissimum est imperfectionis argumentum. Praeterea, etiamsi cognitio mea semper magis & magis augeatur, nihilominus intelligo nunquam illam idcirco fore actu infinitam, quia nunquam eo devenietur, ut majoris adhuc incrementi non sit capax; Deum autem ita judico esse actu infinitum, ut nihil ejus perfectioni addi possit. Ac denique percipio esse objectivum ideae non a solo esse potentiali, quod proprie loquendo nihil est, sed tantummodo ab actuali sive formali posse produci.

Neque profecto quicquam est in his omnibus, quod diligenter attendenti non sit lumine naturali manifestum; sed quia, cùm minus attendo, & rerum sensibilium imagines mentis aciem excaecant, non ita facile recordor cur idea entis me perfectioris necessariò ab ente aliquo procedat quod sit revera perfectius, ulte[48]rius quaerere libet an ego ipse habens illam ideam esse possem, si tale ens nullum existeret.

[26.] But perhaps I am something greater than I myself might understand, and all those perfections which I attribute to God are in some mode in me potentially, even if they themselves had not yet come out and they would not be reduced to act. For I am now getting to know that my cognition is gradually becoming greater, and I do not see what would be an obstacle thereto that it would thus increase more and more into the infinite; and I also do not see why—the cognition having thus increased—I could with the help of it not get all the remaining perfections of God; and finally, I do not see why the potentiality for producing these perfections, if it is already in me, would not suffice to produce the idea of them.

[27.] But none of these things can be the case. For first, granted that it be true that my cognition is gradually becoming greater, and that many things are in me potentially that are not yet in me actually, still none of these things pertains to the idea of God—in which surely nothing at all is potential. For this itself—to increase gradually—is a most certain argument for imperfection. Moreover, even if my cognition were always to increase more and more, I nonetheless understand that it will never therefore be actually infinite, because it will never be achieved by it that it would not be capable of even greater increase. But I so judge that God is actually infinite that nothing could be added to his perfection. And finally, I perceive that the objective being of an idea cannot be produced by potential being alone, which is—properly speaking—nothing, but rather can the objective being of an idea be produced only by actual or formal being.

[28.] And in fact there is not anything whatsoever in all these things that would not be manifest by the natural light to one who is diligently paying attention. But because when I pay less attention, and the images of sensible things blind the vision of the mind, I do not then so easily remember why the idea of a being more perfect than me would necessarily proceed from a being that really and truly be more perfect than me, it is fitting to ask, in addition, whether I—*I* myself as one having this idea—could be if no such being did exist.

Nempe a quo essem? A me scilicet, vel a parentibus, vel ab aliis quibuslibet Deo minus perfectis; nihil enim ipso perfectius, nec etiam aeque perfectum, cogitari aut fingi potest.

Atqui, si a me essem, nec dubitarem, nec optarem, nec omnino quicquam mihi deesset; omnes enim perfectiones quarum idea aliqua in me est, mihi dedissem, atque ita ipsemet Deus essem. Nec putare debeo illa forsan quae mihi desunt difficilius acquiri posse, quàm illa quae jam in me sunt; nam contrà, manifestum est longe difficilius fuisse me, hoc est rem sive substantiam cogitantem, ex nihilo emergere, quàm multarum rerum quas ignoro cognitiones, quae tantùm istius substantiae accidentia sunt, acquirere. Ac certe, si majus illud a me haberem, non mihi illa saltem, quae facilius haberi possunt, denegassem, sed neque etiam ulla alia ex iis, quae in ideâ Dei contineri percipio; quia nempe nulla difficiliora factu mihi videntur; si quae autem difficiliora factu essent, certe etiam mihi difficiliora viderentur, siquidem reliqua quae habeo, a me haberem, quoniam in illis potentiam meam terminari experirer.

Neque vim harum rationum effugio, si supponam me forte semper fuisse ut nunc sum, tanquam si inde sequeretur, nullum existentiae meae authorem esse quaerendum. Quoniam enim omne tempus vitae in [49] partes innumeras dividi potest, quarum singulae a reliquis nullo modo dependent, ex eo quòd paulo ante fuerim, non sequitur me nunc debere esse, nisi aliqua causa me quasi rursus creet ad hoc momentum, hoc est me conservet. Perspicuum enim est attendenti ad temporis naturam, eâdem plane vi & actione opus esse ad rem quamlibet singulis

[29.] From whom, then, would I be? Scil., from myself, or from my parents, or from whatever other things less perfect than God. For nothing more perfect than him, nor even any-thing equally as perfect as he, can be cogitated or feigned.

[30.] But if I were from me, neither would I doubt, nor would I wish, nor would anything at all be lacking in me. For I would have given to me all the perfections of which there is some idea in me, and thus would I myself be God. And I must not think that those things which are lacking in me can perhaps be more difficult to acquire than those things which are in me now. For — on the contrary — it is manifest that it would have been more difficult by far that I, that is, a cogitating thing or a cogitating substance, emerge from nothing than that I acquire the cogni-tions of many things of which I am ignorant, which cognitions are only the accidents of that substance. And if I were to have that greater thing — that I as a cogitating thing or substance had emerged from nothing — from me, I would certainly not have denied to me at least those things which can be had more easi-ly, but nor would I have denied to me even any other things of those which I perceive to be contained in the idea of God, because surely none of these things seems to me to be more difficult to make. But if they were more difficult to make, cer-tainly they would also seem to me to be more difficult, if I did indeed have the remaining things that I have from me, because I would know by experience that my power terminates in them.

[31.] And I do not escape the force of these arguments if I were to suppose that I have perhaps always been just as I am now, as if it would therefrom follow that about no author of my existence is to be asked. For because every lifetime can be divided into innumerable parts, each one of which in no way depends on the others, it does not follow from thence that I had been shortly before, that I must be now, unless some cause were — as it were — to create me again at this moment, that is, to preserve me. For it is perspicuous to one who is paying at-tention to the nature of time that plainly the same power and action are needed to preserve anything whatever at the individual

momentis quibus durat conservandam, quâ opus esset ad eandem de novo creandam, si nondum existeret; adeo ut conservationem solâ ratione a creatione differre, sit etiam unum ex
iis quae lumine naturali manifesta sunt.

Itaque debeo nunc interrogare me ipsum, an habeam aliquam
vim per quam possim efficere ut ego ille, qui jam sum, paulo
post etiam sim futurus: nam, cùm nihil aliud sim quàm res cogitans, vel saltem cùm de eâ tantùm meî parte praecise nunc agam
quae est res cogitans, si quae talis vis in me esset, ejus proculdubio conscius essem. Sed & nullam esse experior, & ex hoc
ipso evidentissime cognosco me ab aliquo ente a me diverso
pendere.

Forte verò illud ens non est Deus, sumque vel a parentibus
productus, vel a quibuslibet aliis causis Deo minus perfectis.
Imo, ut jam ante dixi, perspicuum est tantumdem ad minimum
esse debere in causâ quantum est in effectu; & idcirco, cùm sim
res cogitans, ideamque quandam Dei in me habens, qualiscun-
que tandem meî causa assignetur, illam etiam esse rem cogitantem, & omnium perfectionum, quas Deo tribuo, ideam habere
fatendum est. Potestque de illâ rursus quaeri, an sit a se, vel
ab aliâ. Nam si a se, patet ex dictis illam ipsam Deum esse,
quia nempe, [50] cùm vim habeat per se existendi, habet proculdubio etiam vim possidendi actu omnes perfectiones quarum
ideam in se habet, hoc est omnes quas in Deo esse concipio.
Si autem sit ab aliâ, rursus eodem modo de hac alterâ quaeretur,
an sit a se, vel ab aliâ, donec tandem ad causam ultimam deveniatur, quae erit Deus.

Satis enim apertum est nullum hîc dari posse progressum in
infinitum, praesertim cùm non tantùm de causâ, quae me olim
produxit, hîc agam, sed maxime etiam de illâ quae me tempore
praesenti conservat.

moments at which it endures which would be needed to create the same thing from anew if it did not yet exist. Hence, that preservation differs from creation solely by a distinction of reason would also be one of the things that are manifest by the natural light.

[32.] And thus I must now ask me myself whether I would have some power through which I could effect that I—as that *I* who I am now—am also going to be a little later on. For since I be nothing other than a cogitating thing—or at least since I be now dealing with precisely only the part of me that is a cogitating thing—, I would without doubt be conscious of it if there were such a power in me. But I also know by experience that there is none, and from thence itself I cognize most evidently that I depend on some being different from me.

[33.] Yet perhaps this being is not God, and I have been produced by my parents or by whatever other causes less perfect than God. But just as I have already said before, it is perspicuous that there must be at a minimum just as much [reality] in the cause as there is in the effect. And therefore it is to be conceded that, since I be a cogitating thing—and having in me some idea of God—, whatever kind of cause of me would, finally, be assigned, it is also a cogitating thing, and that this cause has the idea of all the perfections that I attribute to God. And again, it can be asked of this cause whether it would be from itself, or from another cause. For if this cause would be from itself, it is obvious from the things that have been said that it itself is God, namely, because—since it would have the power of existing through itself—without doubt it also has the power of possessing actually all the perfections the ideas of which it has in itself, that is, all the perfections that I conceive to be in God. But if this cause would be from another, it will in the same manner again be asked of this other cause whether it would be from itself, or from another cause, until it would, finally, come down to the ultimate cause: which will be God.

[34.] For it is satisfactorily overt that no infinite regress can be given here, especially since I be here dealing not only with the cause that has once produced me, but also—maximally—with that cause which preserves me at the present time.

Nec fingi potest plures forte causas partiales ad me efficiendum concurrisse, & ab unâ ideam unius ex perfectionibus quas Deo tribuo, ab aliâ ideam alterius me accepisse, adeo ut omnes quidem illae perfectiones alicubi in universo reperiantur, sed non omnes simul junctae in uno aliquo, qui sit Deus. Nam contrà, unitas, simplicitas, sive inseparabilitas eorum omnium quae in Deo sunt, una est ex praecipuis perfectionibus quas in eo esse intelligo. Nec certe istius omnium ejus perfectionum unitatis idea in me potuit poni ab ullâ causâ, a quâ etiam aliarum perfectionum ideas non habuerim: neque enim efficere potuit ut illas simul junctas & inseparabiles intelligerem, nisi simul effecerit ut quaenam illae essent agnoscerem.

Quantum denique ad parentes attinet, ut omnia vera sint quae de illis unquam putavi, non tamen profecto illi me conservant, nec etiam ullo modo me, quatenus sum res cogitans, effecerunt; sed tantùm dispositiones quasdam in eâ materiâ posuerunt, cui me, hoc est mentem, quam solam nunc pro me acci[51]pio, inesse judicavi. Ac proinde hîc nulla de iis difficultas esse potest; sed omnino est concludendum, ex hoc solo quòd existam, quaedamque idea entis perfectissimi, hoc est Dei, in me sit, evidentissime demonstrari Deum etiam existere.

Superest tantùm ut examinem quâ ratione ideam istam a Deo accepi; neque enim illam sensibus hausi, nec unquam non expectanti mihi advenit, ut solent rerum sensibilium ideae, cùm istae res externis sensuum organis occurrunt, vel occurrere videntur; nec etiam a me efficta est, nam nihil ab illâ detrahere, nihil illi superaddere plane possum; ac proinde superest ut mihi sit innata, quemadmodum etiam mihi est innata idea meî ipsius.

Et sane non mirum est Deum, me creando, ideam illam mihi indidisse, ut esset tanquam nota artificis operi suo impressa;

[35.] And it cannot be feigned that several partial causes have perhaps concurred to effect me, and that from one I have received the idea of one of the perfections that I attribute to God and from another the idea of another, so that all these perfections would surely be found somewhere in the universe, but not all joined together in some one being, who would be God. For—on the contrary—the unity, the simplicity, or the inseparability of all the things that are in God is one of the foremost perfections that I understand to be in him. And the idea of this unity of all his perfections certainly could not have been posited in me by any cause from which I had not also had the ideas of the other perfections. For it could not have effected that I would understand these perfections as joined together and inseparable unless it simultaneously had effected that I would recognize which perfections they would be.

[36.] Finally, as far as it pertains to my parents, even if all the things that I have ever thought about them would be true, they still do not in fact preserve me, and they have also not effected me, in so far as I am a cogitating thing, in any manner. Rather have they only posited certain dispositions in that matter in which I have judged that I, that is, a mind—which alone I now accept as me—, am. And therefore there can be no difficulty concerning them here. Rather is it completely to be concluded from thence alone that I were to exist, and that an idea of a most perfect being, that is, of God, were to be in me, that it is very evidently demonstrated that God also exists.

[37.] There remains only that I would examine how I have received this idea from God. For I have not derived it from the senses, and it has never come to me as one who is not expecting it, as the ideas of sensible things usually then do when these things occur—or seem to occur—to the external organs of the senses. Nor also has it been feigned by me, for plainly I can subtract nothing from it and add nothing to it. And therefore it remains that this idea would be innate in me, just as the idea of me myself is also innate in me.

[38.] And it is surely not surprising that in creating me God has given this idea into me in order that it might be like the

nec etiam opus est ut nota illa sit aliqua res ab opere ipso diversa. Sed ex hoc uno quòd Deus me creavit, valde credibile est me quodammodo ad imaginem & similitudinem ejus factum esse, illamque similitudinem, in quâ Dei idea continetur, a me percipi per eandem facultatem, per quam ego ipse a me percipior: hoc est, dum in meipsum mentis aciem converto, non modo intelligo me esse rem incompletam & ab alio dependentem, remque ad majora & majora sive meliora indefinite aspirantem; sed simul etiam intelligo illum, a quo pendeo, majora ista omnia non indefinite & potentiâ tantùm, sed reipsâ infinite in se habere, atque ita Deum esse. Totaque vis argumenti in eo est, quòd agnoscam fieri non posse [52] ut existam talis naturae qualis sum, nempe ideam Dei in me habens, nisi revera Deus etiam existeret, Deus, inquam, ille idem cujus idea in me est, hoc est, habens omnes illas perfectiones, quas ego non comprehendere, sed quocunque modo attingere cogitatione possum, & nullis plane defectibus obnoxius. Ex quibus satis patet illum fallacem esse non posse; omnem enim fraudem & deceptionem a defectu aliquo pendere, lumine naturali manifestum est.

Sed priusquam hoc diligentius examinem, simulque in alias veritates quae inde colligi possunt inquiram, placet hîc aliquandiu in ipsius Dei contemplatione immorari, ejus attributa apud me expendere, & immensi hujus luminis pulchritudinem, quantum caligantis ingenii mei acies ferre poterit, intueri, admirari, adorare. Ut enim in hac solâ divinae majestatis contemplatione summam alterius vitae foelicitatem consistere fide credimus, ita etiam jam ex eâdem, licet multo minus perfectâ, maximam, cujus in hac vitâ capaces simus, voluptatem percipi posse experimur.

mark of an artificer impressed on his work. And there is also no need that that mark would be something different from the work itself. But from this one thing — that God has created me — it is very credible that I have in some manner been made in his image and likeness, and that that likeness, in which the idea of God is contained, is perceived by me through the same faculty through which *I* myself am perceived by me: that is, when I turn the vision of the mind into myself, not only do I then understand that I am a thing incomplete and dependent on another, and a thing indefinitely aspiring to greater and greater, or better, things, but simultaneously I also understand that he on whom I depend has all these greater things in him not just indefinitely and potentially, but rather according to the thing itself infinitely, and thus that he is God. And the total force of the argument lies therein that I would recognize that it cannot happen that I would exist of such a nature of which I am, namely, having the idea of God in me, unless God did also really and truly exist: God, I say, he, the same one of whom the idea is in me, that is, having all those perfections which *I* cannot comprehend, but to which I can in some way attain by cogitation, and being subject to no defects at all. From which things it is obvious enough that God cannot be a deceiver. For it is manifest by the natural light that all fraud and deception depend on some defect.

[39.] But before I were to examine this more diligently and simultaneously were to inquire into the other truths that can be gathered therefrom, it is here fitting to pause for a while in the contemplation of God himself, to reflect within me on his attributes and to intuit, to admire and to adore the beauty of his immense light, so far as the vision of my darkened mind will be able to bear it. For just as we believe by faith that the highest felicity of the other life consists solely in this contemplation of the divine majesty, so also do we know by experience that the maximal pleasure of which we would be capable in this life can now be perceived from the same — it is granted — much less perfect contemplation.

MEDITATIO IV.

De vero & falso.

Ita me his diebus assuefeci in mente a sensibus abducendâ, tamque accurate animadverti perpauca [53] esse quae de rebus corporeis vere percipiantur, multoque plura de mente humanâ, multo adhuc plura de Deo cognosci, ut jam absque ullâ difficultate cogitationem a rebus imaginabilibus ad intelligibiles tantùm, atque ab omni materiâ secretas, convertam. Et sane multò magis distinctam habeo ideam mentis humanae, quatenus est res cogitans, non extensa in longum, latum, & profundum, nec aliud quid a corpore habens, quàm ideam ullius rei corporeae. Cùmque attendo me dubitare, sive esse rem incompletam & dependentem, adeo clara & distincta idea entis independentis & completi, hoc est Dei, mihi occurrit; & ex hoc uno quòd talis idea in me sit, sive quòd ego ideam illam habens existam, adeo manifeste concludo Deum etiam existere, atque ab illo singulis momentis totam existentiam meam dependere, ut nihil evidentius, nihil certius ab humano ingenio cognosci posse confidam. Jamque videre videor aliquam viam per quam ab istâ contemplatione veri Dei, in quo nempe sunt omnes thesauri scientiarum & sapientiae absconditi, ad caeterarum rerum cognitionem deveniatur.

In primis enim agnosco fieri non posse ut ille me unquam fallat; in omni enim fallaciâ vel deceptione aliquid imperfec-

MEDITATION IV.

Concerning the true and the false.

[1.] In these days I have thus accustomed myself to leading the mind away from the senses, and I have so accurately noticed that there are very few things about corporeal things that be perceived truly, and that many more things about the human mind — and still many more things about God — are cognized, that now I shall without any difficulty turn cogitation from imaginable things to intelligible things only, and ones separate from all matter. And I have indeed a much more distinct idea of the human mind, in so far as it is a cogitating thing — not extended in length, breadth and depth, and not having anything else from body —, than I have a distinct idea of any corporeal thing. And when I pay attention thereto that I doubt, or that I am a thing incomplete and dependent, then there occurs to me the clear and distinct idea of an independent and complete being, that is, of God. And from this one thing — that there would be such an idea in me, or that *I* would exist as one having this idea — I so manifestly conclude that God also exists, and that my whole existence depends on him at individual moments, that I might be confident that nothing more evident and nothing more certain can be cognized by the human mind. And now I seem to see a way by which one might get from that contemplation of the true God — in whom, namely, all the treasures of the sciences and of wisdom are hidden — to the cognition of other things.

[2.] For among the first things that I recognize is that it cannot happen that God would ever deceive me. For in all fallacy

151

tionis reperitur; & quamvis posse fallere, nonnullum esse videatur acuminis aut potentiae argumentum, proculdubio velle fallere, vel malitiam vel imbecillitatem testatur, nec proinde in Deum cadit.

Deinde experior quandam in me esse judicandi facultatem, quam certe, ut & reliqua omnia quae in me [54] sunt, a Deo accepi; cùmque ille nolit me fallere, talem profecto non dedit, ut, dum eâ recte utor, possim unquam errare.

Nec ullum de hac re dubium superesset, nisi inde sequi videretur, me igitur errare nunquam posse; nam si quodcunque in me est, a Deo habeo, nec ullam ille mihi dederit errandi facultatem, non videor posse unquam errare. Atque ita prorsus, quamdiu de Deo tantùm cogito, totusque in eum me converto, nullam erroris aut falsitatis causam deprehendo; sed, postmodum ad me reversus, experior me tamen innumeris erroribus esse obnoxium, quorum causam inquirens animadverto non tantùm Dei, sive entis summè perfecti, realem & positivam, sed etiam, ut ita loquar, nihili, sive ejus quod ab omni perfectione summè abest, negativam quandam ideam mihi obversari, & me tanquam medium quid inter Deum & nihil, sive inter summum ens & non ens ita esse constitutum, ut, quatenus a summo ente sum creatus, nihil quidem in me sit, per quod fallar aut in errorem inducar, sed quatenus etiam quodammodo de nihilo, sive de non ente, participo, hoc est quatenus non sum ipse summum ens, desuntque mihi quam plurima, non adeo mirum esse quòd fallar. Atque ita certe intelligo errorem, quatenus error est, non esse quid reale quod a Deo dependeat, sed tantummodo esse defectum; nec proinde ad errandum mihi opus esse aliquâ facultate in hunc finem a Deo tributâ, sed contingere ut errem, ex eo quòd facultas verum judicandi, quam ab illo habeo, non sit in me infinita.

or deception is to be found some imperfection. And although to be able to deceive would seem to be an argument for sharpness of wit or power, to will to deceive attests without doubt to malice or weakness and therefore does not befit God.

[3.] Next, I know by experience that there is a certain faculty of judging in me which—like all the other things too that are in me—I have certainly received from God. And since God does not will to deceive me, he has in fact not given to me a faculty such that I could ever then err when I use it correctly.

[4.] And there would not remain any doubt about this matter if it did not seem to follow therefrom that I can, then, never err. For if I have whatever is in me from God, and he would not have given to me any faculty of erring, I do not seem to be able ever to err. And thus, in a word, so long as I cogitate only about God, and I as a whole turn myself to him, I find no cause of error or of falsity. But I know by experience that, soon after I have reverted to cogitating about me, I am nevertheless subject to innumerable errors, inquiring into the cause of which I notice that there is before me not only a real and positive idea of God, or of a most highly perfect being, but also —as I would so speak—a certain negative idea of nothing, or of that which is most highly absent from all perfection, and that I am so constituted to be—as it were—a middle something between God and nothing, or between the highest being and nonbeing, that in so far as I have been created by the highest being, there were surely nothing in me by which I might be deceived or induced to error, but that in so far as I also participate in some mode in nothing or in non-being, that is, in so far as I am not the highest being himself and very many things are lacking in me, it is not very surprising that I would be deceived. And thus I certainly understand that error, in so far as it is error, is not something real that would depend on God, but rather that it is only a defect; and therefore that to err I do not need some faculty bestowed on me by God to this end, but rather that that I were to err is contingent thereupon that the faculty of judging the true which I have from him be not infinite in me.

Verumtamen hoc nondum omnino satisfacit; non [55] enim error est pura negatio, sed privatio, sive carentia cujusdam cognitionis, quae in me quodammodo esse deberet; atque attendenti ad Dei naturam non videtur fieri posse, ut ille aliquam in me posuerit facultatem, quae non sit in suo genere perfecta, sive quae aliquâ sibi debitâ perfectione sit privata. Nam si, quo peritior est artifex, eo perfectiora opera ab illo proficiscantur, quid potest a summo illo rerum omnium conditore factum esse, quod non sit omnibus numeris absolutum? Nec dubium est quin potuerit Deus me talem creare, ut nunquam fallerer; nec etiam dubium est quin velit semper id quod est optimum: anne ergo melius est me falli quàm non falli?

Dum haec perpendo attentiùs, occurrit primò non mihi esse mirandum, si quaedam a Deo fiant quorum rationes non intelligam; nec de ejus existentiâ ideo esse dubitandum, quòd forte quaedam alia esse experiar, quae quare vel quomodo ab illo facta sint non comprehendo. Cùm enim jam sciam naturam meam esse valde infirmam & limitatam, Dei autem naturam esse immensam, incomprehensibilem, infinitam, ex hoc satis etiam scio innumerabilia illum posse quorum causas ignorem; atque ob hanc unicam rationem totum illud causarum genus, quod a fine peti solet, in rebus Physicis nullum usum habere existimo; non enim absque temeritate me puto posse investigare fines Dei.

Occurrit etiam non unam aliquam creaturam separatim, sed omnem rerum universitatem esse spectandam, quoties an opera Dei perfecta sint inquirimus; quod enim forte non immeritò, si solum esset, valde [56] imperfectum videretur, ut habens in mundo rationem partis est perfectissimum; & quamvis, ex quo

[5.] Yet this account is still not entirely satisfactory. For error is not a pure negation, but rather is it a privation, or a lack, of some cognition that should in some mode be in me. And to one who is paying attention to the nature of God it does not seem to be able to happen that he had posited in me a faculty which would not be perfect in its kind, or which would be deprived of some perfection that should be in it. For if the more skilled the artificer is, the more perfect are the works that were to proceed from him, what can have been made by that highest maker of all things that would not be absolute in all respects? And there is no doubt that God could have created me such that I would never be deceived, and there is also no doubt that he were always to will that which is optimal — the question is: whether therefore it is better that I am deceived than that I am not deceived?

[6.] While I weigh these things more attentively, it occurs to me, first, that it is not something for me to be surprised about if certain things whose reasons I would not understand were to be done by God. And his existence is not therefore to be doubted because I were perhaps to know by experience that there are certain other things that had been made by him, why or how I do not comprehend. For since I were now to know that my nature is very weak and limited, but that the nature of God is immense, incomprehensible and infinite, from this I also satisfactorily know that he can do innumerable things of the causes of which I be ignorant. And for this one reason do I believe that that whole kind of causes which is usually derived from the end has no use in explaining things physical. For not without rashness do I think that I can investigate the ends of God.

[7.] It occurs to me, also, that whenever we inquire as to whether the works of God would be perfect, not some one creature separately, but rather the whole universe of things, is to be regarded. For what would perhaps not without merit seem very imperfect if it were alone is, as having the nature of a part in the world, most perfect. And although from thence that I have willed to doubt all things, I have up until now cognized

de omnibus volui dubitare, nihil adhuc praeter me & Deum existere certò cognovi, non possum tamen, ex quo immensam Dei potentiam animadverti, negare quin multa alia ab illo facta sint, vel saltem fieri possint, adeo ut ego rationem partis in rerum universitate obtineam.

Deinde, ad me propius accedens, & qualesnam sint errores mei (qui soli imperfectionem aliquam in me arguunt) investigans, adverto illos a duabus causis simul concurrentibus dependere, nempe a facultate cognoscendi quae in me est, & a facultate eligendi, sive ab arbitrii libertate, hoc est ab intellectu & simul a voluntate. Nam per solum intellectum percipio tantùm ideas de quibus judicium ferre possum, nec ullus error proprie dictus in eo praecise sic spectato reperitur; quamvis enim innumerae fortasse res existant, quarum ideae nullae in me sunt, non tamen proprie illis privatus, sed negative tantùm destitutus, sum dicendus, quia nempe rationem nullam possum afferre, quâ probem Deum mihi majorem quàm dederit cognoscendi facultatem dare debuisse; atque quantumvis peritum artificem esse intelligam, non tamen ideo puto illum in singulis ex suis operibus omnes perfectiones ponere debuisse, quas in aliquibus ponere potest. Nec verò etiam queri possum, quòd non satis amplam & perfectam voluntatem, sive arbitrii libertatem, a Deo acceperim; nam sane nullis illam limitibus circumscribi experior. Et quod valde notandum mihi videtur, nulla [57] alia in me sunt tam perfecta aut tanta, quin intelligam perfectiora sive majora adhuc esse posse. Nam si, exempli causâ, facultatem intelligendi considero, statim agnosco perexiguam illam & valde finitam in me esse, simulque alterius cujusdam multo majoris, imò maximae atque infinitae, ideam formo, illamque ex hoc ipso quòd ejus ideam formare possim, ad Dei naturam pertinere percipio. Eâdem ratione, si facultatem recordandi vel

nothing certainly except that I and God exist, from thence that I have noticed the immense power of God, I still cannot deny that many other things had been made by him—or at least that they could be made by him—, so that *I* would obtain the nature of a part in the universe of things.

[8.] Coming then more closely to me and investigating of what kind my errors (which alone argue for some imperfection in me) might be, I notice that they depend on two simultaneously concurrent causes, namely, on the faculty of cognizing that is in me and on the faculty of choosing or on the freedom of choice, that is, simultaneously on the intellect and on the will. For through the intellect alone I only perceive the ideas about which I can render a judgment, and no error—properly said—is to be found in it—thus precisely regarded. For although there would perhaps exist innumerable things of which there are no ideas in me, I am still not—properly speaking—to be called "deprived" of these ideas, but rather am I—negatively—to be called only "destitute" of them, because I can surely offer no argument by which I might prove that God ought to have given to me a greater faculty of cognizing than he may have given to me. And however skilled that you will I would understand an artificer to be, I still do not therefore think that he ought to have posited in every single one of his works all the perfections that he can posit in some of them. And I also truly cannot complain that I had received from God a will, or freedom of choice, not satisfactorily ample and perfect, for I indeed know by experience that it is circumscribed by no limits. And which seems to me very much to be noted: there are no other things in me so perfect or so great that I would not understand that they can be yet more perfect or greater. For if I consider the faculty of understanding, for example, I immediately recognize that it is very exiguous and very finite in me, and I simultaneously form the idea of some other faculty of understanding much greater—indeed maximal and infinite—, and from this itself—that I could form the idea of this faculty—I perceive that it pertains to the nature of God. By the same reasoning, if I were to examine the faculty of remembering or

imaginandi, vel quaslibet alias examinem, nullam plane invenio, quam non in me tenuem & circumscriptam, in Deo immensam, esse intelligam. Sola est voluntas, sive arbitrii libertas, quam tantam in me experior, ut nullius majoris ideam apprehendam; adeo ut illa praecipue sit, ratione cujus imaginem quandam & similitudinem Dei me referre intelligo. Nam quamvis major absque comparatione in Deo quàm in me sit, tum ratione cognitionis & potentiae quae illi adjunctae sunt, redduntque ipsam magis firmam & efficacem, tum ratione objecti, quoniam ad plura se extendit, non tamen, in se formaliter & praecise spectata, major videtur; quia tantùm in eo consistit, quòd idem vel facere vel non facere (hoc est affirmare vel negare, prosequi vel fugere) possimus, vel potius in eo tantùm, quòd ad id quod nobis ab intellectu proponitur affirmandum vel negandum, sive prosequendum vel fugiendum, ita feramur, ut a nullâ vi externâ nos ad id determinari sentiamus. Neque enim opus est me in utramque partem ferri posse, ut sim liber, sed contrà, quo magis in unam propendeo, sive quia rationem [58] veri & boni in eâ evidenter intelligo, sive quia Deus intima cogitationis meae ita disponit, tanto liberius illam eligo; nec sane divina gratia, nec naturalis cognitio unquam imminuunt libertatem, sed potius augent & corroborant. Indifferentia autem illa, quam experior, cùm nulla me ratio in unam partem magis quàm in alteram impellit, est infimus gradus libertatis, & nullam in eâ perfectionem, sed tantummodo in cognitione defectum, sive negationem quandam, testatur; nam si semper quid verum & bonum sit clare viderem, nunquam de eo quod esset judicandum vel eligendum deliberarem; atque ita, quamvis plane liber, nunquam tamen indifferens esse possem.

Ex his autem percipio nec vim volendi, quam a Deo habeo, per se spectatam, causam esse errorum meorum, est enim amplissima, atque in suo genere perfecta; neque etiam vim intel-

of imagining—or whatever other ones are fitting—, I plainly find none that I would not understand to be tenuous and circumscribed in me, but immense in God. It is the will alone, or the freedom of choice, which I know by experience as being so great in me that I might apprehend an idea of no greater faculty—so much so that it be above all it by reason of which I understand that I bear the image and likeness of God. For although the will, or the freedom of choice, be without comparison greater in God than in me, both by reason of the cognition and of the power that are joined to it and render it more firm and efficacious, and by reason of the object—because it extends itself to more things—, it still does not seem greater, regarded formally and precisely in itself. The reason is because the will, or the freedom of choice, consists only therein that we could do or not do (that is, affirm or deny, pursue or avoid) the same thing, or better, only therein that we were so to be brought to affirm or to deny, or to pursue or to avoid, that which is proposed to us by the intellect that we would sense that we are determined thereto by no external force. For there is no need that I can be moved to both alternatives in order that I might be free; but rather, on the contrary, the more I tend to one alternative—either because I evidently understand the reason of the true and of the good in it, or because God thus disposes the intimate parts of my cogitation—, the more freely do I choose it. Indeed, neither divine grace nor natural cognition ever diminishes freedom, but rather do they increase and corroborate it. But that indifference which I then experience when there is no reason that impels me to one alternative more than to another is the lowest grade of freedom, and that indifference attests to no perfection in this freedom, but rather only to a defect in cognition, or to some negation. For if I did always see clearly what be true and good, I would never deliberate about that which were to be judged about or chosen. And thus although I plainly could be free, I could still never be indifferent.

[9.] But from these things I perceive that the power of willing which I have from God—regarded by itself—is not the cause of my errors, for that power is most ample, and perfect in its

ligendi, nam quidquid intelligo, cùm a Deo habeam ut intelligam, proculdubio recte intelligo, nec in eo fieri potest ut fallar. Unde ergo nascuntur mei errores? Nempe ex hoc uno quòd, cùm latius pateat voluntas quàm intellectus, illam non intra eosdem limites contineo, sed etiam ad illa quae non intelligo extendo; ad quae cùm sit indifferens, facile a vero & bono deflectit, atque ita & fallor & pecco.

Exempli causâ, cùm examinarem hisce diebus an aliquid in mundo existeret, atque adverterem, ex hoc ipso quòd illud examinarem, evidenter sequi me existere, non potui quidem non judicare illud quod tam clare intelligebam verum esse; non quòd ab ali[59]quâ vi externâ fuerim ad id coactus, sed quia ex magnâ luce in intellectu magna consequuta est propensio in voluntate, atque ita tanto magis sponte & libere illud credidi, quanto minus fui ad istud ipsum indifferens. Nunc autem, non tantùm scio me, quatenus sum res quaedam cogitans, existere, sed praeterea etiam idea quaedam naturae corporeae mihi obversatur, contingitque ut dubitem an natura cogitans quae in me est, vel potius quae ego ipse sum, alia sit ab istâ naturâ corporeâ, vel an ambae idem sint; & suppono nullam adhuc intellectui meo rationem occurrere, quae mihi unum magis quàm aliud persuadeat. Certe ex hoc ipso sum indifferens ad utrumlibet affirmandum vel negandum, vel etiam ad nihil de eâ re judicandum.

Quinimo etiam haec indifferentia non ad ea tantùm se extendit de quibus intellectus nihil plane cognoscit, sed generaliter ad omnia quae ab illo non satis perspicue cognoscuntur eo ipso tempore, quo de iis a voluntate deliberatur: quantumvis enim probabiles conjecturae me trahant in unam partem, sola cognitio quòd sint tantùm conjecturae, non autem certae atque in-

kind. And the cause of my errors is also not the power of understanding, for because I were to have it from God that I would understand, whatever I understand, I understand without doubt correctly. Nor can it happen that I would be deceived in it. Wherefrom therefore do my errors come? Surely from this one thing: that because the will open more widely than the intellect, I do not contain the will within the same limits, but rather do I even extend it to the things that I do not understand. Because the will be indifferent to these things, it easily turns away from the true and the good, and thus both am I deceived and do I sin.

[10.] For example, when in these days I were to examine whether anything would exist in the world, and I were to notice that from thence itself that I were to examine this, it evidently follows that I exist, I cannot indeed then not have judged that that which I so clearly understood was true: not that I had been coerced thereto by some external force, but rather because a great propensity in the will has followed from the great light in the intellect, and thus the more spontaneously and freely I have believed this, the less I have been indifferent to that itself. But now I not only know that I, in so far as I am a cogitating thing, exist, but also, in addition, there is an idea of corporeal nature before me, and it happens that I would doubt whether the cogitating nature that is in me, or better, that *I* myself am, would be another nature different from that corporeal nature, or whether both are the same. And I suppose that as yet there occurs to my intellect no reason that might persuade me of the one possibility more than of the other. From this itself I am certainly indifferent as to whether to affirm or to deny either the one or the other possibility, or even as to whether to judge nothing about this matter.

[11.] Indeed, this indifference even extends itself not only to those things about which the intellect cognizes nothing at all, but also to all the things generally that are not perspicuously enough cognized by it at that time itself at which the will deliberates about them. For although probable conjectures were to pull me to one alternative, the cognition alone that they be

dubitabiles rationes, sufficit ad assensionem meam in contrarium impellendam. Quod satis his diebus sum expertus, cùm illa omnia quae priùs ut vera quam maxime credideram, propter hoc unum quòd de iis aliquo modo posse dubitari deprehendissem, plane falsa esse supposui.

Cùm autem quid verum sit non satis clare & distincte percipio, si quidem a judicio ferendo abstineam, clarum est me recte agere, & non falli. Sed si vel affirmem vel negem, tunc libertate arbitrii non recte utor; atque [60] si in eam partem quae falsa est me convertam, plane fallar; si verò alteram amplectar, casu quidem incidam in veritatem, sed non ideo culpâ carebo, quia lumine naturali manifestum est perceptionem intellectûs praecedere semper debere voluntatis determinationem. Atque in hoc liberi arbitrii non recto usu privatio illa inest quae formam erroris constituit: privatio, inquam, inest in ipsâ operatione, quatenus a me procedit, sed non in facultate quam a Deo accepi, nec etiam in operatione quatenus ab illo dependet.

Neque enim habeo causam ullam conquerendi, quòd Deus mihi non majorem vim intelligendi, sive non majus lumen naturale dederit quàm dedit, quia est de ratione intellectûs finiti ut multa non intelligat, & de ratione intellectûs creati ut sit finitus; estque quòd agam gratias illi, qui mihi nunquam quicquam debuit, pro eo quod largitus est, non autem quòd putem me ab illo iis esse privatum, sive illum mihi ea abstulisse, quae non dedit.

Non habeo etiam causam conquerendi, quòd voluntatem dederit latius patentem quàm intellectum; cùm enim voluntas in

only conjectures—but not certain and indubitable reasons—suffices to impel my assent to the contrary. Which I have satisfactorily gotten to know by experience in these days, since I have supposed all those things which I had previously believed as being as true as maximally as possible to be wholly false because of this one thing: that I had found that they can in some mode be doubted.

[12.] But if I were at least then to refrain from rendering judgment when I do not clearly and distinctly enough perceive what were true, it is clear that I act correctly and that I am not deceived. Yet if I were to affirm or to deny, I do not then correctly use the freedom of choice. And if I were to turn myself to that alternative which is false, I would plainly be deceived. But if I were to embrace the other alternative, I would surely come upon the truth by chance, yet I will not therefore be without fault, because it is manifest by the natural light that the perception of the intellect must always precede the determination of the will. And in this incorrect use of free choice is to be found that privation which has constituted the form of error. The privation is to be found, I say, in the operation itself in so far as it proceeds from me, but not in the faculty that I have received from God, nor even in the operation in so far as it depends on him.

[13.] And indeed I do not have any cause for complaining that God had not given to me a greater power of understanding, or a greater natural light, than he has given to me, because it is of the nature of a finite intellect that it not understand many things, and it is of the nature of a created intellect that it be finite. And it is the case that I would give thanks to him who has never owed me anything for that which he has given to me, but it is not the case that I would think that I have been deprived by him of the things which he has not given to me, or that he has taken them away from me.

[14.] I also do not have any cause for complaining that God had given to me a will opening more widely than the intellect. For since the will were to consist of only one thing, and—

unâ tantùm re, & tanquam in indivisibili consistat, non videtur ferre ejus natura ut quicquam ab illâ demi possit; & sane quo amplior est, tanto majores debeo gratias ejus datori.

Nec denique etiam queri debeo, quòd Deus mecum concurrat ad eliciendos illos actus voluntatis, sive illa judicia, in quibus fallor: illi enim actus sunt omnino veri & boni, quatenus a Deo dependent, & major in me quodammodo perfectio est, quòd illos possim elicere, quàm si non possem. Privatio autem, in quâ solâ ratio [61] formalis falsitatis & culpae consistit, nullo Dei concursu indiget, quia non est res, neque ad illum relata ut causam privatio, sed tantummodo negatio dici debet. Nam sane nulla imperfectio in Deo est, quòd mihi libertatem dederit assentiendi vel non assentiendi quibusdam, quorum claram & distinctam perceptionem in intellectu meo non posuit; sed proculdubio in me imperfectio est, quòd istâ libertate non bene utar, & de iis, quae non recte intelligo, judicium feram. Video tamen fieri a Deo facile potuisse, ut, etiamsi manerem liber, & cognitionis finitae, nunquam tamen errarem: nempe si vel intellectui meo claram & distinctam perceptionem omnium de quibus unquam essem deliberaturus indidisset; vel tantùm si adeo firmiter memoriae impressisset, de nullâ unquam re esse judicandum quam clare & distincte non intelligerem, ut nunquam ejus possem oblivisci. Et facile intelligo me, quatenus rationem habeo totius cujusdam, perfectiorem futurum fuisse quàm nunc sum, si talis a Deo factus essem. Sed non ideo possum negare quin major quodammodo perfectio sit in totâ rerum universitate, quòd quaedam ejus partes ab erroribus immunes non sint, aliae verò sint, quàm si omnes plane similes essent. Et nullum habeo jus conquerendi quòd eam me Deus in mundo personam sustinere voluerit, quae non est omnium praecipua & maxime perfecta.

as it were — of an indivisible thing, its nature does not seem to bear that anything could be taken away from it. And indeed, the more ample the will is, the greater thanks do I owe to its giver.

[15.] Finally, I should also not complain that God would concur with me to elicit those acts of the will, or those judgments, in which I am deceived. For these acts, in so far as they depend on God, are completely true and good, and it is in a certain mode a greater perfection in me that I could elicit them than if I could not do so. But the privation, in which alone the formal nature of falsity and of fault consists, needs no concurrence of God, because the privation is not a thing, and — related to him as its cause — it should be called not "a privation", but rather only "a negation". For it is surely no imperfection in God that he had given to me the freedom of assenting to or of not assenting to certain things of which he has not posited a clear and distinct perception in my intellect. But it is without doubt an imperfection in me that I would not use that freedom well, and that I would render judgment about the things that I do not correctly understand. However, I see that it can have easily been done by God that, even if I would remain free and of finite cognition, I would still never err: namely, if he had given into my intellect a clear and distinct perception of all those things about which I would ever be going to deliberate, or if only he had so firmly impressed in the memory that of nothing that I would not clearly and distinctly understand is ever to be judged that I could never forget it. And I easily understand that, in so far as I have the nature of a certain whole, I would have been going to be more perfect than I am now if I had been made as such by God. But I cannot therefore deny that in a certain mode it be a greater perfection in the total universe of things that certain ones of its parts were not immune from errors, but other ones were so immune, than if all the parts would be wholly similar. And I have no right to complain that God had willed that I play a personal role in the world that is not the foremost and maximally perfect one of all.

Ac praeterea, etiam ut non possim ab erroribus abstinere priori illo modo qui pendet ab evidenti eorum omnium perceptione de quibus est deliberandum, possum tamen illo altero qui pendet ab eo tantùm, [62] quòd recorder, quoties de rei veritate non liquet, a judicio ferendo esse abstinendum; nam, quamvis eam in me infirmitatem esse experiar, ut non possim semper uni & eidem cognitioni defixus inhaerere, possum tamen attentâ & saepius iteratâ meditatione efficere, ut ejusdem, quoties usus exiget, recorder, atque ita habitum quemdam non errandi acquiram.

Quâ in re cùm maxima & praecipua hominis perfectio consistat, non parum me hodiernâ meditatione lucratum esse existimo, quòd erroris & falsitatis causam investigarim. Et sane nulla alia esse potest ab eâ quam explicui; nam quoties voluntatem in judiciis ferendis ita contineo, ut ad ea tantùm se extendat quae illi clare & distincte ab intellectu exhibentur, fieri plane non potest ut errem, quia omnis clara & distincta perceptio proculdubio est aliquid, ac proinde a nihilo esse non potest, sed necessariò Deum authorem habet, Deum, inquam, illum summe perfectum, quem fallacem esse repugnat; ideoque proculdubio est vera. Nec hodie tantùm didici quid mihi sit cavendum ut nunquam fallar, sed simul etiam quid agendum ut assequar veritatem; assequar enim illam profecto, si tantùm ad omnia quae perfecte intelligo satis attendam, atque illa a reliquis, quae confusius & obscurius apprehendo, secernam. Cui rei diligenter imposterum operam dabo. [63]

[16.] And besides, even if I could not refrain from errors by that prior mode, which depends on an evident perception of all those things about which is to be deliberated, I can still do so by that other mode, which depends only thereupon that I would remember, whenever the truth of a matter is not transparent, that from rendering judgment is to be refrained. For although I were to know by experience that there is in me the weakness that I could not always inhere fixed in one and the same cognition, by attentive and frequently repeated meditation I can still effect that I might remember it whenever the need requires me to do so — and thus I might acquire a certain habit of not erring.

[17.] Because the maximal and foremost perfection of the human being were to consist in this — in having acquired a certain habit of not erring — , I think that I have gained not a little by today's meditation, in that I had investigated the cause of error and of falsity. And there can surely be no other cause of error and of falsity than the one that I have explicated. For whenever I so contain the will in the judgments to be rendered that it were to extend itself only to the things that are clearly and distinctly exhibited to it by the intellect, it cannot happen at all that I would err, because every clear and distinct perception is without doubt something, and therefore it cannot be from nothing, but rather does it necessarily have God as its author: that most highly perfect God, I say, whom it contradicts to be a deceiver. And therefore every clear and distinct perception is without doubt true. Nor have I today learned only against what were to be cautioned by me in order that I might never be deceived, but also I have simultaneously learned what were to be done by me in order that I might reach the truth. For I shall indeed reach the truth, if only I would pay enough attention to all the things that I perfectly understand and I would distinguish these from the other things, which I more confusedly and more obscurely apprehend. At which I shall, henceforth, diligently make an effort.

MEDITATIO V.

De essentiâ rerum materialium;
& iterum de Deo, quòd existat.

Multa mihi supersunt de Dei attributis, multa de meî ipsius sive mentis meae naturâ investiganda; sed illa forte aliàs resumam, jamque nihil magis urgere videtur (postquam animadverti quid cavendum atque agendum sit ad assequendam veritatem), quàm ut ex dubiis, in quae superioribus diebus incidi, coner emergere, videamque an aliquid certi de rebus materialibus haberi possit.

Et quidem, priusquam inquiram an aliquae tales res extra me existant, considerare debeo illarum ideas, quatenus sunt in meâ cogitatione, & videre quaenam ex iis sint distinctae, quaenam confusae.

Nempe distincte imaginor quantitatem, quam vulgo Philosophi appellant continuam, sive ejus quantitatis aut potius rei quantae extensionem in longum, latum & profundum; numero in eâ varias partes; quaslibet istis partibus magnitudines, figuras, situs, & motus locales, motibusque istis quaslibet durationes assigno.

Nec tantùm illa, sic in genere spectata, mihi plane nota & perspecta sunt, sed praeterea etiam particularia innumera de figuris, de numero, de motu, & similibus, attendendo percipio, quorum veritas adeo aperta [64] est & naturae meae con-

168

MEDITATION V.

Concerning the essence of material things;
and again concerning God, that he exist.

[1.] There remain to be investigated by me many things concerning the attributes of God, and many things concerning me myself or the nature of my mind. But I shall perhaps resume these things at another time, and now nothing seems to be more urgent (after I have noticed against what were to be cautioned and what were to be done in order to reach the truth) than that I might try to emerge from the doubts into which I have gone in the previous days and that I might see whether something certain concerning material things could be had.

[2.] And before I shall inquire as to whether any such things would exist outside me, I must surely consider the ideas of these things, in so far as they are in my cogitation, and see which of these ideas would be distinct and which of them would be confused.

[3.] Of course I distinctly imagine the quantity that philosophers commonly call "continuous", or the extension of the quantity — or rather the extension of the thing quantified — in length, breadth and depth; in it I enumerate various parts; to these parts I assign whatever magnitudes, figures, positions and local movements, and to these movements I assign whatever durations.

[4.] Not only are these things — thus regarded in general — plainly known and transparent to me, but also by paying attention I perceive, in addition, innumerable particulars concerning figures, concerning number, concerning movement and concerning similar things, particulars whose truth is so overt and

sentanea, ut, dum illa primùm detego, non tam videar aliquid
novi addiscere, quàm eorum quae jam ante sciebam reminisci,
sive ad ea primùm advertere, quae dudum quidem in me erant, licet non prius in illa obtutum mentis convertissem.

Quodque hîc maxime considerandum puto, invenio apud me
innumeras ideas quarumdam rerum, quae, etiam si extra me
fortasse nullibi existant, non tamen dici possunt nihil esse; &
quamvis a me quodammodo ad arbitrium cogitentur, non tamen a me finguntur, sed suas habent veras & immutabiles
naturas. Ut cùm, exempli causâ, triangulum imaginor, etsi fortasse talis figura nullibi gentium extra cogitationem meam existat, nec unquam extiterit, est tamen profecto determinata quaedam ejus natura, sive essentia, sive forma, immutabilis &
aeterna, quae a me non efficta est, nec a mente meâ dependet;
ut patet ex eo quòd demonstrari possint variae proprietates de
isto triangulo, nempe quòd ejus tres anguli sint aequales duobus rectis, quòd maximo ejus angulo maximum latus subten-
datur, & similes, quas velim nolim clare nunc agnosco, etiamsi de iis nullo modo antea cogitaverim, cùm triangulum
imaginatus sum, nec proinde a me fuerint effictae.

Neque ad rem attinet, si dicam mihi forte a rebus externis
per organa sensuum istam trianguli ideam advenisse, quia nempe
corpora triangularem figuram habentia interdum vidi; possum
enim alias innumeras figuras excogitare, de quibus nulla suspicio esse potest quòd mihi unquam per sensus illapsae sint,
& tamen [65] varias de iis, non minus quàm de triangulo,
proprietates demonstrare. Quae sane omnes sunt verae, quandoquidem a me clare cognoscuntur, ideoque aliquid sunt, non
merum nihil: patet enim illud omne quod verum est esse ali-

consentaneous to my nature that when I first detect them I would then seem not so much to learn something new as to remember things that I already knew before, or to notice for the first time things that were surely already in me for a long time although I had not previously turned the gaze of the mind to them.

[5.] And what I think is maximally to be considered here is that I find within me innumerable ideas of certain things which, even if they would perhaps exist nowhere outside me, still cannot be said to be nothing. And although they would in a certain manner be cogitated by me at will, they are still not feigned by me, but rather do they have their own true and immutable natures. So that when I imagine a triangle, for example, even if such a figure would perhaps exist nowhere in the world outside my cogitation — nor would it have ever existed — , there still is in fact a certain determinate nature or essence or form of it, immutable and eternal, which has not been feigned by me, nor does it depend on my mind: as is obvious from thence that various properties could be demonstrated about this triangle, namely, that its three angles be equal to two right ones, that the maximum side be opposite to its maximum angle, and similar things, which properties — whether I would want to or not want to — I now clearly recognize, even if I previously would in no way have then cogitated about them when I have imagined the triangle, nor would they therefore have been feigned by me.

[6.] And it does not pertain to the matter if I were to say that because I surely have from time to time seen bodies having a triangular figure, that idea of the triangle has perhaps come to me from external things through the organs of the senses. For I can excogitate innumerable other figures about which there can be no suspicion that they had ever slipped into me through the senses, and yet I can demonstrate the various properties of them no less than I can demonstrate those of the triangle. All which properties are surely true, since they are clearly cognized by me; and therefore they are something, and not merely nothing: for it is obvious that all that which is true is something. And I have already demonstrated in great detail that all those

quid; & jam fuse demonstravi illa omnia quae clare cognosco esse vera. Atque quamvis id non demonstrassem, ea certe est natura mentis meae ut nihilominus non possem iis non assentiri, saltem quamdiu ea clare percipio; meminique me semper, etiam ante hoc tempus, cùm sensuum objectis quam maxime inhaererem, ejusmodi veritates, quae nempe de figuris, aut numeris, aliisve ad Arithmeticam vel Geometriam vel in genere ad puram atque abstractam Mathesim pertinentibus, evidenter agnoscebam, pro omnium certissimis habuisse.

Jam verò si ex eo solo, quòd alicujus rei ideam possim ex cogitatione meâ depromere, sequitur ea omnia, quae ad illam rem pertinere clare & distincte percipio, revera ad illam pertinere, nunquid inde haberi etiam potest argumentum, quo Dei existentia probetur? Certe ejus ideam, nempe entis summe perfecti, non minus apud me invenio, quàm ideam cujusvis figurae aut numeri; nec minus clare & distincte intelligo ad ejus naturam pertinere ut semper existat, quàm id quod de aliquâ figurâ aut numero demonstro ad ejus figurae aut numeri naturam etiam pertinere; ac proinde, quamvis non omnia, quae superioribus hisce diebus meditatus sum, vera essent, in eodem ad minimum certitudinis gradu esse deberet apud me Dei existen[66]tia, in quo fuerunt hactenus Mathematicae veritates.

Quanquam sane hoc primâ fronte non est omnino perspicuum, sed quandam sophismatis speciem refert. Cùm enim assuetus sim in omnibus aliis rebus existentiam ab essentiâ distinguere, facile mihi persuadeo illam etiam ab essentiâ Dei sejungi posse, atque ita Deum ut non existentem cogitari. Sed tamen diligentius attendenti fit manifestum, non magis posse existentiam ab essentiâ Dei separari, quàm ab essentiâ trianguli magnitudinem trium ejus angulorum aequalium duobus

things which I clearly cognize are true. And even if I had not demonstrated this, the nature of my mind is certainly such that I nonetheless could not not assent to these things—at least so long as I clearly perceive them. And I remember that even before this time, when I would inhere as maximally as possible in the objects of the senses, I have always held truths of this mode—which things, namely, of figures or of numbers or of the other things pertaining to arithmetic or geometry or to pure and abstract mathematics in general, I evidently recognized—to be the most certain ones of all.

[7.] But now if from thence alone that I could draw the idea of something from my cogitation, it follows that all the things that I clearly and distinctly perceive to pertain to that thing do really and truly pertain to it, then cannot therefrom also an argument be had by which the existence of God might be proved? I certainly find within me the idea of God, namely, the idea of a most highly perfect being, no less than I do the idea of some figure or number. Nor do I understand less clearly and distinctly that it pertains to his nature that he always exist than that that which I demonstrate of some figure or number also pertains to the nature of this figure or number. And therefore even if not all the things on which I have meditated in these previous days would be true, the existence of God must be within my reach at a minimum in the same grade of certainty in which mathematical truths have hitherto been.

[8.] Yet at first sight this is surely not completely perspicuous, but rather does it bear the look of some sophism. For since I be accustomed to distinguish the existence from the essence in all other things, I easily persuade myself that the existence can also be separated from the essence of God, and hence that God can be cogitated as not existing. But to one who is paying attention more diligently it still becomes manifest that the existence can no more be separated from the essence of God than it can be separated from the essence of a triangle that the magnitude of its three angles is equal to two right ones, or than the

rectis, sive ab ideâ montis ideam vallis: adeo ut non magis repugnet cogitare Deum (hoc est ens summe perfectum) cui desit existentia (hoc est cui desit aliqua perfectio), quàm cogitare montem cui desit vallis.

Verumtamen, ne possim quidem cogitare Deum nisi existentem, ut neque montem sine valle, at certe, ut neque ex eo quòd
cogitem montem cum valle, ideo sequitur aliquem montem in
mundo esse, ita neque ex eo quòd cogitem Deum ut existentem, ideo sequi videtur Deum existere: nullam enim necessita-
tem cogitatio mea rebus imponit; & quemadmodum imaginari
licet equum alatum, etsi nullus equus habeat alas, ita forte Deo
existentiam possum affingere, quamvis nullus Deus existat.

Imo sophisma hîc latet; neque enim, ex eo quòd non possim
cogitare montem nisi cum valle, sequitur alicubi montem &
vallem existere, sed tantùm mon[67]tem & vallem, sive existant, sive non existant, a se mutuo sejungi non posse. Atqui
ex eo quòd non possim cogitare Deum nisi existentem, sequitur
existentiam a Deo esse inseparabilem, ac proinde illum reverà
existere; non quòd mea cogitatio hoc efficiat, sive aliquam neces-
sitatem ulli rei imponat, sed contrà quia ipsius rei, nempe existentiae Dei, necessitas me determinat ad hoc cogitandum: neque enim mihi liberum est Deum absque existentiâ (hoc est ens
summe perfectum absque summâ perfectione) cogitare, ut liberum est equum vel cum alis vel sine alis imaginari.

Neque etiam hîc dici debet, necesse quidem esse ut ponam
Deum existentem, postquam posui illum habere omnes perfectiones, quandoquidem existentia una est ex illis, sed priorem
positionem necessariam non fuisse; ut neque necesse est me putare figuras omnes quadrilateras circulo inscribi, sed posito quòd

idea of a valley can be separated from the idea of a mountain —
so much so that it would be just as contradictory to cogitate
God (that is, a most highly perfect being) in whom existence
would be lacking (that is, in whom a perfection would be lacking) as to cogitate a mountain from which a valley would be
missing.

[9.] Granted, however, that I could not cogitate God except
as existing, just as I could not cogitate a mountain without a
valley, yet as from thence that I would cogitate a mountain with
a valley, it certainly does not therefore follow that there is any
mountain in the world, so also from thence that I would cogitate God as existing, it does not seem therefore to follow that
God exists. For my cogitation imposes no necessity on the things.
And just as it is permitted to imagine a winged horse even if
no horse would have wings, so also can I perhaps feign existence of God although no God would exist.

[10.] But there is a sophism hidden here. For from thence
that I could not cogitate a mountain except with a valley, it
does not follow that a mountain and a valley exist anywhere,
but rather only does it follow that a mountain and a valley —
whether they would exist or whether they would not exist —
cannot mutually be separated from each other. But from thence
that I could not cogitate God except as existing, it does follow
that existence is inseparable from God, and therefore that he
does really and truly exist: not that my cogitation would effect
this, or that it would impose any necessity on anything, but
rather — on the contrary — because the necessity of the thing itself, namely, of the existence of God, determines me to cogitate this. For I am not free to cogitate God without existence
(that is, a most highly perfect being without the highest perfection) as I am free to imagine a horse with wings or without
wings.

[11.] And here it must not be said that while it is necessary
that I would posit God as existing after I have posited that he
has all perfections — since existence is one of these — , yet the
prior positing has not been necessary: just as it is not necessary
that I think that all quadrilateral figures are inscribed in a cir-

hoc putem, necesse erit me fateri rhombum circulo inscribi, quod aperte tamen est falsum. Nam, quamvis non necesse sit ut incidam unquam in ullam de Deo cogitationem, quoties tamen de ente primo & summo libet cogitare, atque ejus ideam tanquam ex mentis meae thesauro depromere, necesse est ut illi omnes perfectiones attribuam, etsi nec omnes tunc enumerem, nec ad singulas attendam: quae necessitas plane sufficit ut postea, cùm animadverto existentiam esse perfectionem, recte concludam ens primum & summum existere: quemadmodum non est necesse me ullum triangulum unquam imaginari, sed quoties volo figuram rectilineam tres tantùm angulos habentem considerare, necesse est ut illi ea tribuam, ex qui[68]bus recte infertur ejus tres angulos non majores esse duobus rectis, etiamsi hoc ipsum tunc non advertam. Cùm verò examino quaenam figurae circulo inscribantur, nullo modo necesse est ut putem omnes quadrilateras ex eo numero esse; imò etiam idipsum nequidem fingere possum, quamdiu nihil volo admittere nisi quod clare & distincte intelligo. Ac proinde magna differentia est inter ejusmodi falsas positiones, & ideas veras mihi ingenitas, quarum prima & praecipua est idea Dei. Nam sane multis modis intelligo illam non esse quid fictitium a cogitatione meâ dependens, sed imaginem verae & immutabilis naturae: ut, primo, quia nulla alia res potest a me excogitari, ad cujus essentiam existentia pertineat, praeter solum Deum; deinde, quia non possum duos aut plures ejusmodi Deos intelligere, & quia, posito quòd jam unus existat, plane videam esse necessarium ut & ante ab aeterno extiterit, & in aeternum sit mansurus; ac denique, quòd multa alia in Deo percipiam, quorum nihil a me detrahi potest nec mutari.

Sed verò, quâcumque tandem utar probandi ratione, semper eò res redit, ut ea me sola plane persuadeant, quae clare

cle, but it having been posited that I would think this, it will be necessary that I admit that a rhombus is inscribed in a circle — which is, however, overtly false. For although it not be necessary that I would ever come upon any cogitation of God, whenever it pleases me to cogitate about the first and highest being, and to draw the idea of him — as it were — out of the thesaurus of my mind, it is still necessary that I were to attribute all perfections to him, even if I did not then enumerate all of them, nor did I pay attention to them as individual things: which necessity plainly suffices so that afterwards, when I notice that existence is a perfection, I might then correctly conclude that the first and highest being exists. In the same way, it is not necessary that I ever imagine any triangle, yet whenever I want to consider a rectilinear figure having only three angles, it is necessary that I would attribute to it those things from which it is correctly inferred that its three angles are not greater than two right ones, even if I did not then notice this itself. But when I examine which figures be inscribed in a circle, it is in no way necessary that I would then think that all quadrilateral ones are of that number. Indeed, I also cannot even feign this itself, so long as I will to admit nothing except what I clearly and distinctly understand. And therefore there is a great difference between false suppositions of this mode, and true ideas inborn in me, of which the first and foremost is the idea of God. For I surely understand in many ways that this idea is not something fictitious depending on my cogitation, but rather an image of a true and immutable nature: as first, because no other thing to whose essence existence would pertain can be excogitated by me besides God alone; then, because I cannot understand two or more Gods of this kind, and because — it having been posited that one God would already exist — I were to see plainly that it is necessary that he had also previously existed from eternity and that he were going to remain into eternity; and finally, because I were to perceive many other things in God, none of which can be taken away or changed by me.

[12.] But finally, whichever argument of proof I would use, truly the matter always goes back thereto that solely the things

& distincte percipio. Et quidem ex iis quae ita percipio, etsi nonnulla unicuique obvia sint, alia verò nonnisi ab iis qui propiùs inspiciunt & diligenter investigant deteguntur, postquam tamen detecta sunt, haec non minus certa quàm illa existimantur. Ut quamvis non tam facile appareat in triangulo rectan[69]gulo quadratum basis aequale esse quadratis laterum, quàm istam basim maximo ejus angulo subtendi, non tamen minùs creditur, postquam semel est perspectum. Quod autem ad Deum attinet, certe nisi praejudiciis obruerer, & rerum sensibilium imagines cogitationem meam omni ex parte obsiderent, nihil illo prius aut facilius agnoscerem; nam quid ex se est apertius, quàm summum ens esse, sive Deum, ad cujus solius essentiam existentia pertinet, existere?

Atque, quamvis mihi attentâ consideratione opus fuerit ad hoc ipsum percipiendum, nunc tamen non modo de eo aeque certus sum ac de omni alio quod certissimum videtur, sed praeterea etiam animadverto caeterarum rerum certitudinem ab hoc ipso ita pendere, ut absque eo nihil unquam perfecte sciri possit.

Etsi enim ejus sim naturae ut, quamdiu aliquid valde clare & distincte percipio, non possim non credere verum esse, quia tamen ejus etiam sum naturae ut non possim obtutum mentis in eandem rem semper defigere ad illam clare percipiendam, recurratque saepe memoria judicii ante facti, cùm non amplius attendo ad rationes propter quas tale quid judicavi, rationes aliae afferri possunt quae me, si Deum ignorarem, facile ab opinione dejicerent, atque ita de nullâ unquam re veram & certam scientiam, sed vagas tantùm & mutabiles opiniones, haberem. Sic, exempli causâ, cùm naturam trianguli considero, evidentissime quidem mihi, utpote Geometriae principiis imbuto, ap-

that I clearly and distinctly perceive might fully persuade me. And although some of the things that I thus perceive would be obvious to everyone, while others, however, are not detected at all except by those people who inspect things more closely and investigate things diligently, after they have been detected, these things are nevertheless thought to be not less certain than those things. So that although in the case of a right-angled triangle it would not so easily appear that the square of the base is equal to the squares of the sides as that this base is opposite to its maximum angle, it is still no less believed after it has once been made transparent. But as for what pertains to God, if I were not overwhelmed by prejudices, and if the images of sensible things did not beset my cogitation from every side, I would certainly recognize nothing prior to, or more easily than, him. For what is more overt from out of itself than that the highest being is, or that God—to whose essence alone existence pertains—exists?

[13.] And although an attentive consideration has been needed for me to perceive this itself, yet now not only am I equally as certain of it as of all else that seems most certain, but also I notice, in addition, that the certitude of the other things so depends on this itself that nothing could ever be known perfectly without it.

[14.] For even if I be of such a nature that so long as I very clearly and distinctly perceive something I could not not believe that it is true, because I am also of such a nature that I could not always fix the gaze of the mind on the same thing in order to perceive it clearly, and because the memory of a judgment previously made would often then recur when I am no longer paying attention to the reasons because of which I have judged such a thing, other reasons can still be offered which—if I were ignorant of God—would easily throw me off from the opinion, and thus would I never have true and certain knowledge of anything, but rather would I ever have only vague and changeable opinions on everything. Thus when I consider the nature of a triangle, for example, it surely then appears most evidently to me—as I am steeped in the principles of geometry—that

paret ejus tres angulos aequales esse duobus rectis, nec possum non credere id verum esse, quamdiu ad [70] ejus demonstrationem attendo; sed statim atque mentis aciem ab illâ deflexi, quantumvis adhuc recorder me illam clarissime perspexisse, facile tamen potest accidere ut dubitem an sit vera, si quidem Deum ignorem. Possum enim mihi persuadere me talem a naturâ factum esse, ut interdum in iis fallar quae me puto quàm evidentissime percipere, cùm praesertim meminerim me saepe multa pro veris & certis habuisse, quae postmodum, aliis rationibus adductus, falsa esse judicavi.

Postquam verò percepi Deum esse, quia simul etiam intellexi caetera omnia ab eo pendere, illumque non esse fallacem; atque inde collegi illa omnia, quae clare & distincte percipio, necessariò esse vera; etiamsi non attendam amplius ad rationes propter quas istud verum esse judicavi, modo tantùm recorder me clare & distincte perspexisse, nulla ratio contraria afferri potest, quae me ad dubitandum impellat, sed veram & certam de hoc habeo scientiam. Neque de hoc tantùm, sed & de reliquis omnibus quae memini me aliquando demonstrasse, ut de Geometricis & similibus. Quid enim nunc mihi opponetur? Mene talem factum esse ut saepe fallar? At jam scio me in iis, quae perspicue intelligo, falli non posse. Mene multa aliàs pro veris & certis habuisse, quae postea falsa esse deprehendi? Atqui nulla ex iis clare & distincte perceperam, sed hujus regulae veritatis ignarus ob alias causas forte credideram, quas postea minus firmas esse detexi. Quid ergo dicetur? Anne (ut nuper mihi objiciebam) me forte somniare, sive illa omnia, quae jam cogito, non magis vera esse quàm ea quae dormienti occurrunt?

its three angles are equal to two right ones, and I cannot not believe that this is true, so long as I pay attention to its demonstration. But as soon as I have turned the vision of the mind away from the demonstration, even though I might then still remember that I have seen through to it most clearly, it can nonetheless easily happen that I would doubt whether it would be true—if I would indeed be ignorant of God. For I can persuade myself that I have been made by nature such that I would from time to time be deceived in the things that I think that I perceive as evidently as possible, especially then when I were to remember that I have often held many things to be true and certain which—led to do so by other reasons—I have afterwards judged to be false.

[15.] But after I have perceived that there is a God, because I have simultaneously also understood that all the other things depend on him and that he is not a deceiver—and I have therefrom gathered that all those things which I clearly and distinctly perceive are necessarily true—, even if I were no longer to be paying attention to the reasons because of which I have judged that this is true, if only I would remember that I have clearly and distinctly perceived it, no contrary reason can be offered that might impel me to doubt it, but rather do I have true and certain knowledge of it. And this is true not only of this, but also of all the remaining things that I remember that I have at some time demonstrated, such as of geometrical and similar things. For what will now be objected to me? Have I been made such that I would often be deceived? But now I know that I cannot be deceived in the things that I perspicuously understand. Have I on other occasions held many things to be true and certain that I have afterwards found to be false? Yet I had clearly and distinctly perceived none of them, but rather had I— ignorant of this rule of truth—perhaps believed for other reasons which I later detected to be less firm. What will therefore be said? That (just as I recently objected to myself) I am perhaps dreaming, or that all those things which I now cogitate are no more true than are the ones that occur to someone who is sleep-

Imò etiam hoc nihil mutat; nam certe, [71] quamvis somniarem, si quid intellectui meo sit evidens, illud omnino est verum.

Atque ita plane video omnis scientiae certitudinem & veritatem ab unâ veri Dei cognitione pendere, adeo ut, priusquam illum nossem, nihil de ullâ aliâ re perfecte scire potuerim. Jam verò innumera, tum de ipso Deo aliisque rebus intellectualibus, tum etiam de omni illâ naturâ corporeâ, quae est purae Matheseos objectum, mihi plane nota & certa esse possunt.

ing? Yet even this changes nothing. For although I were dreaming, if something were evident to my intellect, then it is certainly completely true.

[16.] And thus do I plainly see that the certitude and truth of all knowledge depends on the one cognition of the true God — so much so that before I would know him I could have perfectly known nothing about any other thing. But now innumerable things — both of God himself and of other intellectual things, as well as, too, of all that corporeal nature which is the object of pure mathematics — can be fully known by, and certain to, me.

MEDITATIO VI.

De rerum materialium existentiâ,
& reali mentis a corpore distinctione.

Reliquum est ut examinem an res materiales existant. Et quidem jam ad minimum scio illas, quatenus sunt purae Matheseos objectum, posse existere, quandoquidem ipsas clare & distincte percipio. Non enim dubium est quin Deus sit capax ea omnia efficiendi quae ego sic percipiendi sum capax; nihilque unquam ab illo fieri non posse judicavi, nisi propter hoc quòd illud a me distincte percipi repugnaret. Praeterea ex imaginandi facultate, quâ me uti experior, dum circa res istas materiales versor, sequi videtur illas existere; nam attentius consideranti quidnam sit imaginatio, [72] nihil aliud esse apparet quàm quaedam applicatio facultatis cognoscitivae ad corpus ipsi intime praesens, ac proinde existens.

Quod ut planum fiat, primò examino differentiam quae est inter imaginationem & puram intellectionem. Nempe, exempli causâ, cùm triangulum imaginor, non tantùm intelligo illud esse figuram tribus lineis comprehensam, sed simul etiam istas tres lineas tanquam praesentes acie mentis intueor, atque hoc est quod imaginari appello. Si verò de chiliogono velim cogitare, equidem aeque bene intelligo illud esse figuram constantem mille lateribus, ac intelligo triangulum esse figuram constantem tribus; sed non eodem modo illa mille latera imaginor,

MEDITATION VI.

*Concerning the existence of material things,
and the real distinction of the mind from the body.*

[1.] It remains that I were to examine whether material things would exist. And I now know at a minimum that they can indeed exist, in so far as they are the object of pure mathematics, since I clearly and distinctly perceive them. For there is no doubt that God be capable of effecting all the things that *I* am capable of perceiving thus. And I have judged that there is nothing that cannot ever be made by God — except because of this: that it would contradict being perceived distinctly by me. Moreover, from the faculty of imagining, which I know by experience that I use while I am turned towards these material things, it seems to follow that they exist. For to one who is more attentively considering what it might be, imagination appears to be nothing other than a certain application of the cognitive faculty to a body intimately present to it — and therefore existing.

[2.] In order that this might become plain, I first examine the difference that there is between imagination and pure intellection. Namely, when I imagine a triangle, for example, not only do I then understand that it is a figure bounded by three lines, but also I simultaneously intuit these three lines with the vision of the mind as though they were present, and this is what I call "to imagine". But if I would want to cogitate about a chiliagon, I understand equally as well indeed that it is a figure consisting of a thousand sides as that I understand that a triangle is a figure consisting of three. Yet I do not imagine these thou-

185

sive tanquam praesentia intueor. Et quamvis tunc, propter consuetudinem aliquid semper imaginandi, quoties de re corporeâ
cogito, figuram forte aliquam confuse mihi repraesentem, patet
tamen illam non esse chiliogonum, quia nullâ in re est diversa
ab eâ quam mihi etiam repraesentarem, si de myriogono aliâve
quâvis figurâ plurimorum laterum cogitarem; nec quicquam
juvat ad eas proprietates, quibus chiliogonum ab aliis polygo-
nis differt, agnoscendas. Si verò de pentagono quaestio sit, possum quidem ejus figuram intelligere, sicut figuram chiliogoni,
absque ope imaginationis; sed possum etiam eandem imaginari,
applicando scilicet aciem mentis ad ejus quinque latera, simulque ad aream iis contentam; & manifeste hîc animadverto mihi
pecu[73]liari quâdam animi contentione opus esse ad imaginan-
dum, quâ non utor ad intelligendum: quae nova animi conten-
tio differentiam inter imaginationem & intellectionem puram
clare ostendit.

Ad haec considero istam vim imaginandi quae in me est, prout
differt a vi intelligendi, ad meî ipsius, hoc est ad mentis meae
essentiam non requiri; nam quamvis illa a me abesset, proculdubio manerem nihilominus ille idem qui nunc sum; unde sequi videtur illam ab aliquâ re a me diversâ pendere. Atque facilè
intelligo, si corpus aliquod existat cui mens sit ita conjuncta
ut ad illud veluti inspiciendum pro arbitrio se applicet, fieri posse
ut per hoc ipsum res corporeas imaginer; adeo ut hic modus
cogitandi in eo tantùm a purâ intellectione differat, quòd mens,
dum intelligit, se ad seipsam quodammodo convertat, respiciat-
que aliquam ex ideis quae illi ipsi insunt; dum autem imaginatur,
se convertat ad corpus, & aliquid in eo ideae vel a se intellec-

sand sides in the same manner, or intuit them as though they were present. And although — because of the custom always of imagining something whenever I cogitate about a corporeal thing — I might then perhaps confusedly represent to myself some figure, it is still obvious that this figure is not a chiliagon, because it is in nothing different from the figure that I would also represent to myself if I were to cogitate about a myriagon, or about any other figure that you will of many sides. Nor does it help anything at all towards recognizing the properties by which a chiliagon differs from other polygons. But if the question were about a pentagon, I can surely understand its figure, just as I can understand the figure of a chiliagon, without the help of the imagination. Yet I can also imagine the same figure, scil., by applying the vision of the mind to its five sides and simultaneously to the area contained by them. And here I manifestly notice that for imagining a certain peculiar effort of the mind is needed by me which I do not use for understanding: which new effort of the mind clearly shows the difference between imagination and pure intellection.

[3.] In addition to these things, I consider that this power of imagining which is in me, in so far as it differs from the power of understanding, is not required for the essence of me myself, that is, for the essence of my mind. For although the power of imagining were absent from me, I would without doubt remain nonetheless that same one who I am now: from whence it seems to follow that this power depends on something different from me. And I easily understand that if there were to exist some body to which the mind would so be joined that it might at will apply itself — as it were — to inspect it, it can happen that I would imagine corporeal things through this itself — so much so that this mode of cogitating would differ from pure intellection only therein that the mind, when it understands, would then in some manner turn itself to itself and would regard one of the ideas that are in it itself, but when it imagines, it would then turn itself to the body and would intuit something in it conforming to an idea understood by itself or perceived by the senses. Eas-

tae vel sensu perceptae conforme intueatur. Facilè, inquam, intelligo imaginationem ita perfici posse, siquidem corpus existat; & quia nullus alius modus aeque conveniens occurrit ad illam explicandam, probabiliter inde conjicio corpus existere; sed probabiliter tantùm, & quamvis accurate omnia investigem, nondum tamen video ex eâ naturae corporeae ideâ distinctâ, quam in imaginatione meâ invenio, ullum sumi posse argumentum, quod necessariò concludat aliquod corpus existere. [74]

Soleo verò alia multa imaginari, praeter illam naturam corpoream, quae est purae Matheseos objectum, ut colores, sonos, sapores, dolorem, & similia, sed nulla tam distincte; & quia haec percipio meliùs sensu, a quo videntur ope memoriae ad imaginationem pervenisse, ut commodiùs de ipsis agam, eâdem operâ etiam de sensu est agendum, videndumque an ex iis quae isto cogitandi modo, quem sensum appello, percipiuntur, certum aliquod argumentum pro rerum corporearum existentiâ habere possim.

Et primo quidem apud me hîc repetam quaenam illa sint quae antehac, ut sensu percepta, vera esse putavi, & quas ob causas id putavi; deinde etiam causas expendam propter quas eadem postea in dubium revocavi; ac denique considerabo quid mihi nunc de iisdem sit credendum.

Primo itaque sensi me habere caput, manus, pedes, & membra caetera ex quibus constat illud corpus, quod tanquam meî partem, vel forte etiam tanquam me totum spectabam; sensique hoc corpus inter alia multa corpora versari, a quibus variis commodis vel incommodis affici potest, & commoda ista sensu quodam voluptatis, & incommoda sensu doloris metiebar. Atque,

ily, I say, do I understand that imagination can thus come about, if the body were indeed to exist. And because there occurs to me no other way equally as convenient for explicating imagination, I therefrom conjecture probably that the body exists. But I conjecture this only probably, and although I would accurately investigate all things, I still do not yet see that from the distinct idea of corporeal nature that I find in my imagination any argument can be drawn that would necessarily conclude with the proposition that some body exists.

[4.] Yet besides that corporeal nature which is the object of pure mathematics I am accustomed to imagine many other things — such as colors, sounds, tastes, pain and similar things — , but none so distinctly. And because I perceive these things better by means of the senses — from which they seem to have come through to the imagination with the help of the memory — , in order that I might treat of them more appropriately, with the same effort is also to be dealt with the senses, and it is to be seen whether from the things that are perceived by that mode of cogitating which I call "sensation" I could have a certain argument for the existence of corporeal things.

[5.] And here I shall surely first repeat to myself what those things were which I have previously thought to be true just as they were perceived by the senses, and for what reasons I have thought this; then, I shall also set out the reasons for which I have afterwards called the same things into doubt; and finally, I shall consider what things were now to be believed by me about the same things.

[6.] First then, I have sensed that I have a head, hands, feet and other members of which consists this body that I regarded as a part of me, or even perhaps as me as a whole. And I have sensed that this body is situated among many other bodies, by which various accommodating ones, or incommodious ones, it can be affected; and those accommodating ones I measured by a certain sense of pleasure, and these incommodious ones I measured by a certain sense of pain. And besides pain

praeter dolorem & voluptatem, sentiebam etiam in me famem, sitim, aliosque ejusmodi appetitus; itemque corporeas quasdam propensiones ad hilaritatem, ad tristitiam, ad iram, similesque alios affectus; foris verò, praeter corporum extensionem, & figuras, & [75] motus, sentiebam etiam in illis duritiem, & calorem, aliasque tactiles qualitates; ac praeterea lumen, & colores, & odores, & sapores, & sonos, ex quorum varietate caelum, terram, maria, & reliqua corpora ab invicem distinguebam. Nec sane absque ratione, ob ideas istarum omnium qualitatum quae cogitationi meae se offerebant, & quas solas proprie & immediate sentiebam, putabam me sentire res quasdam a meâ cogitatione plane diversas, nempe corpora a quibus ideae istae procederent; experiebar enim illas absque ullo meo consensu mihi advenire, adeo ut neque possem objectum ullum sentire, quamvis vellem, nisi illud sensûs organo esset praesens, nec possem non sentire cùm erat praesens. Cùmque ideae sensu perceptae essent multo magis vividae & expressae, & suo etiam modo magis distinctae, quàm ullae ex iis quas ipse prudens & sciens meditando effingebam, vel memoriae meae impressas advertebam, fieri non posse videbatur ut a meipso procederent; ideoque supererat ut ab aliis quibusdam rebus advenirent. Quarum rerum cùm nullam aliunde notitiam haberem quàm ex istis ipsis ideis, non poterat aliud mihi venire in mentem quàm illas iis similes esse. Atque etiam quia recordabar me prius usum fuisse sensibus quàm ratione, videbamque ideas quas ipse effingebam non tam expressas esse, quàm illae erant quas sensu percipiebam, & plerumque ex earum partibus componi, facile mihi persuadebam nullam plane me habere in intellectu, quam non prius habuissem in sensu. Non etiam sine ratione corpus illud, quod speciali quodam jure meum ap[76]pellabam, magis ad me pertinere quàm alia ulla arbitrabar: neque enim ab illo poteram unquam sejungi, ut a reliquis;

and pleasure I also sensed hunger, thirst and other appetites of this kind in me. And I also sensed certain corporeal propensities to cheerfulness, to sadness, to anger, and other similar emotions. But from outside I sensed, besides the extension and figures and movements of bodies, hardness and heat and other tactile qualities in these bodies as well. And in addition, I sensed light and colors and odors and tastes and sounds, from whose variety I distinguished the heavens, the earth, the seas and the other bodies, the one from the other. Because of the ideas of all these qualities, which ideas offered themselves to my cogitation and which alone I properly and immediately sensed, I thought surely not without reason that I sensed certain things plainly different from my cogitation, namely, bodies from which these ideas would proceed. For I knew by experience that these ideas come to me without any consent of mine—so much so that I could not sense any object, although I would want to, unless it were present to the organ of sense, nor could I not then sense it when it was present. And since the ideas perceived by the senses were much more vivid and express—and in their own mode even more distinct—than any of those ideas which I myself—prudent and knowing—feigned by meditating or which I noticed as impressed on my memory, it seemed that it cannot happen that they would proceed from me myself. And therefore it remained that these ideas would come to me from some other things. Since I would have no knowledge of these things from elsewhere than from those ideas themselves, nothing else could come to mind for me than that those things are similar to these ideas. And because I remembered that I have been one who has used the senses earlier than reason, and I saw that the ideas that I myself feigned are not as express as were those which I perceived with the senses—and that most of the former are composed of parts of the latter—, I also easily persuaded myself that I have no idea at all in the intellect which I had not previously had in the senses. Also not without reason did I think that this body, which by some special right I called "mine", pertains to me more than any other bodies do: for I could not ever be separated from it, as I could be from the others; I sensed

omnes appetitus & affectus in illo & pro illo sentiebam; ac denique dolorem & titillationem voluptatis in ejus partibus, non autem in aliis extra illud positis, advertebam. Cur verò ex isto nescio quo doloris sensu quaedam animi tristitia, & ex sensu titillationis laetitia quaedam consequatur, curve illa nescio quae vellicatio ventriculi, quam famem voco, me de cibo sumendo admoneat, gutturis verò ariditas de potu, & ita de caeteris, non aliam sane habebam rationem, nisi quia ita doctus sum a naturâ; neque enim ulla plane est affinitas (saltem quam ego intelligam) inter istam vellicationem & cibi sumendi voluntatem, sive inter sensum rei dolorem inferentis, & cogitationem tristitiae ab isto sensu exortae. Sed & reliqua omnia, quae de sensuum objectis judicabam, videbar a naturâ didicisse: priùs enim illa ita se habere mihi persuaseram, quàm rationes ullas quibus hoc ipsum probaretur expendissem.

Postea verò multa paulatim experimenta fidem omnem quam sensibus habueram labefactarunt; nam & interdum turres, quae rotundae visae fuerant è longinquo, quadratae apparebant è propinquo, & statuae permagnae, in eorum fastigiis stantes, non magnae è terrâ spectanti videbantur; & talibus aliis innumeris in rebus sensuum externorum judicia falli deprehendebam. Nec externorum duntaxat, sed etiam interno[77]rum; nam quid dolore intimius esse potest? Atqui audiveram aliquando ab iis, quibus crus aut brachium fuerat abscissum, se sibi videri adhuc interdum dolorem sentire in eâ parte corporis quâ carebant; ideoque etiam in me non plane certum esse videbatur membrum aliquod mihi dolere, quamvis sentirem in eo dolorem. Quibus etiam duas maxime generales dubitandi causas nuper adjeci: prima erat, quòd nulla unquam, dum vigilo, me sentire crediderim, quae non etiam inter dormiendum possim aliquando

all appetites and emotions in it and for it; and finally, I noticed pain and the excitement of pleasure in its parts, but not in the other bodies posited outside it. But why from that — I know not what — sensation of pain a certain sadness of the mind would follow, and why from the sensation of excitement a certain joy would follow, or why that — I know not what — pulling of the stomach which I call "hunger" would warn me about taking in food, but the dryness of the throat would warn me about taking in drink, and thus of the others, I surely had no other reason except: because I have been thus taught by nature. For there is not any affinity at all (at least that *I* would understand) between that pulling and the volition of taking in food, or between the sensation of a thing bringing in pain and the cogitation of sadness arising from that sensation. But I also seemed to have been taught by nature all the other things that I judged about the objects of the senses. For I had persuaded myself that these things are thus before I had weighed out any arguments with which this itself might be proved.

[7.] But afterwards many experiences have little by little weakened all the faith that I had had in the senses. For sometimes both towers that had seemed round from far away appeared square from close up, and very large statues standing on their pinnacles did not seem large to one observing them from the ground. And in innumerable other such things I found that the judgments of the external senses are deceived. And deceived are not only the judgments of the external senses, but also the judgments of the internal senses. For what can be more intimate than pain? And yet I had once heard from those people from whom a leg or an arm had been cut off that it seems to them that they sometimes still sense pain in the part of the body that they lacked. Therefore even in the case of myself it did not seem to be fully certain that some member hurts me, although I would sense pain in it. To which experiences I have also recently added two maximally general reasons for doubting: The first reason was that I had believed that I never sense anything while I am awake that I could not also sometimes think

putare me sentire; cùmque illa, quae sentire mihi videor in somnis, non credam a rebus extra me positis mihi advenire, non
advertebam quare id potius crederem de iis quae sentire mihi
videor vigilando. Altera erat, quòd cùm authorem meae originis adhuc ignorarem, vel saltem ignorare me fingerem, nihil vide-
bam obstare quominus essem naturâ ita constitutus ut fallerer,
etiam in iis quae mihi verissima apparebant. Et quantum ad
rationes quibus antea rerum sensibilium veritatem mihi persuaseram, non difficulter ad illas respondebam. Cùm enim
viderer ad multa impelli a naturâ, quae ratio dissuadebat, non
multùm fidendum esse putabam iis quae a naturâ docentur. Et
quamvis sensuum perceptiones a voluntate meâ non penderent,
non ideo concludendum esse putabam illas a rebus a me diversis procedere, quia forte aliqua esse potest in meipso facultas,
etsi mihi nondum cognita, illarum effectrix.

Nunc autem, postquam incipio meipsum meaeque authorem
originis melius nosse, non quidem omnia, quae habere videor
a sensibus, puto esse temere admit[78]tenda; sed neque etiam
omnia in dubium revocanda.

Et primò, quoniam scio omnia quae clare & distincte intelligo, talia a Deo fieri posse qualia illa intelligo, satis est quòd
possim unam rem absque alterâ clare & distincte intelligere,
ut certus sim unam ab alterâ esse diversam, quia potest saltem
a Deo seorsim poni; & non refert a quâ potentiâ id fiat, ut diversa existimetur; ac proinde, ex hoc ipso quòd sciam me existere,
quòdque interim nihil plane aliud ad naturam sive essentiam
meam pertinere animadvertam, praeter hoc solum quòd sim
res cogitans, recte concludo meam essentiam in hoc uno con-

that I sense while I am sleeping. And since I would not believe that those things which I seem to me to sense in dreams come to me from things posited outside me, I did not notice why I would rather believe this about the things that I seem to me to sense while being awake. The other reason was that since I would still be ignorant of the author of my origin — or at least I were to feign that I am ignorant thereof — , I saw that nothing stands in the way thereof that I had been constituted so by nature that I would be deceived even in the things that appeared to me as most true. And as far as the reasons by which I had before persuaded myself of the truth of sensible things are concerned, I easily responded to them. For since I would seem to be impelled by nature to many things from which reason dissuaded me, I thought that the things that are taught by nature are not much to be trusted. And although the perceptions of the senses might not depend on my will, I did not therefore think that it is to be concluded that they proceed from things different from me, because there can perhaps be some faculty in me myself which is the effecter of them, even if it is not yet known to me.

[8.] But after I am now beginning to know better both me myself and the author of my origin, I think that surely not all the things that I seem to have from the senses are rashly to be admitted. Yet I also think that not all such things are to be called into doubt.

[9.] And first, because I know that all the things that I clearly and distinctly understand can be made by God just as such as I understand them, it is enough that I could clearly and distinctly understand one thing without another thing in order that I might be certain that the one is different from the other: because it can — at least by God — be posited separately. And it does not matter by which power it would happen that the things be thought as being different. And thus from thence itself that I were to know that I exist, and that meanwhile I were to notice that nothing else at all pertains to my nature or essence except this alone — that I were a cogitating thing — , I correctly con-

sistere, quòd sim res cogitans. Et quamvis fortasse (vel potiùs, ut postmodum dicam, pro certo) habeam corpus, quod mihi valde arcte conjunctum est, quia tamen ex unâ parte claram & distinctam habeo ideam meî ipsius, quatenus sum tantùm res cogitans, non extensa, & ex aliâ parte distinctam ideam corporis, quatenus est tantùm res extensa, non cogitans, certum est me a corpore meo revera esse distinctum, & absque illo posse existere.

Praeterea invenio in me facultates specialibus quibusdam modis cogitandi, puta facultates imaginandi & sentiendi, sine quibus totum me possum clare & distincte intelligere, sed non vice versâ illas sine me, hoc est sine substantiâ intelligente cui insint: intellectionem enim nonnullam in suo formali conceptu includunt, unde percipio illas a me, ut modos a re, distingui. Agnosco etiam quasdam alias facultates, ut locum mutandi, varias figuras induendi, & similes, quae quidem non magis quàm praecedentes, absque [79] aliquâ substantiâ cui insint, possunt intelligi, nec proinde etiam absque illâ existere: sed manifestum est has, siquidem existant, inesse debere substantiae corporeae sive extensae, non autem intelligenti, quia nempe aliqua extensio, non autem ulla plane intellectio, in earum claro & distincto conceptu continetur. Jam verò est quidem in me passiva quaedam facultas sentiendi, sive ideas rerum sensibilium recipiendi & cognoscendi, sed ejus nullum usum habere possem, nisi quaedam activa etiam existeret, sive in me, sive in alio, facultas istas ideas producendi vel efficiendi. Atque haec sane in me ipso esse non potest, quia nullam plane intellectionem praesupponit, & me non cooperante, sed saepe etiam invito, ideae istae producuntur: ergo superest ut sit in aliquâ substantiâ a me diversâ, in quâ quoniam omnis realitas vel formaliter

clude that my essence consists in this one thing: that I be a cogitating thing. And although I might perhaps (or rather, as I shall soon afterwards say, for certain) have a body which is very closely joined to me, because I have — on the one hand — a clear and distinct idea of me myself, in so far as I am only a cogitating thing and not an extended one, and because I have — on the other hand — a distinct idea of body, in so far as it is only an extended thing and not a cogitating one, it is still certain that I am really and truly distinct from my body, and that I can exist without it.

[10.] Moreover, I find in me faculties with certain special modes of cogitating — think of the faculties of imagining and sensing — , without which faculties I can clearly and distinctly understand me as a whole, but I cannot — vice versa — understand them without me, that is, without the understanding substance in which they were. For in their formal concept these faculties include some intellection, from whence I perceive that they are distinguished from me just as modes are distinguished from a thing. I also recognize certain other faculties, such as the faculty of changing places, of taking on various figures, and similar ones, which other faculties surely can no more be understood without some substance in which they were than the preceding ones can be, and hence they too cannot exist without it. But it is manifest that these other faculties, if they did indeed exist, must be in a corporeal or extended substance — yet not in an understanding one — , namely, because some extension — yet plainly not any intellection — is contained in the clear and distinct concept of them. But now surely there is in me a certain passive faculty of sensing, or of receiving and cognizing the ideas of sensible things. Yet I would have no use for it unless there did also exist, either in me or in something else, a certain active faculty of producing or effecting these ideas. And surely this active faculty cannot be in me myself, because it plainly presupposes no intellection, and these ideas are then produced when I am not cooperating, but rather often even involuntarily. Therefore it remains that this faculty be in some substance different from me. And because all the reality that

vel eminenter inesse debet, quae est objective in ideis ab istâ facultate productis (ut jam supra animadverti), vel haec substantia est corpus, sive natura corporea, in quâ nempe omnia formaliter continentur quae in ideis objective; vel certe Deus est, vel aliqua creatura corpore nobilior, in quâ continentur eminenter. Atqui, cùm Deus non sit fallax, omnino manifestum est illum nec per se immediate istas ideas mihi immittere, nec etiam mediante aliquâ creaturâ, in quâ earum realitas objectiva, non formaliter, sed eminenter tantùm contineatur. Cùm enim nullam plane facultatem mihi dederit ad hoc agnoscendum, sed contrà magnam [80] propensionem ad credendum illas a rebus corporeis emitti, non video quâ ratione posset intelligi ipsum non esse fallacem, si aliunde quàm a rebus corporeis emitterentur. Ac proinde res corporeae existunt. Non tamen forte omnes tales omnino existunt, quales illas sensu comprehendo, quoniam ista sensuum comprehensio in multis valde obscura est & confusa; sed saltem illa omnia in iis sunt, quae clare & distincte intelligo, id est omnia, generaliter spectata, quae in purae Matheseos objecto comprehenduntur.

Quantum autem attinet ad reliqua quae vel tantùm particularia sunt, ut quòd sol sit talis magnitudinis aut figurae &c., vel minus clare intellecta, ut lumen, sonus, dolor, & similia, quamvis valde dubia & incerta sint, hoc tamen ipsum, quòd Deus non sit fallax, quòdque idcirco fieri non possit ut ulla falsitas in meis opinionibus reperiatur, nisi aliqua etiam sit in me facultas a Deo tributa ad illam emendandam, certam mihi spem ostendit veritatis etiam in iis assequendae. Et sane non dubium est quin ea omnia quae doceor a naturâ aliquid habeant veritatis: per naturam enim, generaliter spectatam, nihil nunc aliud quàm vel Deum, ipsum, vel rerum creatarum coordinationem a Deo

is objectively in the ideas produced by this faculty must be formally or eminently in that substance different from me (just as I have already noticed above): either this substance is a body or a corporeal nature, in which, namely, all the things that are contained objectively in the ideas are contained formally; or certainly this substance is God or some creature more noble than a body, in which, namely, all the things that are contained objectively in the ideas are contained eminently. But since God not be a deceiver, it is completely manifest that he immits these ideas into me neither immediately through himself nor even by means of some mediating creature in which their objective reality might be contained not formally, but rather only eminently. For since he has plainly given to me no faculty with which to recognize this, but rather — on the contrary — a great propensity to believe that these ideas are emitted by corporeal things, I do not see how it could be understood that God is not a deceiver if these ideas would be emitted from elsewhere than from corporeal things. And thus corporeal things do exist. Yet perhaps not all corporeal things exist completely just as such as I comprehend them by means of sensation, because this comprehension of the senses is in many respects very obscure and confused. But at least all those things which I clearly and distinctly understand, that is, all the things — generally regarded — that are encompassed in the object of pure mathematics, are in corporeal things.

[11.] But as for what pertains to the other things, which are only particulars — such as that the sun be of such and such a magnitude or figure, etc. —, or which are less clearly understood — such as light, sound, pain and similar things —, although they might be very dubious and uncertain, this itself — that God not be a deceiver —, and therefore that it could not happen that any falsity would be found in my opinions unless there would also be in me some faculty given by God to emend it, still shows me the certain hope of reaching the truth even in them. And there is surely no doubt that all the things that I am taught by nature would have some truth in them. For by "nature regarded generally" I now understand nothing other than God

institutam intelligo; nec aliud per naturam meam in particulari, quàm complexionem eorum omnium quae mihi a Deo sunt tributa.

Nihil autem est quod me ista natura magis expresse doceat, quàm quòd habeam corpus, cui male est cùm dolorem sentio, quod cibo vel potu indiget, cùm famem aut sitim patior, & similia; nec proinde dubitare debeo, quin aliquid in eo sit veritatis. [81]

Docet etiam natura, per istos sensus doloris, famis, sitis &c., me non tantùm adesse meo corpori ut nauta adest navigio, sed illi arctissime esse conjunctum & quasi permixtum, adeo ut unum quid cum illo componam. Alioqui enim, cùm corpus laeditur, ego, qui nihil aliud sum quàm res cogitans, non sentirem idcirco dolorem, sed puro intellectu laesionem istam perciperem, ut nauta visu percipit si quid in nave frangatur; & cùm corpus cibo vel potu indiget, hoc ipsum expresse intelligerem, non confusos famis & sitis sensus haberem. Nam certe isti sensus sitis, famis, doloris &c., nihil aliud sunt quàm confusi quidam cogitandi modi ab unione & quasi permixtione mentis cum corpore exorti.

Praeterea etiam doceor a naturâ varia circa meum corpus alia corpora existere, ex quibus nonnulla mihi prosequenda sunt, alia fugienda. Et certe, ex eo quòd valde diversos sentiam colores, sonos, odores, sapores, calorem, duritiem, & similia, recte concludo, aliquas esse in corporibus, a quibus variae istae sensuum perceptiones adveniunt, varietates iis respondentes, etiamsi forte iis non similes; atque ex eo quòd quaedam ex illis perceptionibus mihi gratae sint, aliae ingratae, plane certum est meum corpus, sive potius me totum, quatenus ex corpore & mente sum compositus, variis commodis & incommodis a circumjacentibus corporibus affici posse. [82]

himself—or the coordination of created things established by God—, and by "my nature in particular" I understand nothing other than the complex of all the things that have been given to me by God.

[12.] But there is nothing that this nature would teach me more expressly than that I have a body that is then ill when I sense pain, and that then needs food or drink when I suffer hunger or thirst, and similar things. And therefore I should not doubt that there be some truth in this.

[13.] By means of these sensations of pain, hunger, thirst, etc., nature also teaches me that I am not merely present to my body just as a sailor is present in a ship, but rather that I am very closely joined to, and—as it were—thoroughly mixed with, it—so much so that I were to compose one thing with it. For otherwise, when the body is hurt *I*—who am nothing other than a cogitating thing—would then therefore not sense pain, but rather would *I* perceive this damage with the pure intellect, just as a sailor perceives it by sight if something in the ship would be broken. And when the body needs food or drink I would then expressly understand this itself, not have confused sensations of hunger and thirst. For these sensations of thirst, hunger, pain, etc., are certainly nothing other than certain confused modes of cogitating which have arisen from the union and—as it were—thorough mixture of the mind with the body.

[14.] Moreover, I am also taught by nature that various other bodies exist around my body, some of which bodies are to be pursued, and others of which are to be avoided, by me. And from thence that I were to sense very different colors, sounds, odors, tastes, heat, hardness and similar things, I certainly conclude correctly that there are some variations in the bodies from which these various perceptions of the senses come: variations corresponding to—even if perhaps not similar to—the perceptions. And from thence that certain ones of these perceptions be agreeable to me, and others be disagreeable, it is completely certain that my body—or rather I as a whole, in so far as I am a composite of body and mind—can be affected by various things, accommodating and incommodious, from the surrounding bodies.

Multa verò alia sunt quae, etsi videar a naturâ doctus esse, non tamen revera ab ipsâ, sed a consuetudine quâdam inconsiderate judicandi accepi, atque ideo falsa esse facile contingit: ut quòd omne spatium, in quo nihil plane occurrit quod meos sensus moveat, sit vacuum; quòd in corpore, exempli gratiâ, calido aliquid sit plane simile ideae caloris quae in me est, in albo aut viridi sit eadem albedo aut viriditas quam sentio, in amaro aut dulci idem sapor, & sic de caeteris; quòd & astra & turres, & quaevis alia remota corpora ejus sint tantùm magnitudinis & figurae, quam sensibus meis exhibent, & alia ejusmodi. Sed ne quid in hac re non satis distincte percipiam, accuratiùs debeo definire quid proprie intelligam, cùm dico me aliquid doceri a naturâ. Nempe hîc naturam strictiùs sumo, quàm pro complexione eorum omnium quae mihi a Deo tributa sunt; in hac enim complexione multa continentur quae ad mentem solam pertinent, ut quòd percipiam id quod factum est infectum esse non posse, & reliqua omnia quae lumine naturali sunt nota, de quibus hîc non est sermo; multa etiam quae ad solum corpus spectant, ut quòd deorsum tendat, & similia, de quibus etiam non ago, sed de iis tantùm quae mihi, ut composito ex mente & corpore, a Deo tributa sunt. Ideoque haec natura docet quidem ea refugere quae sensum doloris inferunt, & ea prosequi quae sensum voluptatis, & talia; sed non apparet illam praeterea nos docere ut quicquam ex istis sensuum perceptionibus sine praevio intellectûs examine de rebus extra nos positis concludamus, quia de iis verum scire [83] ad mentem solam, non autem ad compositum, videtur pertinere. Ita quamvis stella non magis oculum meum quàm ignis

[15.] But there are many other things that, even if I would seem to have been taught them by nature, I still have really and truly accepted not from it, but rather from a certain custom of judging inconsiderately, and therefore it happens that they are easily false: such as that all space in which there occurs nothing at all that were to move my senses would be empty; for example, that in a hot body there would be something completely similar to the idea of heat that is in me, that in a white or green body there would be the same whiteness or greenness that I sense, that in a bitter or sweet body there would be the same taste, and thus of the other things; also, that the stars and towers, and whatever other remote bodies that you will, would be only of the magnitude and figure that they exhibit to my senses, and other things of this sort. But in order that I might not perceive something in this matter not distinctly enough, I should define more accurately what I would then properly understand when I say that "I am taught something by nature". Here, namely, I take "nature" more strictly than just as the complex of all the things that have been given to me by God. For there are many things contained in this complex that pertain to the mind alone, such as that I were to perceive that that which has been done cannot be made undone, and all the other things that are known by the natural light, concerning which there is no talk here. There are also many things contained in this complex that pertain to the body alone, such as that it were to tend downwards, and similar things, with which I am also not dealing. Rather am I dealing only with the things that have been given by God to me just as a composite of mind and body. This nature, then, teaches me indeed to flee the things that induce a sensation of pain, and to pursue the things that induce a sensation of pleasure, and such things. But it does not appear that this nature teaches us, in addition, that from these perceptions of the senses we should conclude anything about the things posited outside us without the previous examination of the intellect, because to know the true about these things seems to pertain to the mind alone, but not to the composite. Thus although a star would affect my eye no more than the fire of a small torch

exiguae facis afficiat, nulla tamen in eo realis sive positiva propensio est ad credendum illam non esse majorem, sed hoc sine ratione ab ineunte aetate judicavi; & quamvis ad ignem accedens sentio calorem, ut etiam ad eundem nimis prope accedens sentio dolorem, nulla profecto ratio est quae suadeat in igne aliquid esse simile isti calori, ut neque etiam isti dolori, sed tantummodo in eo aliquid esse, quodcunque demum sit, quod istos in nobis sensus caloris vel doloris efficiat; & quamvis etiam in aliquo spatio nihil sit quod moveat sensum, non ideo sequitur in eo nullum esse corpus: sed video me in his aliisque permultis ordinem naturae pervertere esse assuetum, quia nempe sensuum perceptionibus, quae proprie tantùm a naturâ datae sunt ad menti significandum quaenam composito, cujus pars est, commoda sint vel incommoda, & eatenus sunt satis clarae & distinctae, utor tanquam regulis certis ad immediate dignoscendum quaenam sit corporum extra nos positorum essentia, de quâ tamen nihil nisi valde obscure & confuse significant.

Atqui jam ante satis perspexi quâ ratione, non obstante Dei bonitate, judicia mea falsa esse contingat. Sed nova hîc occurrit difficultas circa illa ipsa quae tanquam persequenda vel fugienda mihi a naturâ exhibentur, atque etiam circa internos sensus in quibus errores videor deprehendisse: ut cùm quis, grato cibi alicujus sapore delusus, venenum intus latens assumit. [84] Sed nempe tunc tantùm a naturâ impellitur ad illud appetendum in quo gratus sapor consistit, non autem ad venenum, quod plane ignorat; nihilque hinc aliud concludi potest, quàm naturam istam non esse omnisciam: quod non mirum, quia, cùm homo sit res limitata, non alia illi competit quàm limitatae perfectionis.

would, there is still no real or positive propensity in me to believe that the former is no bigger than the latter, but rather have
I from my youth onwards judged this without reason. And
although I, going to the fire, sense heat, just as I, going too close
to it, also sense pain, there is in fact no reason that would persuade me that there is something in the fire similar to that heat,
just as there is in fact also no reason that would persuade me
that there is something in the fire similar to that pain. Rather
is there only reason for being persuaded that there is something
in the fire — whatever it would finally be — that would effect these
sensations of heat or pain in us. And although there were also
nothing in some space that would move the senses, it does not
follow that therefore there is no body in it. Rather do I see that
in these and in very many other things I have been accustomed
to pervert the order of nature, namely, because I use the perceptions of the senses, which perceptions have — properly
speaking — been given to me by nature only to signify to the mind
which things would be accommodating or incommodious to
the composite of which it is a part, and which perceptions are
to this extent clear and distinct enough, as certain rules for dis-
cerning immediately what the essence of the bodies posited outside us might be — concerning which essence, however, these
perceptions signify only very obscurely and confusedly.

[16.] But now I have already satisfactorily seen through to
how — notwithstanding the goodness of God — it would happen that my judgments are false. Yet here there occurs to me
a new difficulty, a difficulty concerning those things themselves
which are exhibited to me by nature as things to be pursued
or as things to be avoided, and also concerning the internal
senses, in which I seem to have found errors: such as when
someone — deluded by the pleasant taste of some food — then
takes in the poison hidden therein. But then he is indeed impelled by nature only to desire that thing in which there is the
pleasant taste, yet not to desire the poison, of which he is plainly
ignorant. And nothing can therefrom be concluded other than
that this nature is not omniscient: which is not surprising, because since the human being be a limited thing, no nature would
be fitting to that being other than one of limited perfection.

At verò non raro etiam in iis erramus ad quae a naturâ impellimur: ut cùm ii qui aegrotant, potum vel cibum appetunt sibi paulo post nociturum. Dici forsan hîc poterit, illos ob id errare, quòd natura eorum sit corrupta; sed hoc difficultatem non tollit, quia non minus vere homo aegrotus creatura Dei est quàm sanus; nec proinde minus videtur repugnare illum a Deo fallacem naturam habere. Atque ut horologium ex rotis & ponderibus confectum non minus accurate leges omnes naturae observat, cùm male fabricatum est & horas non recte indicat, quàm cùm omni ex parte artificis voto satisfacit: ita, si considerem hominis corpus, quatenus machinamentum quoddam est ex ossibus, nervis, musculis, venis, sanguine & pellibus ita aptum & compositum, ut, etiamsi nulla in eo mens existeret, eosdem tamen haberet omnes motus qui nunc in eo non ab imperio voluntatis nec proinde a mente procedunt, facile agnosco illi aeque naturale fore, si, exempli causâ, hydrope laboret, eam faucium ariditatem pati, quae sitis sensum menti inferre solet, atque etiam ab illâ ejus nervos & reliquas partes ita disponi ut potum sumat ex quo morbus augeatur, quàm, cùm nullum tale in eo vitium est, a simili [85] faucium siccitate moveri ad potum sibi utile assumendum. Et quamvis, respiciens ad praeconceptum horologii usum, dicere possim illud, cùm horas non recte indicat, a naturâ suâ deflectere; atque eodem modo, considerans machinamentum humani corporis tanquam comparatum ad motus qui in eo fieri solent, putem illud etiam a naturâ suâ aberrare, si ejus fauces sint aridae, cùm potus ad ipsius conservationem non prodest; satis tamen animadverto hanc ultimam naturae acceptionem ab alterâ multùm differre: haec enim nihil aliud est quàm denominatio a cogitatione meâ, hominem aegrotum & horologium male fabricatum cum ideâ

[17.] But truly do we not rarely err even in the things to which we are impelled by nature: such as when those people who are sick then desire drink or food that shortly afterwards is going to harm them. Here it will perhaps be able to be said that these people err due thereto that their nature would be corrupt. But this does not remove the difficulty, because a sick human being is no less truly a creature of God than a healthy one is, and therefore it seems to be no less contradictory to suppose that he has a deceptive nature from God. And just as a clock made up of wheels and weights observes all the laws of nature no less accurately then when it has been fabricated badly and does not correctly indicate the hours than then when it satisfies the wish of the artificer in every respect: so too, if I were to consider the body of a human being—in so far as it is a kind of machine so fitted out with and composed of bones, nerves, muscles, veins, blood and skin that, even if no mind would exist in it, it would still have all the same movements which in it now proceed not from the command of the will, and thus not from the mind—, I easily recognize that it will be equally as natural for this body that, if it would suffer from dropsy, for example, it suffers a dryness of the throat which usually brings the sensation of thirst to the mind—and also that its nerves and other parts are so disposed by it that it would take in drink, as a result of which the sickness would become greater—, as that, when there is no such mistake in it, it is then moved by a similar dryness of the throat to take in drink useful to it. And although—regarding the preconceived use of the clock—I could say that when it does not correctly indicate the hours it then turns away from its nature, and in the same mode—considering the machine of the human body as prepared for the movements that usually happen in it—I would think that it too errs off from its nature if its throat would then be dry when drinking is not beneficial to its preservation, still I notice well enough that this last meaning of the expression "nature" differs a lot from the other meaning of the expression: for this last meaning of the expression "nature" is nothing other than a denomination depending on my cogitation—my cogitation comparing a sick human being

hominis sani & horologii recte facti comparante, dependens, rebusque de quibus dicitur extrinseca; per illam verò aliquid intelligo quod revera in rebus reperitur, ac proinde nonnihil habet veritatis.

Ac certe, etiamsi respiciendo ad corpus hydrope laborans, sit tantùm denominatio extrinseca, cùm dicitur ejus natura esse corrupta, ex eo quòd aridas habeat fauces, nec tamen egeat potu; respiciendo tamen ad compositum, sive ad mentem tali corpori unitam, non est pura denominatio, sed verus error naturae, quòd sitiat cùm potus est ipsi nociturus; ideoque hîc remanet inquirendum, quo pacto bonitas Dei non impediat quominus natura sic sumpta sit fallax.

Nempe imprimis hîc adverto magnam esse differentiam inter mentem & corpus, in eo quòd corpus ex naturâ suâ sit semper divisibile, mens autem plane [86] indivisibilis; nam sane cùm hanc considero, sive meipsum quatenus sum tantùm res cogitans, nullas in me partes possum distinguere, sed rem plane unam & integram me esse intelligo; & quamvis toti corpori tota mens unita esse videatur, abscisso tamen pede, vel brachio, vel quâvis aliâ corporis parte, nihil ideo de mente subductum esse cognosco; neque etiam facultates volendi, sentiendi, intelligendi &c. ejus partes dici possunt, quia una & eadem mens est quae vult, quae sentit, quae intelligit. Contrà verò nulla res corporea sive extensa potest a me cogitari, quam non facile in partes cogitatione dividam, atque hoc ipso illam divisibilem esse intelligam: quod unum sufficeret ad me docendum, mentem a corpore omnino esse diversam, si nondum illud aliunde satis scirem.

and a badly fabricated clock with the idea of a healthy human being and of a correctly made clock — and a denomination being extrinsic to the things of which it is said. But by the word "nature" in the other sense I understand something that is really and truly to be found in the things, and therefore it has not no truth in it.

[18.] And certainly even if with respect to the body suffering from dropsy it would be only an extrinsic denomination when from thence that it were to have a dry throat yet would not need a drink, it is then said that "its nature is corrupt", with respect to the composite, or the mind united to such a body, it is still not a pure denomination — but rather a true error of nature — that it would then thirst when drink is going to harm it. Therefore there here remains to be inquired as to how the goodness of God would not prevent the possibility that nature — so taken — be deceptive.

[19.] Now among the first things that I notice here is that there is a great difference between the mind and the body consisting therein that by its nature the body be always divisible, but the mind be completely indivisible. For surely when I consider the mind, or me myself in so far as I am only a cogitating thing, I can then distinguish no parts in me, but rather do I understand that I am plainly a thing one and complete. And although the whole mind would seem to be united to the whole body, I still cognize that, a foot or an arm or whichever other part of the body that you will having been cut off, nothing has therefore been taken away from the mind. And the faculties of willing, of sensing, of understanding, etc., can also not be called its "parts", because it is one and the same mind which wills, which senses and which understands. But — on the contrary — there is no corporeal or extended thing that can be cogitated by me which I might not easily divide into parts by cogitation, and by means of this itself I may understand that it is divisible: which one thing would suffice to teach me that the mind is completely different from the body, if I did not yet satisfactorily know it from elsewhere.

Deinde adverto mentem non ab omnibus corporis partibus immediate affici, sed tantummodo a cerebro, vel forte etiam ab unâ tantùm exiguâ ejus parte, nempe ab eâ in quâ dicitur esse sensus communis; quae, quotiescunque eodem modo est disposita, menti idem exhibet, etiamsi reliquae corporis partes diversis interim modis possint se habere, ut probant innumera experimenta, quae hîc recensere non est opus.

Adverto praeterea eam esse corporis naturam, ut nulla ejus pars possit ab aliâ parte aliquantum remotâ moveri, quin possit etiam moveri eodem modo a quâlibet ex iis quae interjacent, quamvis illa remotior nihil agat. Ut, exempli causâ, in fune A, B, C, D, si [87] trahatur ejus ultima pars D, non alio pacto movebitur prima A, quàm moveri etiam posset, si traheretur una ex intermediis B vel C, & ultima D maneret immota. Nec dissimili ratione, cùm sentio dolorem pedis, docuit me Physica sensum illum fieri ope nervorum per pedem sparsorum, qui, inde ad cerebrum usque funium instar extensi, dum trahuntur in pede, trahunt etiam intimas cerebri partes ad quas pertingunt, quemdamque motum in iis excitant, qui institutus est a naturâ ut mentem afficiat sensu doloris tanquam in pede existentis. Sed quia illi nervi per tibiam, crus, lumbos, dorsum, & collum transire debent, ut a pede ad cerebrum perveniant, potest contingere ut, etiamsi eorum pars, quae est in pede, non attingatur, sed aliqua tantùm ex intermediis, idem plane ille motus fiat in cerebro qui fit pede male affecto, ex quo necesse erit ut mens sentiat eundem dolorem. Et idem de quolibet alio sensu est putandum.

Adverto denique, quandoquidem unusquisque ex motibus, qui fiunt in eâ parte cerebri quae immediate mentem afficit, non

[20.] I then notice that the mind is immediately affected not by all the parts of the body, but rather only by the brain, or even perhaps only by one small part of the brain, namely, by the part in which it is said that the common sense is: which part, as often as it is disposed in the same mode, exhibits the same thing to the mind, even if the other parts of the body could meanwhile have put themselves into different modes — just as innumerable experiments prove, which there is no need to review here.

[21.] In addition, I notice that the nature of the body is such that no part of it could be moved by another part, some distance remote, unless it could also be moved in the same manner by any of the parts that are in between, although the more remote part would do nothing: just as in a cord ABCD, for example, if its last part, D, were to be pulled, the first part, A, will not otherwise be moved than it could also be moved if one of the intermediate parts, B or C, were to be pulled, and the last part, D, were to remain unmoved. And by not dissimilar reasoning, when I sense a pain of the foot, physics has taught me that this sensation then happens by means of nerves distributed throughout the foot, nerves which, extended like cords from there to the brain, when they are pulled in the foot, then also pull the intimate parts of the brain to which they stretch and excite a certain movement in them: which has been established by nature in order that it would affect the mind with a sensation of pain — as it were — existing in the foot. But because these nerves must pass through the tibia, the thigh, the loins, the back and the neck in order that they would come from the foot through to the brain, it can happen that, even if it is not the part of them in the foot, but rather only some one of the intermediate parts of them, which would be touched, plainly that same movement would happen in the brain which happens, the foot having been affected badly: from whence it will be necessary that the mind would sense the same pain. And the same thing is to be thought about any other sensation.

[22.] Finally, I notice that since each and every one of the movements that happen in the part of the brain that immedi-

nisi unum aliquem sensum illi infert, nihil hac in re melius posse excogitari, quàm si eum inferat qui, ex omnibus quos inferre potest, ad hominis sani conservationem quàm maxime & quàm frequentissime conducit. Experientiam autem testari, tales esse omnes sensus nobis a naturâ inditos; ac proinde nihil plane in iis reperiri, quod non Dei potentiam bonitatemque testetur. Ita, exempli causâ, [88] cùm nervi qui sunt in pede vehementer & praeter consuetudinem moventur, ille eorum motus, per spinae dorsi medullam ad intima cerebri pertingens, ibi menti signum dat ad aliquid sentiendum, nempe dolorem tanquam in pede existentem, a quo illa excitatur ad ejus causam, ut pedi infestam, quantum in se est, amovendam. Potuisset verò natura hominis a Deo sic constitui, ut ille idem motus in cerebro quidvis aliud menti exhiberet: nempe vel seipsum, quatenus est in cerebro, vel quatenus est in pede, vel in aliquo ex locis intermediis, vel denique aliud quidlibet; sed nihil aliud ad corporis conservationem aeque conduxisset. Eodem modo, cùm potu indigemus, quaedam inde oritur siccitas in gutture, nervos ejus movens & illorum ope cerebri interiora; hicque motus mentem afficit sensu sitis, quia nihil in toto hoc negotio nobis utilius est scire, quàm quòd potu ad conservationem valetudinis egeamus, & sic de caeteris.

Ex quibus omnino manifestum est, non obstante immensâ Dei bonitate, naturam hominis ut ex mente & corpore compositi non posse non aliquando esse fallacem. Nam si quae causa, non in pede, sed in aliâ quâvis ex partibus per quas nervi a pede ad cerebrum porriguntur, vel etiam in ipso cerebro, eundem plane motum excitet qui solet excitari pede male affecto,

ately affects the mind carries only some one sensation into it, nothing better in the matter can be excogitated than if, of all those which it can carry in, each and every such movement were to carry in the one sensation that is as maximally and as frequently as possible conducive to the preservation of the healthy human being. But I also notice that experience attests thereto that such are all the sensations given into us by nature, and therefore that nothing at all is found in them which would not attest to the power and goodness of God. Thus, for example, when the nerves that are in the foot are moved violently and contrary to custom, this their movement, reaching through the spinal cord to the intimate parts of the brain, there then gives to the mind a signal to sense something, namely, the pain — as it were — existing in the foot, by which the mind is excited to move as much as it is in its power away from the pain's cause as harmful to the foot. But the nature of the human being could have so been constituted by God that this same movement in the brain would exhibit whatever else that you will to the mind: namely, this movement itself in so far as it is in the brain, or this movement itself in so far as it is in the foot or in some one of the intermediate places, or finally, something else whatever. Yet nothing else would have been equally as conducive to the preservation of the body. In the same way, when we need a drink a certain dryness then arises therefrom in the throat, moving its nerves, and by means of them moving the interior parts of the brain. And this movement affects the mind with a sensation of thirst, because in this whole business there is nothing more useful for us to know than that we would need drink for the preservation of health. And thus of the other things.

[23.] From which things it is completely manifest that — notwithstanding the immense goodness of God — the nature of the human being, as the nature of a composite of mind and body, cannot not sometimes be deceptive. For if some cause, not in the foot, but in whichever other one that you will of the parts through which the nerves are extended from the foot to the brain, or even in the brain itself, were to excite fully the same movement which is usually excited by the badly affected foot,

sentietur dolor tanquam in pede, sensusque naturaliter falletur, quia, cùm ille idem motus in cerebro non possit nisi eundem semper sensum menti inferre, multoque frequentius oriri soleat a causâ quae laedit pedem, quàm ab aliâ alibi existente, rationi consenta[89]neum est ut pedis potius quàm alterius partis dolorem menti semper exhibeat. Et si quando faucium ariditas, non ut solet ex eo quòd ad corporis valetudinem potus conducat, sed ex contrariâ aliquâ causâ oriatur, ut in hydropico contingit, longe melius est illam tunc fallere, quàm si contrà semper falleret, cùm corpus est bene constitutum; & sic de reliquis.

Atque haec consideratio plurimum juvat, non modo ut errores omnes quibus natura mea obnoxia est animadvertam, sed etiam ut illos aut emendare aut vitare facile possim. Nam sane, cùm sciam omnes sensus circa ea, quae ad corporis commodum spectant, multo frequentius verum indicare quàm falsum, possimque uti fere semper pluribus ex iis ad eandem rem examinandam, & insuper memoriâ, quae praesentia cum praecedentibus connectit, & intellectu, qui jam omnes errandi causas perspexit; non amplius vereri debeo ne illa, quae mihi quotidie a sensibus exhibentur, sint falsa, sed hyperbolicae superiorum dierum dubitationes, ut risu dignae, sunt explodendae. Praesertim summa illa de somno, quem a vigiliâ non distinguebam; nunc enim adverto permagnum inter utrumque esse discrimen, in eo quòd nunquam insomnia cum reliquis omnibus actionibus vitae a memoriâ conjungantur, ut ea quae vigilanti occurrunt; nam sane, si quis, dum vigilo, mihi derepente appareret, statimque postea dispareret, ut fit in somnis, ita scilicet ut nec unde venisset, nec quo abiret, viderem, non immerito

then the pain will be sensed as if it were in the foot — and the senses will naturally be deceived: because since that same movement in the brain could not but always carry the same sensation into the mind, and it would usually arise much more frequently from a cause that hurts the foot than from another one existing somewhere else, it is consentaneous to reason that it would always exhibit the pain to the mind as the pain of the foot rather than as a pain of another part. And if a dryness of the throat would once arise not — as usual — from thence that drink be conducive to the health of the body, but rather from some contrary cause — just as it happens in the case of the human being with dropsy —, it is far better that it then deceive than if — on the contrary — it would always then deceive when the body is well constituted. And thus of the remaining things.

[24.] And this consideration helps very much, not only in order that I might notice all the errors to which my nature is subject, but also in order that I could easily either emend or avoid them. For because I would know that all the senses indicate the true much more frequently than the false about the things that concern the advantage of the body, and because I could almost always use several of these senses to examine the same thing, and because I could use, in addition, the memory — which connects present things with preceding ones — and the intellect — which has now seen through all the causes of erring —, I should surely no longer fear that those things which are daily exhibited to me by the senses would be false, but rather are the hyperbolic doubts of the last days to be dismissed as worthy of derision — especially the most general one, the one about sleep, which I did not distinguish from being awake. For I now notice that there is a very great difference between the two consisting therein that dreams may never be joined by the memory to all the other actions of life, as are the things that occur to one who is awake. For surely if, while I am awake, someone were suddenly to appear to me and were immediately afterwards to disappear, just as it happens in dreams, so that, scil., I would see neither wherefrom he had come nor whither he might go,

spec[90]trum potius, aut phantasma in cerebro meo effictum, quàm verum hominem esse judicarem. Cùm verò eae res occurrunt, quas distincte, unde, ubi, & quando mihi adveniant, adverto, earumque perceptionem absque ullâ interruptione cum totâ reliquâ vitâ connecto, plane certus sum, non in somnis, sed vigilanti occurrere. Nec de ipsarum veritate debeo vel minimum dubitare, si, postquam omnes sensus, memoriam & intellectum ad illas examinandas convocavi, nihil mihi, quod cum caeteris pugnet, ab ullo ex his nuntietur. Ex eo enim quòd Deus non sit fallax, sequitur omnino in talibus me non falli. Sed quia rerum agendarum necessitas non semper tam accurati examinis moram concedit, fatendum est humanam vitam circa res particulares saepe erroribus esse obnoxiam, & naturae nostrae infirmitas est agnoscenda.

not without merit would I judge that he is a ghost, or a phantasm feigned in my brain, rather than a true human being. But when the things occur concerning which I distinctly notice wherefrom, where and when they would come to me, and I connect the perception of them without any interruption with the whole rest of my life, then am I fully certain that these things occur not in dreams, but rather to one who is awake. Nor should I even at a minimum doubt the truth of these things if, after I have called together all the senses, the memory and the intellect to examine them, nothing were to be announced to me by any of them that would conflict with the others. For from thence that God not be a deceiver, it completely follows that I am not deceived in such things. But because the necessity of the things to be done does not always allow the time for such an accurate examination, it is to be conceded that human life is often subject to errors concerning particular things — and the weakness of our nature is to be recognized.

INDEX

Instructions: "G" = Descartes' 'Greetings to the Men of the Theological Faculty of the Sorbonne'; "P" = *Praefatio ad lectorem*; "S" = *Synopsis sex sequentium Meditationum*; "I"–"VI" = *Meditationes* I–VI; Arabic numbers refer to the numbered paragraphs within the individual meditations; numbers in parentheses give the frequency of occurrence of the terms in the paragraphs. Thus, e.g., "Deus . . . III . . . 25 (3) . . ." indicates that God is mentioned three times in § 25 of Meditation III.

abduco, -duxi, -ductum, -ere (to lead away from): P 6, S 1, 3, IV 1

aberro, -avi, -atum, -are (to aberr): II 4, 10, VI 17

absolutus, -a, -um (absolute): G 6, IV 5

abstineo, -tinui, -tentum, -ere (to abstain): (cf. II 10), IV 12, 16 (2)

abstractus, -a, -um (abstract): V 6

acceptio, -onis, f. (meaning): VI 17

accidens, -dentis, n. (accidents): S 2 (3), III 13, 30

accurate (accurately): G 4–5, P 1, S 2, I 2, 10, IV 1, VI 3, 17

— accuratius (more accurately): VI 15

accuratus, -a, -um (accurate): VI 24

— accuratior, -ius (more accurate): P 2

— accuratissimus, -a, -um (most, very accurate): G 6

acies, -ei, f. (vision): III 28, 38–39, V 14, VI 2 (2)

actio, -onis, f. (action): II 5, III 31, VI 24

activus, -a, -um (active): VI 10

actualis, -e (actual): III 14 (2), 27

actus, -us, m. (act): III 26–27 (3), 33, IV 15 (2)

acumen, -minis, n. (sharpness of wit): IV 2

adventitius, -a, -um (adventicious): III 7 (2), 11

aegroto, -are (to be sick): VI 17

represent more evidently):
II 7

— evidentius explicare (to explicate more evidently): II 9

— evidentius percipere (to perceive more evidently): II 14, 16

— evidentius cognoscere (to cognize more evidently): II 15, IV 1

— multo evidentius efficere (to effect much more evidently): II 15

— quam evidentissime intueri (to intuit most, very evidently): III 4

— evidentissime cognoscere (to cognize most, very evidently): III 32

— evidentissime demonstrare (to demonstrate most, very evidently): III 36

— evidenter intellegere (to intellect evidently): IV 8

— evidenter sequi (to follow evidently): IV 10

— evidenter agnoscere (to recognize evidently): V 6

— evidentissime apparere (to appear most, very evidently): V 14

— quam evidentissime percipere (to perceive most, very evidently): V 14

evidentia, -ae, f. (evidence): G 5

examen, -minis, n. (examination): VI 15, 24

excogito, -avi, -atum, -are (to excogitate): I 6, V 6, 11, VI 22

exhibeo, -hibui, -hibitum, -ere (to exhibit): III 11, 13 (2), 17–18, 20, 25, IV 17, VI 15–16, 20, 22, 24

existentia, -ae, f. (existence): G 2 (2), 6, P 5, S 2–3, 5–6, III 16, 31, IV 1, 6, V 7 (2)–8 (3), 9–10 (3), 11 (3)–12, VI, 4

existo, -stiti, -ere (to exist): (*passim*, but see:) II 3, 6 ('I exist'), III 22 ('God exists'), V 7 ff. ('God exists'), VI 10 ('the world exists')

experientia, -ae, f. (experience): VI 22

experimentum, -i, n. (experience, experiment): VI 7, 20

experior, -pertus sum, -iri (to know by experience): P 6–7, III 8, 26, 30, 32, 39, IV 3–4, 6, 8 (3), 11, 16, VI 1, 6

explicatio, -onis, f. (explication): G 6, P 1, S 2

explico, -avi, -atum, and -ui, -itum, -are (to explicate): P 1, S 3–5, II 5, 9, VI 3

explodo, -plosi, -plosum, -ere (to explode): VI 24

expresse (expressly): VI 12–13

expressus, -a, -um (express): VI 6 (2)

extendo, -tendi, -tensum and tentum, -ere (to extend): IV 8–9, 11, 17

extensio, -onis, f. (extension): I 7, II 2, 12 (2), III 19 (2), 21, V 3, VI 6, 10

extensus, -a, -um (extended): I 7, 9, II 12 (2), III 21 (2), IV 1, VI 9 (2)–10, 19, 21

externus, -a, -um (external): I 12, II 14 (2), III 10, 37, IV 8, 10, V 6, VI 7 (2)

extrinsecus, -a, -um (extrinsic): VI 17–18

intermedius, -a, -um (intermediate): VI 21 (2)–22

internus, -a, -um (internal): VI 7, 16

interruptio, -onis, f. (interruption): VI 24

intima (intimate parts): IV 8, VI 22

intime (intimately): VI 1

intimus, -a, -um (intimate): VI 21

— intimior, -ius (more intimate): VI 7

intueor, -tuitus sum, -eri (to intuit): I 5, III 4 (2), 39, VI 2 (2)–3

inusitatus, -a, -um (unusual): I 6

invenio, -veni, -ventum, -ire (to find): II 6

invito (involuntarily): I 11, (cf. II 9), III 8, VI 10

ira, -ae, f. (anger): VI 6

judicium, -ii, n. (judgment): G 6 (2), P 1, 5–7, I 11, II 7, 14, III 5–6, 12, 19, IV 8, 12, 15 (2)–17, V 14, VI 7, 16

judico, -avi, -atum, -are (to judge): G 2–3, P 1, I 9, II 5, 12–13 (3), 15 (2), III 3–4, 6–9, 25, 27, 36, IV 3–4, 8, 10 (2), 15, V 14 (2)–15, VI 1, 6, 15 (2), 24

jus, juris, n. (right): I 11, IV 15, VI 6

justus, -a, -um (just): G 1 (2)

laesio, -onis, f. (damage): VI 13

laetitia, -ae, f. (joy): VI 6

lapis, -idis, m. (stone, rock): III 14 (4), 21 (2)

lectio, -onis, f. (reading): P 6

Lector, -oris, m. (reader): G 5, P 1, 6–7, S 3

lego, legi, lectum, -ere (to read): P 1, 6 (cf. 7)

Leo X ([Pope] Leo X): G 3

levitas, -atis, f. (levity): I 10

lex, legis, f. (naturae) (law [of nature]): VI 17

liber, -era, -erum (free): G 5, IV 8 (2), 15, V 10 (2)

libere (freely): IV 10

— liberius (more freely): G 5, IV 8

libertas, -atis, f. (liberty): S 2, I 12, IV 8 (5), 12, 15 (2)

limes, -itis, m. (limit): II 10, IV 8–9

limitatus, -a, -um (limited): IV 6, VI 16 (2)

localis, -e (local): V 3

locus, -i, m. (place): P 5, I 7, 9, II 1–2, 5, VI 10, 22

longum, latum, & profundum (length, breadth and depth): III 19, IV 1, V 3

loquor, locutus sum, loqui (to speak): G 5, II 13–14, (cf. III 1)

ludificatio, -onis, f. (playful deception): I 12

lumbus, -i, m. (back): VI 21

lumen, -inis, n. (light): III 19, VI 6, 11

— lumen naturale (the natural light): S 4, III 9 (3), 14–15, 20, 28, 31, 38, IV 12–13, VI 15

— lumen (Dei) (light [of God]): III 39

lux, lucis, f. (light): I 12, II 9, III 24

— lux in intellectu (light in the intellect): IV 10

machina, -ae, f. (machine): S 3, II 5

machinamentum, -i, n. (machine): VI 17 (2)

magnitudo, -inis, f. (size): I 7, 9, II 11 (2), III 19, V 3, 8, VI 11, 15

majestas, -atis, f. (divina) ([divine] majesty): III 39

male (badly): VI 12, 17 (2), 21, 23

malignus, -a, -um (malign): I 12, II 6

malitia, -ae, f. (malice): IV 2

malum, -i, n. (the bad, evil): S 4

manifeste (manifestly): III 24, IV 1, VI 2

manifestus, -a, -um (manifest): G 2, II 9, 11, III 3–4, 14, 28–29, 31, 38, IV 12, V 8, VI 10 (2), 23
  — manifestissimus, -a, -um (most, very manifest): III 4

manus, -us, f. (hand): I 4 (2)–5, 6 (4), 12, II 5, VI 6

mare, -is, n. (sea): VI 6

materia, -ae, f. (matter): III 6, 36, IV 1

materialis, -e (material): S 1, 6, III 19, V, 1, VI, 1 (2)

materialiter (materially): P 4, III 25

Mathematicus, -a, -um (mathematical): V 7

Mathesis, -eos, f. (pura) ([pure] mathematics): V 6, 16, VI 1, 4, 10

maxime (maximally): G 6, S 2–3, I 3, 6, 8, III 11 (2), 25 (5), 34, IV 11, 15, V 5–6, VI 7, 22

maximus, -a, -um (maximal): G 6, S 1, III 21, 39, IV 8, 17, V 5 (2)

Medicina, -ae, f. (medicine): I 8

meditatio, -onis, f. (meditation): P 7 (3), S 2–3, 6, I 12, II 1, 16, IV 16–17

meditatus, -a, -um (meditated): I 10

meditor, -atus sum, -ari (to meditate): P 6, I 10, II 4, V 7, VI 6

medium quid (middle thing): IV 4

medulla, -ae, f. (medulla): VI 22

membrum, -i, n. (member, limb): S 2, I 6, II 5, 7 (2), VI 6–7

memini, -nisse (to remember): V 6, 14–15

memoria, -ae, f. (memory): II 2, 16, IV 15, V 14, VI 4, 6, 24 (3)

mendax (mendacious): II 2

mens, mentis, f. (mind): G 2, 4–6 (3), P 1, 3, 5(2)–6 (2), 7, S 1–2 (9), 3, 6 (3), I 1, 9, 12, II, 3 (2), 5–7, 10, 12 (3)–13 (3), 14–15 (4), 16, III 3–4 (2), 28, 36, 38, IV 1 (3), V 1, 4–6, 11, 14 (2), VI, 2 (2)–3 (3), 6, 13–15 (4), 17 (3)–18, 19 (6)–20 (2), 21 (2)–22 (4), 23 (3)

Metaphysicus, -a, -um (metaphysical): G 5, III 4

Methodus, -i, f. (method): G 4, P 1

minuta & remotiora (minute and more remote things): I 4

modus, -i, m. (mode): G 2 (2), 4–5 (2), 6, P 4–5 (2), 6, S 2 (3)–4, I 8–11, II 5 (2), 12 (3), 14, III 1 (2), 6, 9, 11, 13 (3)–14 (5), 15 (3), 19, 21 (2), 24–27, 31, 33,

(4), 9 (5)–10 (5), 11, 13, 15 (2)–16, 17 (2), 19 (3), 22, 24 (4)

respondens ([cor]responding): VI 14

responsio, -onis, f. (response): (cf. P 7), S 3, 5

revera (really and truly): P 3–4, S 2, 6, I 11, II 7, 9, 14, III 3, 23, 28, 38, V 7, 10, VI 9, 15, 17

revoco, -avi, -atum, -are (to call):
— in dubium revocare (to call into doubt): G 6, I, VI 5, 8

rhombus, -i, m. (rhombus): V 11

ad Romanos (*To the Romans*): G 2

rota, -ae, f. (wheel): VI 17

sacra scriptura (Sacred Scripture): G 2 (3)

saeculum, -i, n. (world): G 2 (2)

sanguis, -inis, m. (blood): I 12, VI 17

sanus, -a, -um (healthy): S 6, VI 17 (2), 22

sapientia, -ae, f. (wisdom): G 6 (2), P 5, IV 1

Sapientia (*Wisdom*): G 2

sapio, -ii, -ere (to know): II 14

sapor, -oris, m. (flavor, taste): II 11 (2), III 19, VI 4, 6, 14–16 (2)

Satyriscus, -i, m. (satyr): I 6

scientia, -ae, f. (science, knowledge): G 4, P 1, S 1, 3, I 1, IV 1, V 14–16, VI 16

scio, -ivi and -ii, -itum, -ire (to know): G 2 (2), 4, 6, P 3, 6, S 2 (2), 4, 6, I 5, 9 (2),

11, II 3, 7, III (3)–4, 25, IV 6 (2), 10, V 4, 13, 15–16, VI 1, 6, 9 (2), 15, 19, 22, 24

scopus, -i, m. (goal): S 6

sensibilis, -e (sensible): III 28, 37, V 12, VI 7, 10

sensus, -us, m. (sense, sensation): G 5, P 3–4, 6, S 1, 3, 6, I 3 (2)–4, 12, II 2–3 (2), 9 (2)–11, 14 (2), 16, III 1 (2), 3, 8, 11–12, 36 (2), IV 1, V 6 (3), VI 3–4 (3), 5–6 (12), 7 (3)–8, 10 (2), 13 (3)–14, 15 (8)–17, 20–21 (3), 22 (3)–23 (2), 24 (3)

sentio, sensi, sensum, -ire (to sense): S 2, I 5, II 5 (2)–6 (3), 8–9 (3), III 1 (2), 7–8, IV 8, VI 6 (9)–7 (6), 10 (2), 12–15 (3), 19 (2), 21 (2)–23

separatus, -a, -um (separate): II 9

separo, -avi, -atum, -are (to separate): V 8

sequor, secutus sum, sequi (to follow): G 5, P 3 (2)–4 (2), S 2 (3), I 11, III 9, 11, 14, 16, 31 (2), IV 4, 10, V 7, 9–10 (2), VI 1, 3, 15, 24

series, -ei, f. (series): P 6, I 10

serio (seriously): P 6, S 6, I 1

siccitas, -atis, f. (dryness): VI 17, 22

significatio, -onis, f. (signification): II 6

significo, -avi, -atum, -are (to signify): VI 15 (2)

signum, -i, n. (sign): S 6, VI 22

similis, -e (similar): III 3, 6, 8,

11 (2), 17, VI 6, 14–15 (2)

similitudo, -inis, f. (similitude, likeness): I 6, III 5, 8, 38 (2), IV 8

simplex (simple): III 4
— simplicissimus, -a, -um (most, very simple): I 8

simplicia (simple things): I 6

simplicitas, -atis, f. (Dei) (the simplicity [of God]): III 35

Siren, -enis, f. (siren): I 6 (cf. III 7)

sitis, -is, f. (thirst): VI 6, 12–13 (3), 17, 22

situs, -us, m. (position): III 19 (2), 21, V 3

Societas, -atis, f. (society): G 6

sol, solis, m. (sun): III 7, 11 (2)

soliditas, -atis, f. (solidity): G 6

solus, -a, -um (alone): I 1, III 16

solutio, -onis, f. (solution): P 7

somnio, -avi, -atum, -are (to dream): I 6, III 10, V 15 (2)

somnium, -ii, n. (dream): I 5 (2), 12 (2), II 6–7, VI 7, 24 (2)

somnus, -i, m. (sleep): I 5 (2), VI 24

sonus, -i, m. (sound): I 12, II 11 (2)–12, III 19, VI 4, 6, 11, 14

sophisma, -atis, n. (sophism): V 8, 10

Sorbona (Sorbonne): G 6

spatium, -ii, n. (space): II 5, VI 15 (2)

specialis, -e (special): VI 6, 10

species, -ei, f. (look): V 8

spectrum, -i, n. (ghost): VI 24

speculativus, -a, -um (speculative): S 4

spes, -ei, f. (hope): S 2, VI 11

spina, -ae, f. (spine): VI 22

spontaneus, -a, -um (spontaneous): III 9

statua, -ae, f. (statue): VI 7

statuo, -ui, -utum, -ere (to establish): II 3, III 2

stella, -ae, f. (star): VI 15

stupor, -oris, m. (stupor): I 5

subjectum, -i, n. (subject): III 5, 14

substantia, -ae, f. (substance): S 2 (5), III 13 (2), 19, 21 (6)–22, 23 (4)–24, 30 (2), VI 10 (5)

subtilitas, -atis, f. (subtlety): II 5

sufficio, -feci, -fectum, -ere (to suffice): III 2, 25

sum, fui, esse (to be): (*passim*, but see:) II 3 (*ego sum, ego existo* [$\underline{I}$ *am*, $\underline{I}$ *exist*]), 6 (ego sum, ego existo [*I am, I exist*])

summe (most, very highly): S 3 (2), I 9, 12, II 3 (2), III 22 (2), 25, IV 4 (2), 17, V 7–8, 10

summus, -a, -um (most high, very high): S 2, III 4, 13, 39, IV 4 (3)–5, V 10–11 (2), 12, VI 24

suppono, -posui, -positum, -ere (to suppose): P 4, S 2, I 10–12, II 2, 6–7 (2), 9, III 31, IV 10–11

sydus (cf. sidus), -eris, n. (star): III 3

Syren, -enis, f. (siren): III 7 (cf. I 6)

tacitus, -a, -um (here: tacitly): II 13

tactilis, -e (tactile): III 19, VI 6

tactio, -onis, f. (taction): II 12

tactus, -us, m. (touch): II 5, 11, 15

tantum (only): P 3 (2), II 6–7, III 32, VI 9 (2), 19

temeritas, -atis, f. (rashness): IV 6

tempus, -oris, n. (time): I 7, III 31 (2), 34, IV 11, V 6

tenebrae, -arum, f. (shadows): I 12, III 24

tenuis (-e) & circumscriptus (-a, -um) (tenuous and circumscribed): IV 8

terra, -ae, f. (earth): I 9, 12, II 1, 3, III 3, 11, VI 6–7

testimonium, -ii, n. (testimony): G 6

Theologi (theologians): G 2

Theologia, -ae, f. (theology): G 2

thesaurus, -i, m. (thesaurus): IV 1, V 11

tibia, -ae, f. (tibia): VI 21

titillatio, -onis, f. (excitement): VI 6 (2)

totalis, -e (total, whole): III 14

totus, -a, -um (whole): G 5 (2), P 6, S 2, I 4 (2), 6 (2), 10, II 5–6, III 14, (cf. 25), 38, IV 1, 4, 6, 15 (2), VI 6, 10, 14, 19 (2), 22, 24

Tractatus, -us, m. (treatise): G 5

triangulum, -i, n. (triangle): V 5 (3)–6 (2), 8, 11–12, 14, VI 2 (2)

tristitia, -ae, f. (sadness): VI 6 (3)

turris, -is, f. (tower): VI 7, 15

ultimus, -a, -um (ultimate, final): III 33, VI 21 (2)

unde, ubi et quando (wherefrom, where and when): VI 24

unio, -onis, f. (mentis cum corpore) (union [of the mind with the body]): VI 13

unitas, -atis, f. (Dei) (the unity [of God]): III 35 (2)

unitus, -a, -um (united): VI 18–19

universalia (universals): I 6

universitas, -atis, f. (rerum) (universe [of things]): IV 7 (2), 15

universum, -i, n. (universe): III 35

unum quid (one something): S 6, VI 13

unus (-a, -um) & integer (-gra, -grum) (one and complete): VI 19

usitate (according to usage): II 13

usitatus, -a, -um (usual): I 5

usus, -us, m. (use, usage): P 1, I 11, II 13, (cf. 14), IV 6, 12, 16, VI 10, 17

utile (the useful): G 2

utilis, -e (useful): S 6, VI 17
— utilior, -ius (more useful): G 4, VI 22

utilitas, -atis, f. (utility): G 6, S 1–2

utor, usus sum, uti (to use): G 5, S 2, IV 3, 12, 15, V 12, VI 1–2, 6, 15, 24

vacuus, -a, -um (empty): VI 15

vagus, -a, -um (vague):
— vagae opiniones (vague opinions): V 14

valetudo, -inis, f. (health): VI 22–23

validus, -a, -um (valid): I 10

vallis, -is, f. (valley): V 8 (2)–9 (2), 10 (3)

SELECTED BIBLIOGRAPHY

The Standard Edition of the Works of Descartes

Descartes, René. *Oeuvres de Descartes* (Vols. I–XIII). Ed. Charles Adam and Paul Tannery. Paris, 1897–1913/ 1957–1958/1964–1976/etc.

Original Editions of the Text of the *Meditationes*

Descartes, René. *Meditationes de prima philosophia, in qua Dei existentia et animae immortalitas demonstratur.* Paris, 1641.

Idem. Meditationes de prima philosophia, in quibus Dei existentia, et animae humanae a corpore distinctio, demonstrantur. Amsterdam, 1642.

Idem. Les Méditations métaphysiques . . . touchant la première philosophie, dans lesquelles l'existence de Dieu, et la distinction réelle entre l'âme et le corps de l'homme, sont démontrées. Paris, 1647.

Standard Editions of the Text of the *Meditationes*

Descartes, René. *Meditationes de prima philosophia . . .,* Oeuvres de Descartes, Vol. VII, pp. 1–90. Ed. Charles Adam and Paul Tannery. Paris, 1904/etc.

Idem. Les Méditations métaphysiques touchant la première philosophie . . ., Oeuvres de Descartes, Vol. IX/1, pp. 1–72. Ed. Charles Adam and Paul Tannery. Paris, 1904/etc.

247

Literature "on" the *Meditationes/Meditations*

Alquié, Ferdinand. *La découverte métaphysique de l'homme chez Descartes.* Paris, 1950/1966.

Balz, Albert G. A. *Cartesian Studies.* New York, 1951.

Beck, Leslie J. *The Metaphysics of Descartes: A Study of the "Meditations".* Oxford/New York, 1965.

Beyssade, Jean-Marie. *La philosophie première de Descartes. Le temps et la cohérence de la métaphysique.* Paris, 1979.

Blanchet, Léon. *Les antécédents historiques du "Je pense, donc je suis."* Paris, 1920.

Bouillier, Francisque. *Histoire de la philosophie cartésienne.* Paris, 1868 (Third Edition; cf. First Edition: *Histoire et critique de la révolution cartésienne.* Lyon, 1842; Second Edition: Paris, 1854).

Butler, R. J. (ed.). *Cartesian Studies.* Oxford, 1972.

Caton, Hiram P. *The Origin of Subjectivity: An Essay on Descartes.* New Haven, Connecticut, 1973.

Cottingham, John. *Descartes.* Cambridge, 1986.

Cronin, Timothy J. *Objective Being in Descartes and in Suarez.* Rome, 1966.

Curley, Edwin M. *Descartes Against the Skeptics.* Cambridge, Massachusetts, 1978.

(Descartes, René.) *Cahiers de Royaumont. Philosophie, No. II: Descartes.* Paris, 1957.

Doney, Willis (ed.). *Descartes: A Collection of Critical Essays.* Garden City, New York, 1967.

Idem (ed.). *Eternal Truths and The Cartesian Circle: A Collection of Studies.* New York/London, 1987.

Frankfurt, Harry G. *Demons, Dreamers, and Madmen: The Defense of Reason in Descartes's "Meditations".* Indianapolis, Indiana, 1970.

Gibson, Alexander Boyce. *The Philosophy of Descartes.* London, 1932/New York, 1967.

Gilson, Étienne. *Études sur le rôle de la pensée médiévale dans la formation du système cartésien. Deuxième partie des Études de philosophie médiévale* (1921), *revue et considérablement augmentée.* Paris, 1930/1951.

Gouhier, Henri. *Essais sur Descartes.* Paris, 1937/1949.

Idem. Les premières pensées de Descartes. Contribution à l'histoire de l'anti-renaissance. Paris, 1958/1979.

Idem. La pensée métaphysique de Descartes. Paris, 1962/1969/1978.

Idem. Cartésianisme et augustinisme au XVIIe siècle. Paris, 1978.

Gueroult, Martial. *Descartes selon l'ordre des raisons.* Paris, 1953/1968.

Idem. Nouvelles réflexions sur la preuve ontologique de Descartes. Paris, 1955.

Halbfaß, Wilhelm. *Descartes' Frage nach der Existenz der Welt. Untersuchungen über die cartesianische Denkpraxis und Metaphysik.* Meisenheim a. G., 1968.

Hamelin, Octave. *Le système de Descartes.* Paris, 1911/1921.

Henrich, Dieter. *Der ontologische Gottesbeweis. Sein Problem und seine Geschichte in der Neuzeit.* Tübingen, 1960.

Hooker, Michael (ed.). *Descartes: Critical and Interpretive Essays.* Baltimore/London, 1978.

Kenny, Anthony. *Descartes: A Study of his Philosophy.* New York, 1968.

Koyré, Alexandre. *Essai sur l'idée de Dieu et les preuves de son existence chez Descartes.* Paris, 1922 (cf. *Descartes und die Scholastik.* Bonn, 1923).

Marion, Jean-Luc. *Sur la théologie blanche de Descartes. Analogie, création des vérités éternelles et fondement.* Paris, 1981.

Idem. Sur le prisme métaphysique de Descartes. Paris, 1986.

Markie, Peter J. *Descartes's Gambit.* Ithaca, New York, 1986.

Marshall, David J. *Prinzipien der Descartes-Exegese.* Freiburg/Munich, 1979.

Röd, Wolfgang. *Descartes. Die innere Genesis des Cartesianischen Systems.* Munich, 1964.

Idem. Descartes' Erste Philosophie. Versuch einer Analyse mit besonderer Berücksichtigung der Cartesianischen Methodologie. Bonn, 1971.

Idem. Descartes. Die Genese des Cartesianischen Rationalismus. Zweite, völlig überarbeitete und erweiterte Auflage (of

Descartes. *Die innere Genesis des Cartesianischen Systems*).
Munich, 1982.

Rodis-Lewis, Geneviève (ed.). *Méthode et métaphysique chez Descartes: Articles en français*. New York/London, 1987.

Eadem (ed.). *La science chez Descartes: Études en français*. New York/London, 1987.

Rorty, Amélie Oksenberg (ed.). *Essays on Descartes' "Meditations"*. Berkeley/Los Angeles/London, 1986.

Russier, Jeanne. *Sagesse cartésienne et religion: Essai sur la connaissance de l'immortalité de l'âme selon Descartes*. Paris, 1958.

Schmidt, Gerhart. *Aufklärung und Metaphysik. Die Neubegründung des Wissens durch Descartes*. Tübingen, 1965.

Sesonske, Alexander, and Fleming, Noel (eds.). *Meta-Meditations: Studies in Descartes*. Belmont, California, 1965.

Smith, Norman Kemp. *Studies in the Cartesian Philosophy*. London, 1902/New York, 1962.

Idem. *New Studies in the Philosophy of Descartes: Descartes as Pioneer*. London/New York, 1952.

Specht, Rainer. *Commercium mentis et corporis. Über Kausalvorstellungen im Cartesianismus*. Stuttgart-Bad Cannstatt, 1966.

Vuillemin, Jules. *Mathématiques et métaphysique chez Descartes*. Paris, 1960.

Williams, Bernard. *Descartes: The Project of Pure Enquiry*. London, 1978.

Wilson, Margaret D. *Descartes*. London, 1978/1982.

On the Life of Descartes

Adam, Charles. *Vie et oeuvres de Descartes. Étude historique* (= Vol. XII, *Oeuvres de Descartes*. Ed. Charles Adam and Paul Tannery. Paris, 1897–1913). Paris, 1910/etc.

Baillet, Adrien. *La vie de Monsieur Des-cartes*. Paris, 1691/Hildesheim, New York, 1972.

Some Bibliographies on the Philosophy of Descartes

Caton, Hiram P. "Bibliography of Descartes Literature, 1960–1970", *The Origin of Subjectivity: An Essay on Descartes*. New Haven, Connecticut, 1973, pp. 223–243.

Chappell, Vere, and Doney, Willis. *Twenty-five Years of Descartes Scholarship, 1960–1984: A Bibliography*. New York/London, 1987.

Doney, Willis. "Bibliography", *Descartes: A Collection of Critical Essays*. Ed. Willis Doney. New York, 1967, pp. 369–386.

Idem. "Some Recent Work on Descartes: A Bibliography", *Philosophy Research Archives*, Vol. 2 (1976–1977), pp. 545–567 (cf. *Descartes: Critical and Interpretive Essays*. Ed. Michael Hooker. Baltimore/London, 1978, pp. 299–312).

Gabbey, A., Marion, J.-L., *et al.* "Descartes", *The Seventeenth Century: Supplement*. Ed. H. G. Hall. (= Vol. 3 A, *A Critical Bibliography of French Literature*. Ed. D. C. Cabeen *et al.*) Syracuse, New York, 1983, pp. 377–419.

Hughes, Robert D. "Liminaire. Le 'cercle' des *Méditations*: un état des recherches récentes" ("Bulletin Cartésien", 7), *Archives de philosophie*, Vol. 41 (1978), pp. 1–12.

Sebba, Gregory. *Bibliographia Cartesiana: A Critical Guide to the Descartes Literature 1800–1960*. The Hague, 1964.

ABOUT THE EDITOR/TRANSLATOR

George Heffernan was Assistant Professor of Philosophy at the University of Notre Dame from 1986 to 1990. He received his B.A. and M.A. degrees from The Catholic University of America and his Ph.D. from the University of Cologne. In preparation for this book Heffernan worked for several years under the direction of Professor Dr. Gerhart Schmidt of the University of Bonn, who is a well-known Descartes specialist. In addition to this edition of the *Meditations on First Philosophy*, Heffernan has also published numerous works in classical phenomenology, including the *Isagoge in die phänomenologische Apophantik* (Phaenomenologica Volume 107). Heffernan is now Associate Professor of Philosophy at Merrimack College.